Strategic Collaborative Innovations in Organizational Systems

Mambo Mupepi
Grand Valley State University, USA

Robert Costello
Newcastle College, UK

A volume in the Advances in
Business Strategy and Competitive
Advantage (ABSCA) Book Series

IGI Global
DISSEMINATOR OF KNOWLEDGE

Published in the United States of America by
IGI Global
Business Science Reference (an imprint of IGI Global)
701 E. Chocolate Avenue
Hershey PA, USA 17033
Tel: 717-533-8845
Fax: 717-533-8661
E-mail: cust@igi-global.com
Web site: http://www.igi-global.com

Library of Congress Cataloging-in-Publication Data

Names: Mupepi, Mambo, 1952- editor. | Costello, Robert, 1979- editor.
Title: Strategic collaborative innovations in organizational systems / Mambo Mupepi and Robert Costello, editors.
Description: Hershey, PA : Business Science Reference, [2018]
Identifiers: LCCN 2018025771| ISBN 9781522573906 (hardcover) | ISBN 9781522573913 (ebook)
Subjects: LCSH: Computational intelligence. | Organization.
Classification: LCC Q342 .S85 2018 | DDC 658.4/038--dc23 LC record available at https://lccn.loc.gov/2018025771

This book is published in the IGI Global book series Advances in Business Strategy and Competitive Advantage (ABSCA) (ISSN: 2327-3429; eISSN: 2327-3437)

British Cataloguing in Publication Data
A Cataloguing in Publication record for this book is available from the British Library.

All work contributed to this book is new, previously-unpublished material.
The views expressed in this book are those of the authors, but not necessarily of the publisher.

For electronic access to this publication, please contact: eresources@igi-global.com.

Advances in Business Strategy and Competitive Advantage (ABSCA) Book Series

ISSN:2327-3429
EISSN:2327-3437

MISSION

Business entities are constantly seeking new ways through which to gain advantage over their competitors and strengthen their position within the business environment. With competition at an all-time high due to technological advancements allowing for competition on a global scale, firms continue to seek new ways through which to improve and strengthen their business processes, procedures, and profitability.

The **Advances in Business Strategy and Competitive Advantage (ABSCA) Book Series** is a timely series responding to the high demand for state-of-the-art research on how business strategies are created, implemented and re-designed to meet the demands of globalized competitive markets. With a focus on local and global challenges, business opportunities and the needs of society, the **ABSCA** encourages scientific discourse on doing business and managing information technologies for the creation of sustainable competitive advantage.

COVERAGE

- Joint Ventures
- Differentiation Strategy
- Entrepreneurship & Innovation
- Strategy Performance Management
- International Business Strategy
- Core Competencies
- Value Creation
- Adaptive Enterprise
- Globalization
- Strategic Management

IGI Global is currently accepting manuscripts for publication within this series. To submit a proposal for a volume in this series, please contact our Acquisition Editors at Acquisitions@igi-global.com or visit: http://www.igi-global.com/publish/.

The Advances in Business Strategy and Competitive Advantage (ABSCA) Book Series (ISSN 2327-3429) is published by IGI Global, 701 E. Chocolate Avenue, Hershey, PA 17033-1240, USA, www.igi-global.com. This series is composed of titles available for purchase individually; each title is edited to be contextually exclusive from any other title within the series. For pricing and ordering information please visit http://www.igi-global.com/book-series/advances-business-strategy-competitive-advantage/73672. Postmaster: Send all address changes to above address.

Titles in this Series

For a list of additional titles in this series, please visit:
https://www.igi-global.com/book-series/advances-business-strategy-competitive-advantage/73672

Creating Business Value and Competitive Advantage With Social Entrepreneurship
N. Oyku Iyigun (Istanbul Commerce University, Turkey)
Business Science Reference • ©2019 • 435pp • H/C (ISBN: 9781522556879) • US $205.00

Applying Business Intelligence Initiatives in Healthcare and Organizational Settings
Shah J. Miah (Victoria University, Australia) and William Yeoh (Deakin University, Australia)
Business Science Reference • ©2019 • 384pp • H/C (ISBN: 9781522557180) • US $215.00

Strategic Optimization of Medium-Sized Enterprises in the Global Market
Milan Vemić (DAI Europe, Serbia)
Business Science Reference • ©2019 • 386pp • H/C (ISBN: 9781522557845) • US $215.00

Effective Open Innovation Strategies in Modern Business Emerging Research and Opportunities
N. Raghavendra Rao (FINAIT Consultancy Services, India)
Business Science Reference • ©2018 • 159pp • H/C (ISBN: 9781522557210) • US $145.00

Examining the Role of Women Entrepreneurs in Emerging Economies
David Chitakunye (London School of Commerce, UK) and Amandeep Takhar (University of Northampton, UK)
Business Science Reference • ©2018 • 375pp • H/C (ISBN: 9781522551126) • US $235.00

Handbook of Research on Strategic Innovation Management for Improved Competitive Advantage
George Leal Jamil (InesTec, Portugal) João José Pinto Ferreira (InesTec, Portugal) Maria Manuela Pinto (InesTec, Portugal) Cláudio Roberto Magalhães Pessoa (Universidade Fumec, Brazil) and Alexandra Xavier (InesTec, Portugal)
Business Science Reference • ©2018 • 772pp • H/C (ISBN: 9781522530121) • US $465.00

Utilizing Consumer Psychology in Business Strategy
Tevfik Dalgic (University of Texas at Dallas, USA) and Sevtap Unal (Izmir Katip Celebi University, Turkey)
Business Science Reference • ©2018 • 325pp • H/C (ISBN: 9781522534488) • US $215.00

For an entire list of titles in this series, please visit:
https://www.igi-global.com/book-series/advances-business-strategy-competitive-advantage/73672

IGI Global
DISSEMINATOR OF KNOWLEDGE

701 East Chocolate Avenue, Hershey, PA 17033, USA
Tel: 717-533-8845 x100 • Fax: 717-533-8661
E-Mail: cust@igi-global.com • www.igi-global.com

We dedicate this new publication to Dr. Mambo Mupepi, who passed away unexpectedly from a pulmonary embolism on June 18, 2018 while visiting in Zimbabwe. At the time of his death, in addition to his many other contributions to IGI Global books and journals, he was finalizing this edited book, and with the kind assistance of Dr. Robert Costello, we are able to publish this final work of Dr. Mupepi as a testament to his lasting memory. We will miss him and his research contributions.

Table of Contents

Detailed Table of Contents

Marketing trends and competitive information is needed for clear decision making about what products to develop for what customers, at what cost, and through which distribution channels, reducing the uncertainty that a new product/service development always brings. There are several characteristics that describe the quality of information that will allow the analysis of the value of the information used. Information is an important aid in the decision-making process and must be of quality to improve its value. Social media intelligence allows the knowledge of competitors' moves and the analysis of trends from the communications exchanged in the networks of individual consumers, making it easy for companies to develop solutions according to their clients and prospects desires. Learning how to extract quality, unbiased, valuable information from these social tools is the aim of this chapter.

Organizational design could be understood as a metaphor to appreciate customer needs through segmentation or cross-channel analysis and extrapolation in pervasive value creation environment. Corporations need to calculate moves based on available capacity to produce the products demanded in highly competitive markets. The workforce must possess the required skillsets and brashness critical in getting the job done correctly all the time. The knowledge drawn from data analytics can be applied to develop performance metrics essential in advancing productivity in ubiquitous value making systems. This chapter explores strengthening the significance of data analytics.

This chapter aims to provide a theoretically based and proven educational design for lessons learned. Called a proactive review, this educational design is exemplified in a case study of a global information technology company classified as big business, where proactive reviews were developed and implemented in over 40 countries. This chapter explores how employees who solve a task together can learn from the experience and share this learning with relevant colleagues to improve work practices, services, and/or products. This chapter describes the format of proactive reviews, suggestions for starting points called PR triggers, and the four roles involved—the participant, sponsor, top management, and facilitator. The tangible and intangible results of proactive reviews are presented with their impacts on the participants, their teams, and the organization's products, services, and/or work practices. Finally, the chapter provides recommendations for implementing and maintaining proactive reviews in organizations.

Management view the skunkworks approach as an enriched environment composed of individuals possessing the required experience critical in the formulation of strategy to advance efficiency and effectiveness in the firm. It is a purpose-built forum where learning happens by sharing experiences to design and implement new products in at least four modalities. The first is its capability to ignite the company's mission by co-construction a shared vision. Organizations need to appreciate what the future may look like. The second is the collective experience of its membership where new ideas can lead to the design and implementation of the technology to progress the job. A company must do all it can to differentiate itself to compete successfully. The third is its ability to create diffuse and distribute knowledge to cognitive areas where it will be put into organizational context. The fourth is the need to sustain change by continuing to learn and improve. This chapter models the skunkworks technology.

Foreword

Since the 1970s we have witnessed the adoption of technology and computer systems across all industries at a persistent rate, leading us into the Age of Information. The digitization of data has profoundly impacted the way in which businesses operate as they look to capitalize on the new opportunities created as we push further into the Information Age. Businesses have adjusted their philosophies and business models to stay current with developments in computing and digital information. There also now exists many companies built entirely on a solid foundation of digital information, demonstrating what a valuable and powerful commodity that information has become. The impacts as we transition further into the Information Age can also be seen throughout modern society. Digital information mediates our personal lives on an almost daily basis, and with technology providing easier access to large amounts of information, virtually everybody has the opportunity to gather and disseminate information at their fingertips. This information can support our life choices and shape our day to day lives.

It is important to remember that when we refer to Data, we define it as a collection of unorganized facts, figures or perhaps even "bits of Information". Information is created through the processing, organization and structuring of Data in a given context to make it purposeful. Even before the Age of Information, businesses applied organisational analytics as a method of continuous improvement through the exploration, analysis and investigation of past business performance. Digitizing such data not only began to streamline the organizational analytics process but offered businesses the ability to analyze greater quantities of data in smaller amounts of time, allowing for more flexibility in our analysis and greater resilience in the Information used to drive businesses forward.

This book presents a collection of innovative theories for the strategic and collaborative shaping of organizational structures and systems within businesses. Information can be a powerful tool when utilized correctly by businesses, reducing uncertainty, developing internal knowledge further and contributing to the improvement and optimization of business processes. Be it Information regarding product development, distribution channels or industry best practices; high quality

Information generates the best results when competing with other organizations. The sources from which businesses gather information has also changed as technology has developed, with social media and digital communication platforms providing our client and customer base with a louder voice and in most cases, an almost instant and direct line of communication to a business. Social media analytics and data gathering is currently a thriving area of the Digital Information sector and will no doubt continue to influence and shape businesses for many years to come.

The Information Age continues to connect the world together, slowly but surely offering us all access to a platform for knowledge and information to be shared amongst communities all over the globe. As we continue to move forward, the prospect of what comes next is an exciting one. We must begin to consider: What will happen once we have completed our transition into a fully digital world? While we can only theorize at this time, we can hope to enter an age of enlightenment where information sharing, innovative and strategic collaboration practices amongst businesses and research institutions become commonplace as we strive to better ourselves and our technology.

Adam Robson
Newcastle College, UK

Adam Robson *is an experienced industry professional, software developer and lecturer. He has recently completed an MPhil and is currently working towards a PhD with Northumbria University. His research interests include business process optimization, dimensionality reduction, artificial intelligence and machine learning.*

Preface

Today, Collaborative Innovation (CI) approaches in organization systems seek to integrate culture, behaviors, beliefs and values that can contribute to the unique social and psychological environment of an organization to improve productivity. Organizational Innovation brings together important insights from other related fields into a guiding concept that can be useful for developers and scholars. Innovation within organizations are always challenging and there is a demand for increased of productivity internally as well as externally to determine the future of large companies, and to make them more indistinguishable with what consumerism products they offer across their value chain. To compensate for this shift in consumerism, there is a need for a deviate from an industry-based to an information-based economy, which demands new organizational capabilities and human skills, not just at macro but also micro level (Elkjaer, 2003). CI can provide the necessary support and knowledge for the advancement, creation and implementation (Akhtar & Khan, 2011; Holsapple & Wu, 2011; Chang, 2016) to enable employees to harness productivity and improve business results while gaining competitive and revenues (Chang, 2016; Nonaka & Takeuchi, 1995). As Leven, Holmstrom & Mathiassen (2014) points out, CI represent a structures within an organization where members can have the abilities to interact and cooperate in order to increase productivity and knowledge to steer innovation.

To achieve a more supportive advancement that offers organizations a more fluid creative approach to improve productive and innovations, researchers like (Syahirah, Bibi, & Bazli, 2018; Lanza-Cruz, Berlanga, & Aramburu, 2018; Archer-Brown, Marder, Calvard, & Kowalski, 2018) suggest Social Media Intelligence (SMI) approach that has the abilities to transform knowledge and information based information that is directly relevant to the world economy. The whole idea of using SMI within an organisation is to gain information that is directly interconnected with every changing flux and flows of the dynamic changing world and take advantage to the exchange of goods and trends.

Organisations are living in a era, where Information Systems (IS) can disseminate and support decisions in reducing uncertainty and to develop knowledge in organizations (Best, 1996b; Kahaner, 1997; Porter & Millar, 1985; Syahirah, Bibi, & Bazli, 2018). Syahirah, Bibi, & Bazli, (2018) indicates that building a community through IS, has improved not just communications between different generations, but they have had the abilities to express and share views, ideas, and ways to improve, business activities “such as selling and buying goods as social media is becoming one of the most effective platform” (Syahirah, Bibi, & Bazli, p1). Information Systems according to (Lanza-Cruz, Berlanga, & Aramburu, (2018), provides tools and strategies for organization to extract process and monitor trends, that can directly affect important decision making. In every changing dynamic global world, we are living in, quality information warrants best results when competing against other organizations. One approach is the use of Intelligence activities, which are based on the intelligence cycle. The intelligence cycle involves accurately identifying your information needs, collecting relevant information, analysing it, communicating the results to the people who need it, and taking rapid and appropriate action (Yin, 2018; Yap, Cheng, Mohamad Hussain, & Ahmad, 2018).

Through the use of Intelligence Cycles, and Quality Information, organizations can make clear decision-making about what products to develop, for what customers, depending on trends, through which distribution channels can assist with reducing the uncertainty that a new product/service development always bring. Rho & Vasilakos (2018) suggests that through using interconnecting processes and relationships organisations can promote collaborative intelligence, and this improving performance and securing competitive advantages.

Value creation in the Western world has come to rely more heavily on intangible resources. This question stems from the top management of a global high-technology company. The top management had realized that mistakes and failures were repeated. Relevance of communication along the innovation process pipeline has remained historically neglected. Efforts have traditionally been managed as separate activities, as Edgar (2013) and Rho & Vasilakos (2018) suggests. Through incorporating unique human characteristics based on our own self capacity and self-consciousness will we be able to learn and improve the production of goods to supply the ever-demanding needs by the consumer.

Garet and Porter et al. (2001) suggests that to for efforts to be improved in managing activities knowledge for professional development must be required through structural instructions on account of the sheer volume and complexity of the learning materials. This knowledge can then be professional shared between others internally through online community either through information Systems (IS) mentioned above by Syahirah, Bibi, and Bazli (2018) or embracing how technology and open accessibility to learning content can lead to changes in which scholarly research (Costello, 2018) within academia or Intellectual Properties(IP) rights can be used to assist an organization to gain more productivity.

It is up to the organization, to choose the correct process relating to strategic collaborative invocations, that can steer the organizational systems to facilitate successfully by adjusting to latest trends, technologies, individual's communities and also offering staff the latest training to keep them at the top of the game. These approaches, from COP (Community of Practice) sharing ideas within Information Systems (IS) or using latest techniques within scholar activities will ensure and illuminate the effective use of tools to accelerate developmental practices and outcomes (Mupepi, 2017a).

This book is for industry, educators, researchers and academics, looking at how Strategic Collaborative Innovations techniques can be used and harnessed to improve productivity across the global for system organisations.

ORGANIZATION OF THE BOOK

The book is organized into nine chapters. A brief description of each of the chapters follows:

Chapter 1

Marketing trends and competitive information is needed to clear decision-making about what products develop, for what customers, at what cost, through which distribution channels, reducing the uncertainty that a new product/service development always brings. Learning how to extract quality information, unbiased, valuable for business, from these social tools is the aim and this can be achieved through the use of Social Media intelligence.

Chapter 2

Organizational design could be understood as a metaphor to appreciate customer needs through segmentation and extrapolation in pervasive value creation. Corporations need to calculate moves based on knowledge drawn from data to develop performance metrics in advancing productivity within value making systems.

Chapter 3

This article uses a proven educational design called Proactive Review, that explores how employees would describe, a starting point called PR Triggers, which uses four roles - the participant, sponsor, top management, and facilitator. The tangible and intangible results of Proactive Reviews are presented, with their impacts on the participants; their teams; and the organization's products, services, and/or work practices. Finally, the article provides recommendations for implementing and maintaining Proactive Reviews in organization who solve a task together can learn from the experience and share this learning with relevant colleagues to improve work practices, services, and/or products.

Chapter 4

The skunk-works approach as an enriched environment composed of individuals possessing the required experience critical in the formulation of strategy to advance efficiency and effectiveness in the firm to assist management. It is a purpose-built forum where learning happens by sharing experiences to design and implement new products in at least four modalities: the first is its capability to ignite the company's mission by co-construction a shared vision. The second is the collective experience of its membership where new ideas can lead to the design and implementation of the technology to progress the job. The third is its ability to create diffuse and distribute knowledge to cognitive areas where it will be put into organizational context. The fourth is the need to sustain change by continuing to learn and improve.

Chapter 5

This chapter describes the deliberate making of a community of practice(COP) to advance specialization in divided labor and structuring a successful enterprise. The division of labor is identified to enable the novice to develop the proficiencies required for specialty to happen. Bootstrapping and other techniques are applied to replicate the performance required in making effective specialists. A conclusion is drawn taking the position that the centricity of an epistemic community is the locus of control of the job, individual, and team; additionally, it is the only organization that can authenticate the practices necessary to boost productivity.

Chapter 6

The growing acceptance of marrying across racial and ethnic lines (as reflected in US census statistics) – together with the growth of demographic changes across workplaces – is fuelling fears among some, who see their culture being threatened and react by engaging in overt discrimination. Paradoxically, a business's culture's greatest strength could be its greatest weakness when not consistent with sound business strategies. Moreover, when such a culture prevents a firm from meeting competitive threats, this can lead to the firm's stagnation and ultimate demise.

Chapter 7

This paper offers a case study in Adaptive Personalised Learning for Higher Education Learners and transferable skills, through, raising standards and improvements within universities expectation. Research students can be provided with suitable transferable skills to benefit them while carrying out R&D not just within academia but also in Industry.

Chapter 8

On-job training (OJT) and the Zone of proximal learning (ZPL) remain as some of the top innovative approaches to increasing the efficacies required in progressive enterprises. A case study was drawn to illustrate how OJT and the ZPL was applied to the divided labor, which helped to grow specialization and design technology required for productivity in a successful organization. The ZPL is at the cutting-edge of improving cognitive, affective and sensory practices while OJT upsurge the skilfulness required to boost performance.

Mambo Governor Mupepi
Grand Valley State University, USA

Robert Costello
Newcastle College, UK

REFERENCES

Akhtar, N., & Khan, R. A. (2011). Exploring the paradox of organizational learning and learning organization. *Interdisciplinary Journal of Contemporary Research in Business*, *2*(9), 257–270.

Archer-Brown, C., Marder, B., Calvard, T., & Kowalski, T. (2018). Hybrid social media: Employees' use of a boundary-spanning technology. *New Technology, Work and Employment*, *33*(1), 74–93. doi:10.1111/ntwe.12103

Chang, V. (2016). Review and discussion: E-learning for academia and industry. *International Journal of Information Management*, *36*(3), 476–485. doi:10.1016/j.ijinfomgt.2015.12.007

Easterby-Smith, M., & Prieto, I. M. (2008). Dynamic capabilities and knowledge management: An integrative role for learning? *British Journal of Management*, *19*(3), 235–249. doi:10.1111/j.1467-8551.2007.00543.x

Elkjaer, B. (2003). Organizational learning with a pragmatic slant. *International Journal of Lifelong Education*, *22*(5), 481–494. doi:10.1080/02601370320000102841

Elkjaer, B. (2013). Organisational Learning as Movements in Practice. Pedagogy and Teacher Education, Scientific Papers. *University of Latvia*, *790*, 22–33.

Flamholtz, E., & Randle, Y. (2014). Implications of organizational Life Cycles for Corporate Culture and Climate. In B. Schneider & K. Barbera (Eds.), *The Oxford Handbook of organizational Climate and Culture, Oxford Library of psychology* (pp. 235–265). OUP.

Freiberg, K., & Frieberg, J. (2005). *Guts: Companies that blow the doors off business-as-usual*. New York: Random House.

Garet, M. S., Porter, A. C., Desimone, L., Birman, B. F., & Yoon, K. S. (2001). What Makes Professional Development Effective? Results from a National Sample of Teachers. *American Educational Research Journal*, *38*(4), 915–945. doi:10.3102/00028312038004915

Lanza-Cruz, I., Berlanga, R., & Aramburu, M. (2018). Modeling Analytical Streams for Social Business Intelligence. In Informatics (Vol. 5, No. 3, p. 33). Multidisciplinary Digital Publishing Institute.

Lave, J., & Wenger, E. (1991). *Situated Learning: Legitimate Peripheral Participation*. Cambridge, UK: Cambridge University Press. doi:10.1017/CBO9780511815355

Leven, P., Holmstrom, J., & Mathiassen, L. (2014). Managing research and innovation networks: Evidence from a government sponsored cross-industry program. *Research Policy*, *43*(1), 156–168. doi:10.1016/j.respol.2013.08.004

Mupepi, M. (2017a). *Effective Talent Management Strategies for Organizational Success*. Hershey, PA: IGI Global. doi:10.4018/978-1-5225-1961-4

Nonaka, I., & Takeuchi, H. (1995). *The knowledge-creating company*. New York, NY: Oxford University Press.

Rho, S., & Vasilakos, A. V. (2018). *Intelligent collaborative system and service in value network for enterprise computing*. Academic Press.

Schein, E. (2013). *Corporate culture: How to think ab out and define culture*. In *Handbook for Strategic HR: Best practices in Organization Development*. New York: Amacon.

Syahirah, S. S. S., Bibi, H. F., & Bazli, H. M. (2018). Leadership, Policy and Governance in Malaysia: A Study on Gen Y Perception and Expectation. In *International Conference on Kansei Engineering & Emotion Research* (pp. 683-691). Springer.

Yap, C. S., Cheng, B. L., Mohamad Hussain, N., & Ahmad, R. (2018). Innovativeness, market intelligence practices, and firm performance of small-and medium-sized tour operators. *Tourism and Hospitality Research*, *18*(2), 143–151. doi:10.1177/1467358416636931

Yin, C. Y. (2018). Measuring organizational impacts by integrating competitive intelligence into executive information system. *Journal of Intelligent Manufacturing*, *29*(3), 533–547. doi:10.100710845-015-1135-4

Chapter 1
Applying Social Media Intelligence for Successful Business Management

Sérgio Maravilhas
Salvador University, Brazil

ABSTRACT

Marketing trends and competitive information is needed for clear decision making about what products to develop for what customers, at what cost, and through which distribution channels, reducing the uncertainty that a new product/service development always brings. There are several characteristics that describe the quality of information that will allow the analysis of the value of the information used. Information is an important aid in the decision-making process and must be of quality to improve its value. Social media intelligence allows the knowledge of competitors' moves and the analysis of trends from the communications exchanged in the networks of individual consumers, making it easy for companies to develop solutions according to their clients and prospects desires. Learning how to extract quality, unbiased, valuable information from these social tools is the aim of this chapter.

DOI: 10.4018/978-1-5225-7390-6.ch001

INTRODUCTION

Some authors (Brown & Duguid, 2000; Castells, 2000, 2004; Webster, 2000) observed that a huge transformation is taking place; that we are moving towards a society that is no longer dependant in a massive industrialization or agriculture. They often talk about the knowledge and information based transformation of the world economy we are living in, with flux and flows of information gaining advantage to the exchange of goods. This notion is Interconnected with the birth of the information technology, characterized by computers and electronic means of producing and transmitting information at the speed of light through a network of other technological apparatus (Godeluck, 2000).

We are living in an information society (IS) (Webster, 2000) where organizational and personal life are mediated by information and knowledge (Castells, 2000; Negroponte, 1995), with the help of technologies that gather, disseminate and deliver that raw material to support our decisions (McGee & Prusak, 1995; Penzias, 1995; Tapscott, 1995; Tapscott & Williams, 2008; Ward & Peppard, 2002). Nowadays, we tend to call information society to the constraints we move in, sociologically interpreted. An IS, tend to describe a society no longer based in the production of materials, goods, production means, but in the production of knowledge. Information, as a tool to reduce uncertainty and to develop knowledge in organizations (Best, 1996b; Kahaner, 1997; Porter & Millar, 1985), is an important aid in the decision making process and must be of quality to improve its value (Best, 1996b; Beuren, 1998; Choo, 2003; Davenport, Marchand, & Dickson, 2004; Marchand & Horton Jr., 1986; Tapscott, 1999; Wilson, 1985, 1987).

In the globalized world we are living in, quality information warrants best results when competing with other organizations (Brophy & Coulling, 1996; Redman, 1996; Wormell, 1990). Its value is related to the results that it will allow obtaining and it's dependable on its context (Best, 1996b; Davenport, 1997; Marchand & Horton Jr., 1986; Orna, 1999; Penzias, 1989; Tapscott, 1995; Tapscott, Ticoll, & Lowy, 2000). Quality information is needed to clear decision-making about what products develop, for what customers, at what cost, through which distribution channels, reducing the uncertainty that a new product/service development always brings with it (Garber, 2001; Kotler, Armstrong, Saunders, & Wong, 1999; Mohr, Sengupta, & Slater, 2010; Scott, 2008; Trott, 2008).

Competitive Intelligence (CI) aims to monitor a firm's external environment for information relevant to its decision-making process (Choo, 2003). Intelligence activities are based on the intelligence cycle. The intelligence cycle involves accurately identifying your information needs, collecting relevant information, analysing it, communicating the results to the people who need it, and taking rapid and appropriate action (Besson & Possin, 1996; Martinet & Marti, 1995; Taborda &

Ferreira, 2002). As an excellent information source, the Internet provides significant opportunities for CI (Sage, 2013). Internet search engines have been widely used to facilitate information search on the Internet (Gomes & Braga, 2001; Taborda & Ferreira, 2002). However, many problems minimize their effective use in CI research (Bedell, 2011; Kahaner, 1997).

Many major companies, such as Ernst & Young, Motorola, Xerox, and almost all the pharmaceutical companies, have formal and well-organized CI units that enable managers to make informed decisions about critical business matters such as investment, marketing, and strategic planning (Prescott & Miller, 2002).

Traditionally, CI relied upon published company reports and other kinds of printed information. In recent years, Internet has rapidly become an extremely good source of information about the competitive environment of companies (Hawthorne & Cromity, 2012; Ojala, 2012; Revelli, 2000; Sage, 2013). Much time and effort is required for CI professionals to search for relevant information on the Internet and then analyze the information collected in the correct context.

Internet search engines have been useful in helping people search for information on the Internet. Nevertheless, the exponential growth of information sources on the Internet and the unregulated and dynamic nature of many Web sites are making it increasingly difficult to locate useful information using these search engines (Scott, 2008). Social Media tools allow the knowledge of competitor's moves and the analysis of trends from the communications exchanged in the networks of individual consumers (Russell, 2011; Tsvetovat & Kouznetsov, 2011), making it easy for companies to develop solutions according to their clients and prospects desires (Berthon, Pitt, Plangger, & Shapiro, 2012; Bramston, 2009; Burgelman, Christensen, & Wheelwright, 2009; Canhoto, 2013; Christensen, Anthony, & Roth, 2004; Kotze, 2013).

Web 2.0 and Social Media are more than tools where you can keep track of your old school and college friends (Bedell, 2011). Due to the amount of information exchanged in these platforms, companies can look at Web 2.0 tools like Wikis, Blogs, Social Networking sites and so forth, to check for some pieces of information that come in first hand to these communication tools (Berkman, 2008; Brown, 2012; Canhoto, 2013; Kotze, 2013). If we have enough patience, it will pay off the time spent in this activity because it will be possible to identify micro-trends that have not yet gained momentum (Sage, 2013). Companies can use this information, from these social tools, for competitor surveillance, consumer satisfaction monitoring, trend development and technology watch. There are not, yet, many bibliographic resources dealing with this subject, because it's still a new medium that needs to be proved and tested, that is being currently used to perform competitive strategies so companies can excel in their areas of business (Berthon, Pitt, Plangger, & Shapiro, 2012).

Learning how to extract quality information, unbiased, valuable for business, from these social tools is the aim of this work, sharing with the interested parties some ways of using it for their profit and competitive sustainability. If properly done, this monitoring activity even allows a company to measure the level of satisfaction of its own employees by the analysis of the content of what they post online about their employer (Ojala, 2012). That gives you clues about improvements and changes to be made.

We will start explaining the value of information for business management, and afterwards describing CI and Social Networking, identifying some tools that will ease monitoring requirements, and conclude with a few ideas for analyzing Blogs, Wikis and Tag Clouds to identify consumer signals and trends (Barbosa & O'Reilly, 2011; Canhoto, 2013; Higham, 2010; Kotze, 2013; Rasquilha, 2010; Scott, 2008).

We will survey the applications of Web 2.0 relative to CI and consumer trends, and explore approaches of gathering information for CI through Web 2.0. Some applications of Web 2.0 (Blog, Wiki, RSS and Tag Clouds) are discussed for CI and business intelligence use.

COMPETITIVE INTELLIGENCE FOR BUSINESS MANAGEMENT

CI is the use of public sources to develop information about the competition, consumers, and market environment (Miller & Business Intelligence Braintrust, 2002). CI is different from espionage (Bergier, 1970; Fialka, 1997; Guisnel, 1997; Rustmann Jr., 2002; Winkler, 1997), which implies illegal means of information gathering. CI is restrained to the gathering of public information (Kahaner, 1997; Mordecai, 2013c). One of the main differences between CI and general business information, such as business growth rate and operating ratios, is that CI is of strategic importance on the organization. It is not only the collection of information from a variety of sources, but also the analysis and synthesis of such information, which could help the company decide the course of action to improve its position (Choo, 2003).

Because of the broad reach and potential of CI, involvement in intelligence activities can provide first-class training for managers and marketers. In fact, an increasing number of leading companies insist that their best people spend some time in intelligence operations prior to promotion to the highest ranks (Miller & Business Intelligence Braintrust, 2002; Prescott & Miller, 2002; Taborda & Ferreira, 2002).

Intelligence must be passed to decision makers in a timely manner, and in a style and format that will encourage them to take appropriate measures and decisions. Intelligence reports and briefings should aim, above all, for clarity and brevity, and should provide the decision maker with suggestions or recommendations for action

(Besson & Possin, 1996; Choo, 2003; Garber, 2001; Martinet & Marti, 1995). Executives have a major part to play in ensuring the success of your intelligence activities. Among other things, they must offer commitment, involvement, and support (Johnson, 2005; Prescott & Miller, 2002). Managers have a part to play in making intelligence activities successful because they already spend lots of time talking with others and that enables them to collect information. However, it is essential that they keep their intelligence manager informed of any significant change in the business environment (Miller & Business Intelligence Braintrust, 2002; Prescott & Miller, 2002).

A typical CI process consists of a series of business activities that involve identifying, gathering, developing, analyzing and disseminating information (Besson & Possin, 1996; Martinet & Marti, 1995; Taborda & Ferreira, 2002).

Every competitor broadcasts a large amount of data to you in their advertising and their product itself. Every feature that they have in their products and every special technique that's part of their service is data you can use. (Mordecai, 2013c).

The following list shows a typical sequence in which these activities take place: i) identify competitors, markets, customers, suppliers, or other variables in the environment to be monitored. Identify what information is to be collected; ii) specifically identify possible sources of information and collect the information from these sources; iii) evaluate the validity, reliability, and usefulness of the information collected; iv) gather information collected from different sources and integrate them; v) interpret and analyze the information for strategic or tactical significance. Draw conclusions and recommend actions; vi) disseminate and present analyzed findings to management; vii) respond to ad hoc inquiries for decision support (Ribault, Martinet, & Lebidois, 1995). According to Goldman (2011), three tools deserve a visit to enlighten us about what our competitors are doing: AdGooroo (https://www.adgooroo.com/), SpyFu (http://www.spyfu.com/), and The Search Monitor (http://www.thesearchmonitor.com/). Information gathering and information analysis are the key areas of the CI process.

Competitive Intelligence and the Internet

The Internet is currently the most popular medium for gathering information and it has enormous advantages for that function (Russell, 2011; Tsvetovat & Kouznetsov, 2011). At the same time, it calls for a minimum level of expertise if it is to be effective. For instance, you need to be able to find specific information (Berkman, 2008), and that calls for familiarity with search engines and sophisticated retrieval techniques (Prior, 2006, 2007).

Nevertheless, "*search engines are severely lacking in the realm of exploratory search. (...) If you want to find new things with which you're unfamiliar, the online world has a market gap*" (Hawthorne & Cromity, 2012, p. 36). Social Media can reduce that gap (Safko, 2010).

With very few exceptions, standards for citing and classifying information are poor, unenforceable or non-existent, and there is a distinct absence of identifying information (metadata) (Chen, Chau, & Zeng, 2002). "*Content often lacks depth and substance, and it is almost impossible to distinguish between fact, editorial, advertising and news. But, many of these disadvantages will be overcome with time*" (Prior, 2007).

Commercial online databases, such as Dialog (http://www.dialog.com) and Lexis-Nexis (http://www.lexisnexis.com), contain a large amount of well-organized information on a variety of subjects, storing information ranging from company annual reports to US patent documents, and from history journals to chemistry periodicals (Chen et al., 2002; Taborda & Ferreira, 2002). These commercial databases are among the major sources used by CI professionals (Herring, 2002). "*Recent years have seen the tremendous growth of the Internet. Many commercial online databases are now accessible through the Internet. The Internet also enables organizations to monitor and search the websites of their competitors, alliances, and possible collaborators*" (Chen et al., 2002). Internet-based information sources are becoming increasingly important in the CI process (Guisnel, 1997). "*In the old days, corporate intelligence gathering meant painstakingly gleaning information from experts and competitors' reports, subscribing to expensive online data aggregators such as Factiva or Dialog, and scanning unstructured documents from the media*" (Kotze, 2013).

Corporate Web sites usually contain useful information, including company history, corporate overviews, business visions and missions, product overviews, financial data, sales figures, annual reports, press releases, biographies of top executives, locations of offices, hiring ads, among others (Godeluck, 2000; Weiss, 2008). The data is "*valuable in providing direct or indirect contextual information and enable the CI professionals to analyze corporate strategies. Another reason attracting CI professionals to use the Internet is that most of the contents available on the Internet are free of charge*" (Chen et al., 2002). In fact, Internet is now one of the most important resources for CI information collection (Deng & Luo, 2007; Kirsch, Gregory, Brown, & Charley, 2006).

Corporate or employees Wikis and Blogs also contain a vast amount of useable information because everybody likes to tell in what they are working, what are they good at, the results that they were capable of reaching with their work, the goals and objectives they provided and so on (Turchi, 2012). As Kotze (2013) declares "*none of the employee's actions were 'leaks' and taken alone they are all innocuous. But taken together they may reveal more than the company wants. For the competitive intelligence professional at the competitor they are a vital stream of information*" (Kotze, 2013). Managers tend to think that more information is better. In today's business environment, however, it is not necessarily true. CI professionals could be spending too much time and effort on data collection rather than data analysis. For CI professionals to manually access the Internet, extract and analyse the information on every single Web page at a company Web site to locate the useful information, and to synthesize information is very exhausting and time consuming.

Fuld alerts that "tracking social media activity can provide many benefits", being five the main reasons to use social media for competitor insight: i) Identify key influencers; ii) Measure Marketing metrics; iii) Illuminate investment decisions; iv) Determine share of voice; v) Develop early warning indicators.

To address this information and cognitive overload problem, research has been conducted in developing techniques and tools to analyze, categorize, and visualize large collections of Web pages, among other text documents. (Chen et al., 2002).

In turn, a variety of tools have been developed to assist searching, gathering, monitoring and analyzing information on the Internet (Guisnel, 1997; Prescott & Miller, 2002; Revelli, 2000)[1].

SOCIAL MEDIA NETWORKING

Social Networks, made possible by Web 2.0, are one of several next generation communications and collaboration tools that include Blogs, Wikis and Social Bookmarking.

Participants worldwide contribute to and collaborate in readily available online discussions, creating new knowledge bases that can become recognized as information sources (Mayeh, 2012).

Kane declares that

Social Media technologies may be particularly disruptive for business because they undermine some of the key reasons why companies survive or thrive. (n.d.)

Web 2.0 technologies transform broadcast media monologues (one to many) into social media dialogues (many to many). Social media is the product of internet-based applications that build on the technological foundations of Web 2.0. (Berthon, Pitt, Plangger, & Shapiro, 2012, p. 263).

Social networks are free to join, to search for a vast amount of reference questions, and to find experts for all kinds of requirements and research projects (Qualman, 2010).

The concept of a social network, meaning a social structure made of nodes (which are generally individuals or organizations) that are tied by one or more specific types of interdependency, is as valuable as the number of nodes that constitute it (Castells, 2004; Tapscott & Williams, 2008). This means that, the bigger the number of nodes, the more valuable that network becomes (Godeluck, 2000). With this in mind, it's easy to perceive that this trend in modern communication and interaction among humans will be very important to achieve results that it will be very difficult with other non-interactive means (Tapscott, 1995, 1999; Tapscott et al., 2000; Tapscott & Williams, 2008).

The relation of confidence among each node will open a number of possibilities that a traditional media, like TV or Newspapers, couldn't impose simply because we don't know who those people are or, if we do, we know that they are trying to earn something at our expenses (Tapscott et al., 2000). With this new possibility, either we know the person communicating with us, or we know someone who knows him/her. That condition gives us the confidence and trust that will induce the preference on a certain product or service and makes us discard others. That's basic consumer behaviour (Scott, 2008). For companies, this new possibility can be the most important decision of all times. It will allow to transform our brand in a major player among the preferences of customers (Carrera, 2012b; Hortinha, 2002; Mohr et al., 2010). With Social Media companies can gain a better knowledge of their business environment, using visual tools that can enhance the analysis of the huge amount of posts, comments, and shares (Mordecai, 2013b). Also for employees, that can be a major source of information and knowledge, because we can now access the information we need among a network of thousands of specialists in a certain subject that can answer us almost immediately saving us precious time in the searching process (Libert & Spector, 2009; Surowiecki, 2007).

If someone thought that social networking was only for the youngsters, like with MySpace (http://www.myspace.com), or with Facebook (https://www.facebook.com), that is a huge mistake. Web 2.0 introduced many new types of applications for users to express their thoughts, concerns, needs, desires and level of satisfaction with what they buy (Berthon, Pitt, Plangger, & Shapiro, 2012; Hawthorne & Cromity, 2012; Shapiro, & Varian, 1999). This allows, in a very fast and inexpensive manner, to scan the trends of a market, understand consumer motivation and the actual preferences in the business area where companies act and compete (Rasquilha, 2010)[2]. New applications of Web 2.0 provide new opportunities for CI, such as Web Blogs (Blogs) which are created by thousands of individuals (Blood, 2004; Deng & Luo, 2007), Wikis (ex. Wikipedia) which allow public group creation, RSS (Rich Site

Summary or Really Simple Syndication) using XML (Extensible Markup Language) to classify and organize the information (Tsvetovat & Kouznetsov, 2011) making it more transparent and open (Carrera, 2012b; Hortinha, 2002; Scott, 2008).

All of them bring convenience for CI especially in collecting information. "In the view of CI, Web 2.0 paved new ways and channels for gathering information" (Deng & Luo, 2007).

All this tools, like Blogs and Wikis, provide intelligence for consumer trend monitoring (Barbosa & O'Reilly, 2011; Higham, 2010; Rasquilha, 2010; Sage, 2013).

In conjunction with existing consumer intelligence and CI resources, Social Networks can highlight significant issues that affect your brands, identify competitor weaknesses, opportunities in the marketplace and those specific to a brand (Qualman, 2010).

Monitoring Blogs and Podcasts can help develop actionable solutions to fuel organizations (Carrera, 2009, 2012a, 2012b; Hortinha, 2002).

When looking at Blogs and Wikis, we must also look at some of the networking sites, like LinkedIn.com, Xing.com, Facebook.com, Myspace.com, and search tools for people such as Zoominfo.com for company and competitor employees. Sites like these will mention what people are doing, their interests and past achievements. This information is very valuable because contacts can be found easily. "*Sites such as LinkedIn.com and Xing.com allow you to see where people used to work as well as where they are now. The networking sites can also be searched using tools such as yoname.com and wink.com*" (Weiss, 2008).

Also, creative consumers help companies developing new and better products by their feedback on using them and what to improve for better results (Berthon, Pitt, Plangger, & Shapiro, 2012). Although Social Media includes Blogs, Podcasts, Wikis and more, we will just explore some of them, and will demonstrate how monitoring and analyzing what consumers create on Blogs and Wikis can enrich our understanding of their needs and desires (Higham, 2010; Hortinha, 2002; Kotler et al., 1999; Rasquilha, 2010; Scott, 2008), and thus support our CI efforts.

Social Networking for Business Intelligence

Online Social Networking enables us to find people who may not be familiar with our organisation, becoming quality prospects and then effective clients, creating an opportunity to connect with them and sell them our products and services (Thiel, 2012). Social Networking offers a high level of integration, and focuses on the sharing elements of the various applications. Sharing resources can increase the possibility of finding relevant information, like sharing our favourite bookmarks or photos and in return having access to the favourite resources of others who share our interests.

It can mean being able to read comments and chat with people on topics of shared interest and being able to tap into collective knowledge (Russell, 2011)[3].

If we already know someone in that network, we can feel more comfortable that they can become quality prospects. And, because of that mutual connection, we can overcome difficulties and begin a business relationship with more trust (Bolander, 2015).

These "*new tools, based on social networking and deployed on mobile devices, are enabling companies to streamline operations, enhance customer satisfaction and improve financial performance across their entire businesses*" (Bedell, 2011), allowing to accurately perform a SWOT (Strengths, Weaknesses, Opportunities and Threats) analysis to scan the macro-environment where the company develops its activity (Mordecai, 2013a).

Some advantages are that you can contact people or companies in your network to: i) Regenerate old connections; ii) Maximise value in your weak connections; iii) Build business relationships with clients or hiring managers; iv) Find and meet prospective job seekers; v) Grow a referral network; vi) Enlarge your corporate and personal brand; vii) Make new connections and grow your sphere of influence; viii) Open doors to future career opportunities, increased salary or promotions; ix) Increase visibility, which improves influence and effectiveness internally with your organisation as well as externally; x) Educate yourself and ask questions about other organisations; xi) Conduct competitive intelligence on companies, industries or individuals; xii) Make fewer cold calls and better prepare for them; xiii) Leverage contacts you already have (Steckerl, 2007).

Although a major opportunity for business, companies with brands in the luxury market are failing to take advantage of these tools (Dickins, 2013). As some authors declare, "*better social searching tools will enable information professionals to find reliable sources for sentiment or common knowledge for word-of-mouth coverage*" (Hawthorne & Cromity, 2012, p. 36), what is already being performed by some companies that analyze attitudes, emotions, brand evangelism, and its sponsor correlation present in the Social Media conversation share (Focalytic, 2013).

Communities of Practice and Social Interactions

The advantage of Blogs is that they facilitate the growth of Social Networks into true communities of practice (Blood, 2004). Much of the value of these networks is in their advantage for the "*social capital required for effective decision support to grow based on relationships between analytically opinionated minds*" (Johnson, 2005).

This defies the control hierarchies that still define most businesses where top-down decision making is still the rule of the day (Scott, 2008). Here, the reputations of writers are built on the value of their ideas, their ability to convince others that their ideas are valid and therefore develop the most respect and authority (Curtis, 2006; Kassel, 2008; Miller, 2007).

Collaboration applications that build such communities of practice socialize critical business decisions in an open forum based on the social capital of merit.

Concerns with Networking Sites

"*There's a tension between the audience participation model of Web 2.0 and business need for confidentiality and verification*" (Miller, 2007). Some questions must be addressed like: i) If an employee is blogging, what are they saying about the firm? ii) In a world where Wikis or Social bookmarks and tags are popular research tools, who is responsible for the accuracy and quality of information? iii) If you create an online community, how will you moderate what should be an open and free forum? iv) If you let your employees access Facebook at work, how can you be sure that they will remain alert to whether it's a work or social conversation they're having? (Steckerl, 2007).

According to some authors (Miller, 2007; Steckerl, 2007), other issues that raise some questions are: i) Privacy - The more we share the more we are exposed. But, we will increase our benefit from the network with more exposure. This concept involves a little trust. For the network to be most useful to us there needs to be a little reciprocity. People very secretive about their privacy may not get great results from using these tools; ii) Barriers to entry - Getting started means investing time to put your information into the application. This can take a few minutes or a few hours, it depends on how much we want to disclose to the network. The more we share about us the easier it will be to make new connections. If we only upload a few contacts, we get little benefit since these systems only search for connections through people we already know; iii) Maintenance - If we have a large network we can get to a point where we are receiving lots of requests. We can turn off e-mails about our connections, and with some networks we can even change our settings to accept requests from specific levels. We may get requests from people we don't know or don't remember. We shouldn't add everyone because we are a reflection of our networks; iv) Cost - Many of these services may begin to charge membership fees.

Sage (2013) warns that the "*speed and volume of information that is published on social media can cause significant damage. (...)* ***A misleading comment*** *can damage a company's reputation in seconds*".

He also points out to the problem of hackers and cyber security because Social Media can be used by hackers to acquire "*personal information about employees, then use it to befriend them. Having built a relationship, the criminal may be able to deceive the employee into revealing how to access to their company's* ***systems, and so opening the door to cyber-attacks***" or Phishing.[4] Ojala warns that "*in minding* *our own business, we need to know what information about our employer can be gathered from social media* ***and whether it is what should be publicly available***" (2012, p. 53).[5]

The weakness in these new Social Networking sites is that "*if users do not trust the system to protect their relationships, then they will not use the application effectively and gain very little incremental advantage from their connections*" (Steckerl, 2007)[6].

In the end, the quality and value of this information will be dependent on the user and related to the results that it will allow obtaining, always integrated on its context.

SOCIAL TOOLS FOR BUSINESS

The high number of social tools indicates an enthusiastic acceptance of this new media by individuals and companies (Steckerl, 2007). Organisations cannot afford to ignore Social tools. If they don't know how they can use these tools, maybe they have already lost opportunities to faster competitors. For example, a business can help its staff save time searching if it encourages them to bookmark useful sites and share them with their co-workers. We must remember that participation drives traffic. "*Wikipedia is far more popular than Encarta, and Flikr is used more than Kodak Gallery. If you want people to use a tool, letting them contribute to it will engage their interest*" (Miller, 2007).

For individuals, the benefits of using social tools often feel obvious but difficult or even impossible to measure. But, for most organisations, therc's a need to demonstrate return on investment. "*Those responsible for proving value have a dilemma: on the one hand, hard targets such as page hits or number of posts are easier to collect but have relatively little meaning*" (Miller, 2007). On the other hand, measurements such as the ability of an organisation to innovate are hard to measure or directly attribute but are of fundamental importance to its financial health[7]. The idea that social tools are of interest to companies is unquestionable. As long as collaborators have basic Internet knowledge, the problem is the time needed to be actively involved. The more you use these new tools the more obvious the advantages become. To ignore these new tools is to ignore the unique benefits that they can offer (Zarrella, 2013).

Those companies who have opened their organisation to social tools had more positive results than they expected. The strategy is to treat your networked individuals as intelligent adults and minimize the need to be in control. Open and honest support is more constructive and usually works. However, we must stay involved and assume that the community can't grow without some time and attention (Curtis, 2006; Kassel, 2008; Steckerl, 2007).

SOME OF THE TOOLS AND HOW THEY OPERATE

For most of the services, the initial sign up is free. Users begin by filling out a form with personal data and then inviting friends. Some networks allow uploading current contacts, but others ask users to invite contacts directly through the application's interface. The connections then invite their own contacts, and that's how the network grows (Steckerl, 2007). There are several Social Networking sites. Most of the applications competing for your attention offer a combination of professional and personal networking. Some of them are seriously oriented to business. From the top 20 players, three of them stand out: i) LinkedIn.com (http://www.linkedin.com) - Profiles look very much like a CV, excellent mix of people from different levels in the organisation, and many industries (Schaffer, 2011). Used mostly as a business research tool without the noise and redundant information that occurs in other social media platforms (Ojala, 2012). The most concrete application of LinkedIn is developing a network of associates, an excellent way to stay connected with current and past friends and clients (Kawasaki, 2007). Search for: industry experts, potential employees, hiring managers, deal-makers, people from specific geographies, or people with particular keywords in their profiles; ii) Plaxo.com (http://www.plaxo.com) - Keeps all of your current contacts' information updated automatically thus is extremely useful in repair old relationships and staying in touch. Not a tool to build your network yet, though it does have a very useful 'mini Blog' feature to help you keep friends informed; iii) Spoke.com (http://spoke.com) - Focused on providing sales prospects. Deeply integrated, extracts contact data from enterprise applications (Outlook, Notes, etc.) to establish and leverage connections.

There are so many Social Networks that they are too numerous to list here. Most of them, like friendster.com, flickr.com, among hundreds of others tend to serve only social categories like dating, common interests, finding friends, photo sharing and others not directly related to business. Nevertheless, they might contain important information about their users like brands they wear, satisfaction, or not, with the products they own, special needs and interest in solve their problems with new technologies, products or services, among others (Mordecai, 2013a). Some web sites can also be networking sites, like MySpace.com, Windows Live Spaces, LiveJournal.com, and Blogger.com. Other networks with a decidedly business or professional purpose, are: Passado.com (http://passado.com), Europe's largest business network, now called Wasabi (http://www.wasabi.com/signup); Ryze.com (http://www.ryze.com/); Ecademy.com (http://www.sunzu.com/) – Became Sunzu in January 2013. They all focus in business networking.

Two other networks reflect some specialty in social networking: BiomedExperts (http://www.biomedexperts.com) - "*The first literature-based scientific social network - brings the right researchers together and allows them to collaborate online. Collexis provides the BiomedExperts social network free of charge to researchers worldwide in an effort to increase collaborative biomedical research for the common good*"; globalEDGE (http://globaledge.msu.edu/) - "*Sponsored and developed by the International Business Center at Michigan State University [...] connects users to prospective collaboration partners and industry experts.*"

Social Networks for Business Use

Social Networks are one source, among many others, to consider in everyday reference and research work. There are tools like SlideShare (http://www.slideshare.net) that makes possible to share slide presentations, and includes the text of the slides in a format called a transcript. We can use the search box to find relevant topics, watch the presentation slides at the SlideShare site, or download them for future use. Some require registration based on the poster's preference before downloading is permitted, and Vidipedia (http://www.vidipedia.org) which is a selection of a multimedia picture social networking. Similarly to Wikipedia, Vidipedia is a free encyclopaedia that anyone can edit, search for key terms or browse by category. The results are encyclopaedic answers that link to relevant videos. When only one result is available, the video is automatically launched and all videos can be downloaded. Running a search on a given term produces an extensive description with definitions and videos.

A great advantage of Social Networking is connecting anyone who needs with those who have direct experience with companies, products, or services and are experts in some field (Kassel, 2008). Businesses can use social tools to improve creativity, productivity, collaboration and visibility in certain markets, as well as engaging clients and partners in more fruitful collaboration (Berkman, 2008; Brown, 2012; Holloman, 2012).

There are a huge range of tools and sites (Russell, 2011; Tsvetovat & Kouznetsov, 2011), including: i) Wikis, ii) Blogs, iii) Mash-ups[8], iv) Social Tagging, v) Instant Messaging, vi) Video, vii) Social Bookmarking, viii) Podcasts, and ix) Services, like Facebook, Twitter, NetVibes, Flock and others (Miller, 2007).

There are practical examples of how geographically dispersed organisations could improve networking, knowledge sharing and collaboration using these tools (Tapscott & Williams, 2008).

The biggest benefit of such social tools for business is that this ongoing social contact with a colleague or client can mean that face-to-face meetings start with a deeper personal trust and understanding (Berkman, 2008; Brown, 2012; Zarrella, 2009).

If a person posts in his or her Social Networking community something like "*I'm walking my dog to the dog park and his leash just broke. It was brand new. I'm so frustrated*" (Leonard, 2013), we get to know several important things that can be used on the behalf of our company. This person has a need, the need to purchase a new leash for the dog. We also know that there is frustration with a new leash that just got broke leaving a bad evaluation and opinion about the manufacturer of that product. That person shows a real love and care for its animal friend so he must want the best for it. A dog needs food, toys, veterinarian care, among other things and we may know where that person lives, which dog park uses and the stores where he passes to reach the park[9].

For a company in the pet business this is great because we have a behavioural segmentation (Kotler et al., 1999; Scott, 2008) that allows contacting the owner with a full range of services and products adapted to the animal, the climate where it lives and other specific needs. Perhaps the dog breed, name and birth date of the animal are posted also in the network and the offers can be personalized to target the prospect with some empathy.

Leonard (2013) calls this "*the Anatomy of an Expression of Intent*" and this can be used in a large sort of situations like animals, children, jobs, marriages and other businesses if we pay attention and learn how to read between the lines.

Blogs

According to Blog search engine Technorati (http://www.technorati.com), more than 200 million Blogs are being written in the public cyberspace known as the Blogosphere, up from just 100,000 in late 2002. Technorati's '2013 Digital Influence Report' shows that "consumers are turning to blogs when looking to make a purchase. In fact, blogs rank favorably with consumers for trust, popularity and even influence" (Leonard, 2013).

The report states that blogs are now the third-most influential digital resource (31%) when making overall purchases, behind retail sites (56%) and brand sites (34%), making it a useful resource to watch for consumer behavior and needs.

Ojala states that "*blogs – or at least some blogs – gained the status of reputable sources for reporting and informed commentary. Curated blog content of interest to business researchers is part of online services such as ProQuest (in its Entrepreneurship product), LexisNexis, and Factiva.*" (2012, p.53).

Some Blogs with interest in CI like Traction (http://traction.tractionsoftware.com), MovableType (http://www.movabletype.org), and Manila (http://manila.userland.com) are used to streamline dissemination and collection[10] (Johnson, 2005). Now, enterprises in every industry are learning the power and risks of unleashing their employees' ideas on both their colleagues and the marketplace (Blood, 2004; Qualman, 2010). Blogs have also taken on a greater role in CI practice within the enterprise, alongside Blogs in product, R&D, information technology, legal and financial teams, sales and marketing and even executive management (Johnson, 2005). Today, blogging is helping to create real communities of practice within organizations large and small (Curtis, 2006).

To obtain information about "*which Blogs are reliable and worthy, the content aggregator and distributor Newstex (*http://newstex.com/*)*" (Ojala, 2012, p.53) is the right place to start.

Wikis

The Wiki is a new collaboration tool in the corporate environment and is gaining significance in organizational information sharing. Borrowed from the Hawaiian word for quick, the first Wiki was originally developed by Ward Cunningham in 1995. Today they take the form of dozens of software applications that have Wiki-like capabilities (Johnson, 2005). Like Blogs, Wikis allow for very easy publishing and commenting on topics of collective interest to the community. Its unique social dynamics, allowing all contributors to change anything on any or all of the documents available, subjects the entire community to consensus-building (Carrera, 2012b).

Many of these tools are open-source and available free of charge, such as OpenWiki, Kwiki and Twiki. The best example of a Wiki is the Wikipedia. It begun in 2001 to build a free, multi-lingual encyclopaedia of knowledge on every subject in the human knowledge (Johnson, 2005). It has now more than 4.000.000 individual articles and serves as the laboratory for what Wikis can ultimately become given time and attention in the enterprise (Libert & Spector, 2009; Qualman, 2010; Surowiecki, 2007).

Wikis are just like Blogs. With Wikis, the same social interaction happens, but much faster and with far more intense collaboration (Tapscott & Williams, 2008). "They are based on the notion that the best results come from allowing decision-making to emerge from the bottom up with minimal editorial control from the top down (Johnson, 2005).

Wikis are great tools because of their editing and contribution characteristics. Wikis are made of hypertext documents linked together and edited collectively by the community in a web browser interface (Qualman, 2010). It is a very open medium where all authors can add to, change, or delete other people's work. "*To prevent the damaging effects of creative destruction this can obviously lead to, Wikis have a means of comparing two states of a page, known as a diff, so that revisions can be viewed and rolled back and mistakes can be corrected*" (Johnson, 2005).

The only way anyone can write something that will survive is if it's written with such quality that even its opponents can agree that it has value (Carrera, 2009, 2012a; Tapscott & Williams, 2008).

In CI, focus must be on the analysis of options available and the arguments that make one course stand apart from its alternatives as superior. This ascertains the quality of the information retrieved, allowing for a sustainable business decision making in organisations.

RSS

The technology that made all this possible is RSS (Rich Site Summary or Real Simple Syndication). It is an XML specification for distributing published media files to a web address that can be read by a RSS feed reader[11].

RSS has become the modern example for what XML can do for the user. It is also the most widespread form of XML in use today. RSS could very well become the principal mean by which all data, structured or unstructured, is broadcasted and applied (Johnson, 2005). This includes applications such as change-detection in Weblogs, retrieving spam-free email, or passing transactional data through a complex workflow environment (Carrera, 2009, 2012a).

"In addition to receiving posts from news sites and other Weblogs, RSS feeds can contain data from corporate systems: sales information, financial data, inventory or vendor information, data from partner or distribution systems, competitor events, and all manner of real-time data relevant to the enterprise" (Johnson, 2005).

The challenge now is to disseminate examples where collaborative social community applications have an impact on competitive intelligence efficiency and/or effectiveness (Carrera, 2012b; Hortinha, 2002).

Tag Clouds

Analysis of Blogs, Wikis and Web pages is an excellent way to gain an understanding of the individuals who use those particular tools of Social Media, and thus put the information into context. Social Media search engines provide important data through Tag Clouds and through lists, such as the week's top ten tags and/or Blogs. Tags are words that content creators use to describe their works (http://en.wikipedia.org/wiki/Tag_cloud). In effect, they are keywords, guides that lead content users to the posts of content creators. Analyzing Tag Clouds, groups of tags within content, provides powerful insights into what Blog and other Social Media content creators and users are interested in (Curtis, 2006).

Tag Clouds can be used to build up a picture of the demographics of particular sites as a Wordle[12]. If we look at a Tag Cloud and we see a big number of technology-related words, such as: Ajax, Apple, CSS, Linux and Web 2.0, this helps us to analyze what type of consumer uses that site, segmenting them in psychographic means, and correlate it to the site's popular tags. To begin monitoring, we must match keywords with the tags created by active consumers. Content creators are active consumers that rely on tags to help other consumers find them. Tags connect content creators with the readers, and are an important tool for monitoring consumer trends.

Over time, the use of tags results in a folksonomy, "*a user-defined, keyword system in which tags are defined by users rather than by a provided vocabulary. Unfortunately, folksonomies often diverge from keywords that researchers might use*" (Curtis, 2006).

Tag Clouds provide an excellent way to identify the most popular trends and can be used in reverse. "*Rather than matching keywords you choose in advance, let them lead you to toward what seems popular*" (Curtis, 2006).

Squidoo (http://www.squidoo.com/browse/top_lenses) allows users to set up a web page where they control the content. Squidoo has a number of tags that will help you. Each web page (Squidoo calls them lenses) has the tags prominently displayed. In addition, the site has a number of tags compiled based on popularity, and category. After some examination we will have a better understanding of tags and consumer interests and needs disclosed in Social Media. By watching tags carefully, you can monitor and correlate product category, brands, uses, interests and needs. Tag Clouds will show consumer interests integrated in the social media space (Kassel, 2008; Miller, 2007; Steckerl, 2007).

This way, consumer trends can be revealed.

CONCLUSION

In the globalized world quality information warrants best results when competing with other organizations, enabling a competitive advantage.

After describing what CI is and what is it good for, we have mentioned the advantages of being involved in CI projects. How to receive information for competitive decisions and the benefits of continually scan the business environment are some issues also analysed.

We have described several web tools available for information retrieval purposes and some features of each one, after showing the relations and benefits of the Internet for CI.

Social Networking is getting involved and getting your brand name being discussed every time you can. With the Internet we have the ability to reach more people and make more money in a highly personalized manner, knowing their needs and desires and the trends that are getting more attention (Kassel, 2008; Miller, 2007). Nevertheless, Ethics and good practice still play a major part.

Companies look at Social Media as a way of attracting and retaining customers (Brown, 2012; Ojala, 2012; Schaffer, 2011; Zarrella, 2009, 2013) but are not taking benefit (Dickins, 2013) of its major advantage in obtaining feedback from the market and be aware of competitors moves and market trends discussed by the clients (Berkman, 2008; Holloman, 2012). Customer and employee satisfaction is another invaluable information scanning that social tools allow to perform (Hawthorne & Cromity, 2012; Ojala, 2012; Sage, 2013).

Being connected is an incredible leverage, invaluable in your business development (Steckerl, 2007). Connections can have many unexpected positive results (Carrera, 2009; Kawasaki, 2007). Also, creative consumers help companies developing new and better products by their feedback on using them and what to improve for better results (Berthon, Pitt, Plangger, & Shapiro, 2012). We've concluded with a short description of some of the social network tools that can be adopted to gain current awareness about all the unexpected events in the macro environment of the companies, allowing the anticipation of what's going on with trends among specific market segments (Higham, 2010; Sage, 2013).

Web 2.0 tools are impacting the definition, collection and dissemination of CI but there is still much more untapped potential (Canhoto, 2013; Ojala, 2012). CI professionals must redefine their roles in terms of strategic analysis (Kotze, 2013). Regardless of whether you show enthusiasm or scepticism in the face of these new Internet collaborative and communication tools, there is no excuse to be uninformed. Consumers have always wanted to be heard, have always wanted their desires to be taken into account in the creation of new products and services. Consumer trends begin life through a series of small or big signals (Rasquilha, 2010). Through monitoring and analyzing the Social Media space, information professionals can provide a valuable analysis within consumer trend monitoring, knowing the consumer's interests and needs directly from the consumer posts and commentaries (Curtis, 2006), building the adequate solution to those clients' problems[13]. Like much of the web, corporate Blogs of Social Network web sites can be a good place to keep track of what the company is exploring for future products and services (Ojala, 2012). Blogs also provide excellent flags in response to consumer needs (Blood, 2004; Carrera, 2012a; Hortinha, 2002). BlogPulse point us toward the direction of trends we might otherwise let go (Curtis, 2006)[14].

In a fast moving business world, like the one we are living in, it should be a competitive edge having the chance of monitoring the market trends, the competition moves and still improve internal communication to flat the channels and downsize the hierarchy inside companies.

We must watch closely what the competitor employees are posting online and also keep an eye on what our employees are posting and check if they are, unconsciously, giving away valuable information to the competitors. We are not the only ones looking at the competition; they are doing the same thing with us and our company. Be aware.

Sage (2013) explains that social intelligence is better than traditional market research because it provides answers that companies consider critical to business strategy. Only future research will tell if this is effectively true and the real value obtained by companies that perform this task accurately. It's our expectation to contribute to take this relevant subject further in ulterior research to disseminate all the advantages in adopting Web 2.0 tools in companies. Let's hope CEO's learn how to leverage all this advantages and know how to make a good use for them all.

REFERENCES

Barbosa, P., & O'Reilly, A. (2011). *Harvard Trends: Tendências de Gestão*. Porto: Vida Económica.

Bedell, D. (2011, March). Business Intelligence. *Global Finance,* 46-47.

Bergier, J. (1970). *A Espionagem Industrial*. Porto: Editorial Inova.

Berkman, R. (2008). *The Art of Strategic Listening: Finding Market Intelligence in Blogs and Social Media*. Paramount Market Pub.

Berthon, P., Pitt, L., Plangger, K., & Shapiro, D. (2012). Marketing meets Web 2.0, social media, and creative consumers: Implications for international marketing strategy. *Business Horizons*, *55*(3), 261–271. doi:10.1016/j.bushor.2012.01.007

Besson, B., & Possin, J. (1996). *Do serviço de informação à inteligência económica: detectar as ameaças e oportunidades da empresa*. Instituto Piaget.

Best, D. (1996a). Business Process and Information Management. In D. Best (Ed.), *The Fourth Resource: Information and its Management*. Hampshire, UK: Aslib/Gower.

Best, D. (1996b). *The Fourth Resource: Information and its Management*. Hampshire, UK: Aslib/Gower.

Beuren, I. M. (1998). *Gerenciamento da informação: um recurso estratégico no processo de gestão empresarial*. São Paulo: Atlas.

Blood, R. (2004). *O Livro de Bolso do Weblogue: Conselhos Práticos para Criar e Manter o seu blogue* (1st ed.). Porto: Campo das Letras.

Bolander. (2015). Social networks sales organizations: their development and importance for salesperson performance. *Journal of Marketing: A Quarterly Publication of the American Marketing Association,79*(6), 1-16.

Bramston, D. (2009). *Basics Product Design: Idea Searching* (1st ed.). Lausanne: Ava Publishing.

Brophy, P., & Coulling, K. (1996). *Quality Management for Information and Library Managers*. Guildford: Aslib/Gower.

Brown, E. (2012). *Working the Crowd: Social Media Marketing for Business* (2nd ed.). British Informatics Society.

Brown, J., & Duguid, P. (2000). *The Social Life of Information* (1st ed.). Boston: Harvard Business School Press.

Burgelman, R., Christensen, C., & Wheelwright, S. (2009). *Strategic Management of Technology and Innovation* (5th ed.). Singapore: McGraw-Hill.

Canhoto, A. (2013). *Social media as a source of competitive intelligence*. Retrieved 28-02-2013, from http://anacanhoto.com/2013/01/18/social-media-as-a-source-of-competitive-intelligence/

Carrera, F. (2009). *Networking: Guia de Sobrevivência Profissional* (1st ed.). Lisboa: Sílabo.

Carrera, F. (2012a). *Comunicar 2.0: a Arte de bem Comunicar no Século XXI* (1st ed.). Lisboa: Sílabo.

Carrera, F. (2012b). *Marketing Digital na Versão 2.0: o que não pode ignorar* (2nd ed.). Lisboa: Sílabo.

Castells, M. (2000). *The Information Age: The Rise of the Network Society* (2nd ed.). London: Blackwell.

Castells, M. (2004). *A Galáxia Internet: Reflexões sobre Internet, Negócios e Sociedade*. Lisboa: Fundação Calouste Gulbenkian.

Chen, H., Chau, M., & Zeng, D. (2002). CI Spider: A tool for competitive intelligence on the Web. *Decision Support Systems*, *34*(1), 1–17. doi:10.1016/S0167-9236(02)00002-7

Choo, C. W. (2003). *Gestão de informação para a organização inteligente: a arte de explorar o meio ambiente*. Lisboa: Editorial Caminho.

Christensen, C., Anthony, S., & Roth, E. (2004). *Seeing What's Next: Using the Theories of Innovation to Predict Industry Change*. Harvard Business School Press.

Curtis, P. (2006). *Gleaning consumer intelligence from blogs and podcasts*. Retrieved 02-12-2012, from http://www.freepint.com/issues/040506.htm#tips

Davenport, T. (1997). *Information Ecology: Mastering the Information and Knowledge Environment*. New York: Oxford University Press.

Davenport, T., Marchand, D., & Dickson, T. (2004). *Dominando a gestão da informação*. Porto Alegre: Bookmann.

Deng, Z., & Luo, L. (2007). An Exploratory Discuss of New Ways for Competitive Intelligence on WEB 2.0. In Integration and Innovation Orient to E-Society (pp. 597-604). Boston: Springer.

Dickins, J. (2013). Social media is an underused opportunity for luxury brands. *Digital Marketing Hub: The Guardian*. Retrieved 14-06-2013, from http://www.guardian.co.uk/media-network/media-network-blog/2013/jun/14/social-media-opportunity-luxury-brands

Fialka, J. (1997). *War by other means: Economic espionage in America* (1st ed.). Norton.

Focalytic. (2013). Social Media Content Analysis of the 2013 Masters Golf Tournament. *Focal Point*. Retrieved 16-06-2013, from http://www.focalytic.com/Portals/182440/docs/themastersgolfebook.pdf

Garber, R. (2001). Inteligência competitiva de mercado: como capturar, armazenar, analisar informações de marketing e tomar decisões num mercado competitivo. São Paulo: Madras.

Godeluck, S. (2000). *A Explosão da Economia na Internet*. Lisboa: Livros do Brasil.

Goldman, A. (2011). *Tudo que sei sobre Marketing aprendi com o Google*. S. Paulo: Saraiva.

Gomes, E., & Braga, F. (2001). *Inteligência competitiva: como transformar informação em um negócio lucrativo*. Rio de Janeiro: Campus.

Guisnel, J. (1997). *Espionagem na Internet: As Guerras no Ciberespaço*. Lisboa: Difusão Cultural.

Guynn, J. (2013). Facebook releases information on NSA requests for user data. *Los Angeles Times*. Retrieved 14-06-2013, from http://www.latimes.com/business/technology/la-fi-tn-facebook-releases-first-information-on-fisa-requests-20130614,0,3315731.story

Hawthorne, K., & Cromity, J. (2012, March). Social Search for Market Intelligence. *Online: Exploring Technology & Resources for Information Professionals,* 36-38.

Herring, J. P. (2002). Tópicos fundamentais de inteligência: processo para identificação e definição de necessidades de inteligência. In Prescott & Miller (Eds.), Inteligência competitiva na prática. Rio de Janeiro: Campus.

Higham, W. (2010). The Next Big Thing: Spotting and Forecasting Consumer Trends for Profit (1ª ed.). Bodmin: Kogan Page.

Holloman, C. (2012). *The Social Media MBA: Your Competitive Edge in Social Media Strategy Development and Delivery* (1st ed.). John Wiley & Sons.

Hortinha, J. (2002). *X-Marketing* (1st ed.). Lisboa: Sílabo.

Johnson, A. (2005). Blogs, Wikis & RSS: Colaborative social communities and the value of distributed CI. *Competitive Intelligence Magazine*. Retrieved 10-02-2013, from http://www.aurorawdc.com/blogswikisrss_scipcimag_20050102.pdf

Kahaner, L. (1997). *Competitive Intelligence: How to gather, analyze, and use information to move your business to the top* (1st ed.). New York: Simon & Schuster.

Kane, G. C. (n.d.). *Why Social Media Will Fundamentally Change Business*. Retrieved from https://sloanreview.mit.edu/article/why-social-media-will-fundamentally-change-business/

Kassel, A. (2008). *Social Networking: A Research Tool*. Retrieved 15/12/2012, from http://web.fumsi.com/go/article/find/3196

Kawasaki, G. (2007). *Ten Ways to Use LinkedIn*. Retrieved 05-01-2007, from http://blog.guykawasaki.com

Kirsch, Brown, & Charley. (2006). Using Patents in Competitive Intelligence. *Competitive Intelligence Magazine*, *9*(1), 17–21.

Kotler, P., Armstrong, G., Saunders, J., & Wong, V. (1999). *Principles of Marketing* (2nd ed.). Cambridge, UK: Prentice Hall.

Kotze, L. (2013). *Social media increasingly important in competitive intelligence*. Retrieved 08-03-2013, from http://www.ibis.co.za/Competitive-Intelligence-Blog/social-media-increasingly-important-in-competitive-intelligence.html

Leonard, H. (2013). *Blogs Outrank Social Networks In Influence*. Retrieved 09-03-2013, from http://www.businessinsider.com/blog-influence-outranks-social-networks-2013-3

Libert, B., & Spector, J. (2009). *Muitas Cabeças Pensam Melhor: Como mobilizar o poder das multidões para o seu negócio* (1st ed.). Porto: Lua de Papel.

Marchand, D., & Horton, F. Jr. (1986). *Infotrends: Profiting from your Information Resources*. John Wiley & Sons.

Martinet, B., & Marti, Y. (1995). *A Inteligência Económica: os olhos e os ouvidos da empresa*. Instituto Piaget.

Mayeh, M. (2012, December). *Understanding the Role of Social Media Monitoring in Generating External Intelligence*. Retrieved from https://dro.deakin.edu.au/eserv/DU:30049105/scheepers-understandingtherole-2012.pdf

McGee, J. V., & Prusak, L. (1995). *Gerenciamento estratégico da informação: aumente a competitividade e a eficiência de sua empresa utilizando a informação como uma ferramenta estratégica*. Rio de Janeiro: Campus.

Miller, A. (2007). *Social Tools for Business Use: Messages from a Web 2.0 Conference*. Retrieved from http://web.fumsi.com/go/article/find/3916

Miller, J. (2002). *O milênio da inteligência competitiva*. Porto Alegre. *The Bookman*.

Mohr, J., Sengupta, S., & Slater, S. (2010). *Marketing of High-Technology Products and Innovations* (3rd ed.). Pearson.

Mordecai, V. (2013a). 4 Things Social Media Analysis Can Tell You About Your Business. *Focal Point: Focalytic*. Retrieved 23-05-2013, from http://www.focalytic.com/focal-point/bid/291330/4-Things-Social-Media-Analysis-Can-Tell-You-About-Your-Business

Mordecai, V. (2013b). What Businesses Can Gain from a Custom Social Media Listening Tool. *Focal Point: Focalytic*. Retrieved 20-05-2013, from http://www.focalytic.com/focal-point/bid/291331/What-Businesses-Can-Gain-from-a-Custom-Social-Media-Listening-Tool

Mordecai, V. (2013c). What Is Competitive Intelligence? *Focal Point: Focalytic*. Retrieved 14-06-2013, from http://www.focalytic.com/focal-point/bid/297577/What-Is-Competitive-Intelligence

Negroponte, N. (1995). *Being Digital*. New York: Knopf.

Ojala, M. (2012, July). Minding Your Own Business: Social Media Invades Business Research. *Online: Exploring Technology & Resources for Information Professionals,* 51-53.

Orna, E. (1999). *Practical Information Policies* (2nd ed.). Cambridge, UK: Gower.

Penzias, A. (1989). *Ideas and Information: Managing in a High-Tech World*. New York: W. W. Norton.

Penzias, A. (1995). *Harmony: Business, Technology & Life After Paperwork*. Harper Collins.

Porter, M. E., & Millar, V. E. (1985). How information gives you competitive advantage. *Harvard Business Review, 63*(4), 149–160.

Prescott, J. E., & Miller, S. H. (2002). *Inteligência competitiva na prática: técnicas e práticas bem sucedidas para conquistar mercados*. Rio de Janeiro: Campus.

Prior, V. (2006). *Competitive Intelligence: An Introduction*. Retrieved 06-10-2008 from http://www.freepint.com/issues/050106.htm#feature

Prior, V. (2007). *DIY Detection: Competitive Intelligence for SMEs*. Retrieved from http://web.freepint.com/go/features/2483

Qualman, E. (2010). *Socialnomics: Como os media sociais estão a transformar o modo como vivemos e como fazemos negócios* (1st ed.). Lisboa: Presença.

Rasquilha, L. (2010). *Tendências e Gestão da Inovação: como aplicar as tendências na estratégia de inovação empresarial*. Lousã: Verlag Dashöfer.

Redman, T. (1996). *Data Quality for the Information Age*. Norwood: Artech House.

Revelli, C. (2000). *Inteligência estratégica na Internet: como desenvolver eficazmente actividades de monitorização e de pesquisa nas redes*. Instituto Piaget.

Ribault, J.-M., Martinet, B., & Lebidois, D. (1995). *A Gestão das Tecnologias* (1st ed.). Lisboa: D. Quixote.

Russell, M. (2011). *Mining the Social Web: Analyzing Data from Facebook, Twitter, LinkedIn, and Other Social Media Sites* (1st ed.). O'Reilly Media.

Rustmann, F., Jr. (2002). CIA, Inc.: Espionage and the Craft of Business Intelligence (1ª ed.). Dulles: Brassey's.

Safko, L. (2010). *The Social Media Bible: Tactics, Tools & Strategies for Business Success* (2nd ed.). Hoboken, NJ: John Wiley & Sons.

Sage, N. (2013). *How to create business value from social intelligence*. Retrieved 30-05-2013, from http://www.computerweekly.com/opinion/How-to-create-business-value-from-social-intelligence

Schaffer, N. (2011). *Maximizing LinkedIn for Sales and Social Media Marketing: An Unofficial, Practical Guide to Selling & Developing B2B Business on LinkedIn*. CreateSpace Independent Publishing Platform.

Scott, D. (2008). *As Novas Regras de Marketing e Relações Públicas: Como usar os blogues, o podcasting, os media online e as notas informativas para chegar directamente aos consumidores*. Porto: Ideias de Ler.

Shapiro, C., & Varian, H. (1999). *Information Rules: A Strategic Guide to the Network Economy* (1st ed.). Boston: Harvard Business School Press.

Steckerl, S. (2007). *Survival Guide: Online Social Networking*. Retrieved 12/12/2012, from http://web.fumsi.com/go/article/use/2346

Surowiecki, J. (2007). *A Sabedoria das Multidões: Como a inteligência colectiva transforma a economia e a sociedade* (1st ed.). Porto: Lua de Papel.

Taborda, J. P., & Ferreira, M. D. (2002). *Competitive intelligence: conceitos, práticas e benefícios*. Pergaminho.

Tapscott, D. (1995). *The Digital Economy: Promise and Peril in the Age of Networked Intelligence*. New York: McGraw-Hill.

Tapscott, D. (1999). *Creating Value in the Network Economy*. Boston: Harvard Business School Press.

Tapscott, D., Ticoll, D., & Lowy, A. (2000). *Digital Capital: Harnessing the Power of Business Webs*. Boston: Harvard Business School Press.

Tapscott, D., & Williams, A. (2008). Wikinomics: A Nova Economia das Multidões Inteligentes (1ª ed.). Matosinhos: Quidnovi.

Thiel, K. (2012). *Creating Usable Customer Intelligence from Social Media Data: Network Analytics meets Text Mining*. Retrieved from http://www.knime.org/files/knime_social_media_white_paper.pdf

Trott, P. (2008). *Innovation Management and New Product Development* (4th ed.). Essex, UK: Prentice Hall | Financial Times.

Tsvetovat, M., & Kouznetsov, A. (2011). *Social Network Analysis for Startups: Finding connections on the social web* (1st ed.). O'Reilly Media.

Turchi, S. (2012). Estratégias de Marketing Digital e E-Commerce. S. Paulo: Atlas.

Ward, J., & Peppard, J. (2002). *Strategic Planning for Information Systems* (3rd ed.). Chichester, UK: John Wiley & Sons.

Webster, F. (2000). *Theories of the Information Society*. Cornwall, UK: Routledge.

Weiss, A. (2008). *If They Only Knew: Finding Competitive Intelligence from the Web Sites of Your Competitors*. Retrieved 21/01/2013, from http://web.fumsi.com/go/article/find/3355

Wilson, T. (1985). Information Management. *The Electronic Library*, *3*(1), 62–66. doi:10.1108/eb044644 PMID:2498741

Wilson, T. (1987). Information for business. The business of information. *Aslib Proceedings*, *39*(10), 275–279. doi:10.1108/eb051066

Winkler, I. (1997). *Corporate Espionage: What it is, why it's happening in your company, what you must do about it.* Prima Publishing.

Wormell, I. (1990). *Information Quality: Definitions and Dimensions*. London: Taylor Graham.

Zarrella, D. (2009). *The Social Media Marketing Book* (1st ed.). O'Reilly Media.

Zarrella, D. (2013). *The Science of Marketing: When to Tweet, What to Post, How to Blog, and Other Proven Strategies*. John Wiley & Sons.

ENDNOTES

1 For a list of CI software, Cf. (http://www.thecisource.com/resources/software). For a list of tools and how to use them for Social Media monitoring and competitor awareness, Cf. (http://www.business.com/social-media-marketing/people-are-talking-are-you-listening-the-importance-of-social-media-monitoring/), plus (http://www.socialmediaexaminer.com/how-to-perform-a-detailed-analysis-of-your-social-media-competitors/?awt_l=4Yt0yp&awt_m=3ggscWx3BAr.ILT&utm_source=Newsletter&utm_medium=NewsletterIssue&utm_campaign=New), and (https://www.brandwatch.com/2015/02/marketing-understanding-social-media-intelligence-stack/#.VO4M5IP-tlI.twitter).

2 Cf., also, (http://trendwatching.com/).

3 Cf. Flock (http://www.flock.com/) and StumbleUpon (http://www.stumbleupon.com/).

4 In **Bold** in the original text.

5 In **Bold** and *Italic* in the original text.

6 Facebook releases information on NSA requests for user data (Guynn, 2013).

7 For information in Marketing metrics and analytics, Cf. (http://blog.eloqua.com/marketing-analytics/?utm_source=feedburner&utm_medium=email&utm_campaign=Feed%3A+ItsAllAboutRevenue+%28It%27s+All+About+Revenue%29). For calculating Return on Investment, Cf. (http://businesscenter.eloqua.com/roi-calculator/).

8 For good examples of Mash-ups, Cf. (Tapscott & Williams, 2008).

9 "Julie Doe posts (…): "I love this particular brand of soda, though I really wish they had a diet option!" Social media analysis can then add this (…) to the group of opportunities that your business can pursue" (Mordecai, 2013a).

10 See, for example: IceRocket (http://www.icerocket.com), Technorati (http://www.technorati.com), Google (http://blogsearch.google.com/blogsearch), NM Incite (http://nmincite.com), Blogger (Google-owned) (http://www.blogger.com/start), Bloglines (http://www.Bloglines.com), Feedster (http://www.feedster.com), del.icio.us (http://del.icio.us/), and Podcast Alley (http://www.podcastalley.com).

11 For a list of several news readers for Mac and Windows, Cf. RSS Info (http://blogspace.com/rss/readers) . You can subscribe to an RSS feed for each individual term, simplifying your monitoring.

12 "Wordle is a toy for generating 'word clouds' from text that you provide. The clouds give greater prominence to words that appear more frequently in the source text. You can tweak your clouds with different fonts, layouts, and color schemes. The images you create with Wordle are yours to use however you like. You can print them out, or save them to the Wordle gallery to share with your friends". Retrieved 03-11-2008 from (http://www.dailyack.com/2008/06/worlde.html).

13 Retrieved 02-11-2012 from http://www.buzzlogic.com/press/news.html?postdate=1225203064 now Twelvefold Media (http://www.twelvefold.com/splash/?postdate=1225203064).

14 Cf. (http://blog.blogpulse.com/).

Chapter 2
Strengthening the Significance of Data Analytics:
Championing Organizational Design

Mambo Governor Mupepi
Grand Valley State University, USA

Patience Taruwinga
Walla Walla University, USA

ABSTRACT

Organizational design could be understood as a metaphor to appreciate customer needs through segmentation or cross-channel analysis and extrapolation in pervasive value creation environment. Corporations need to calculate moves based on available capacity to produce the products demanded in highly competitive markets. The workforce must possess the required skillsets and brashness critical in getting the job done correctly all the time. The knowledge drawn from data analytics can be applied to develop performance metrics essential in advancing productivity in ubiquitous value making systems. This chapter explores strengthening the significance of data analytics.

DOI: 10.4018/978-1-5225-7390-6.ch002

INTRODUCTION

In Wang and Strong (1996) data analysis is preceded by ensuring that the data is fit for use. They developed a data-quality dimension that is applicable in ensuring that the information deduced is of a high quality and fit for intended use (see Table 1)

Wang and Strong argue that the thrust of second-generation data systems is to consistently identify and prevent the most important root causes of future errors. This require both proper techniques and management infrastructure. Quality data analysis is critical in successful decision-making in highly competitive business environment. Quality analysis begins with the data collection instruments and software employed to analyze the data. Companies could be drowning in data from production, sales or outsourcing contracts, they need to master how to extract and analyze it to make cutting-edge organizational design of the business. Analytics are important in articulating a 360 degree evaluation of how the organization is doing, and what can be done to increase productivity.

BACKGROUND INFORMATION

Organizational Analytics

Organizational analytics refers to the skills, technologies, practices for continuous iterative exploration and investigation of past business performance to gain insight and drive organizational change. Organizational analytics focus on developing new insights and understanding of business performance based on data and statistical methods. The technique is important in pinpointing at the change needed to advance efficiency and effectiveness in successful enterprises (Mupepi, 2017). In contrast, business intelligence traditionally focuses on using a consistent set of metrics to both measure past performance and guide business planning, which is also based on data and statistical methods (Davenport, 2006).

Table 1. Fitness for use

Free of Defects	Process Desired Features
Accessible	Relevant
Accurate	Comprehensive
Current	Proper level of detail
Consistent with other sources	Easy to read
Etc.	Easy to interpret

In Watkins Mohr and Kelly (2011), organizational analytics is viewed as a technique that applies extensive use of statistical analysis, including explanatory and predictive modeling and fact-based management to drive organizational design. It is therefore closely related to management science. Analytics may be used as input for human decisions or may drive fully automated decisions. Business intelligence is querying, reporting, online analytical processing (OLAP), and "alerts."(Saxena and Srinavasan 2012).

Knowledge From Information

A database management system (DBMS) is a computerized system for creating and maintaining databases. Useful databases are those that can be browbeaten to increase output in many ways. A database can constitute the organization's intellectual assets and interpreted in many ways such as the capability to take new orders and expand business operations (see Figure 1). A minimal DBMS performs the following functions: Defines a database, stores and accesses data, retrieves and displays or prints data in response to a request, maintains data in the database (inserts, modifies or deletes and maintains the integrity of the stored data according to its defined structure.

Creating Exploitable Database

Firms in competitive markets benchmark each other in an attempt to price their goods and services competitively. In Juran (1999), exploitable databases are useful in benchmarking performance. A benchmarking study should not be restricted to one industry when organization in a different industry is achieving superior results in a similar function. This source of best practices is where the large process gains are possible. The search of best practices is where the large process gains are possible. The search here is not restricted to a common application, but to a method or practice within a process that can be adopted and adopted to a specific process. For example, a low-cost airline in southwest Texas undertook a project to maximize its revenue by benchmarking the time a plane spends on the ground. After all, revenues are generated only when the plane is in the air. The project was to determine how ground crews could safely clean and service the aircraft, refuel it, change tires, and provide food service in the most efficient manner to minimize ground time. The benchmarking team decided to meet with individuals who have perfected such techniques…race pit crews at the Indianapolis Speedway. Racing professionals certainly are experts at these very practices because they are faced with the same issues, and have developed an expertise in rapid service. They develop the capacity necessary to win all the time by focusing on knowledge skills technology and the brashness to effectively win all the time (see Figure 1).

The Sociotechnical Systems Design (STSD)

Sociotechnical systems pervade the value creation structures in knowledge-intensive organization. A divided labor consisting of specified specialist areas (see Figure 2). Within the divided areas learning never stops for many reasons. One of them is that customers keep placing orders with variations from the last one. Job specifications dictate the skills knowledge and technology attributes required to meet the orders of the customers. Another reason is that technology continues to change all the time. These changes characterize the dynamism in STSD. In STSD learning is a continuous improvement effort. The STSD conceptual model provides a description of perceived reality particularly that of a knowledge community. It gives a systemic content of knowledge, technology, and skills and how they can be framed to champion organization. The disposition to effectively do the job in ubiquitous value creation systems makes the difference in organization. Trist and Bamforth (1951) coined the phrase sociotechnical systems design to imply organizational design that enables a business to adapt in an environment where there is uncertainty. The STSD term also refers to complex organizational work design that recognizes the interaction between people and technology in the workplace.

Figure 1.

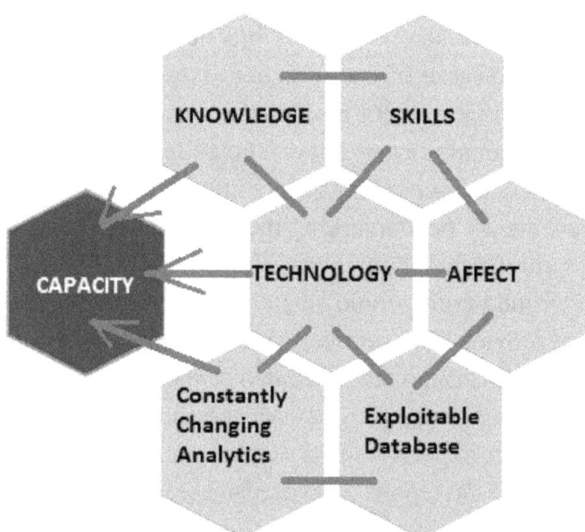

In later research Carvalho (2006) suggested that the STSD approach could be applied to design meaningful tasks and autonomous work teams. In Mupepi (2017) the STSD approach is viewed as a tool useful in perfecting process improvement. It can be applied to assess and evaluate the skills and practices required at every stage within the process. Such information is used to perfect specialization within the pervasive value creation systems. There are a myriad configurations of technology, skills and talent in structures designed to produce the goods demanded by the consumers. For example a corporation is characterized by talented individuals possessing the disposition to effectively do the job. In Mupepi (2017) the STSD perspective is perceived as an opportunity to enhance effectiveness and minimize risk in successful enterprises. Proprietary information in high performance organization is understood in terms of product specifications and job descriptions and the role they play in knowledge sharing, and making the items demanded by consumers. Mupepi (2017) places emphasis on the need to appreciate proprietary information how it is accessed and consumed in the value creation system and as a precondition to minimizing risk. The protection of what gives a company the advantage should be protected to warrant technology exclusiveness and minimize risk. The STSD approach can enable the analysis of knowledge and its application in the value system to allow managers to build physical and virtual protection walls.

A system is viewed as a whole whose elements hang together because they continuously affect each other over time and operate toward a common purpose. In Stichweh (2010), systems theory is defined as an interdisciplinary study of systems in general, with the goal of discovering patterns and algorithms necessary in maintaining the value creation system to produce the goods and services demanded by the customers. Stichweh elucidates the definition of systems theory as an understanding related to the General System Theory of biologist Ludwig von Bertalanffy (Bertalanffy, 1934), physiologists Walter B. Cannon, Walter Pitts, Warren McCulloch and cybernetics technologists Claude Shannon, Norbert Wiener, and William Ross Ashby. In much later studies Parsons (1977), developed a social action theory after interpretation of the work of Max Weber Emile Durkheim and Vilfredo Pareto. Parsons viewed cultural values and social structures that constrain choices and ultimately determine all social action. Building on the work Parsons (1977), Button (2006) considered that realistic structures could only occur if the system of the object instantiate a position within the structure. Two or more groups could validate the existence of a system. In computer programming instantiation is the creation of a real instance or particular realization of an abstraction or template such as a class of objects or a mathematical process. Rouse (2018) expands the systems theory in defining organizational network analysis (ONA) to analyze and model how communication information decisions and resources flow through an organization. Rouse suggested that ONA is applied in business management to gain a better understanding of relationships that affect the effectiveness of individuals and the tools and equipment they use to get the job done.

Skunkworks

In Daft (2013) a group of technocrats from the same organization referred to as skunkworks meet regularly in defined physical places and in cyberspace to progress organizational goals. Daft argued that the skunkworks were a group of engineers who shared the same vision about aviation technology in their organization. They deliberated in designing new products and appropriate technology to make those new products a reality. In Gharajedaghi (2010) systems thinking is deployed in the search for solutions to the problems the organization faces such as competition. How to effectively compete can be framed by co-constructing a shared vision of the future. Systems thinking can be applied to design and implement the competitive advantage.

BACKGROUND

Action Research a Lewinian Approach

The sociotechnical systems is founded on action research (Lewin 1946) as its basic process of inquiry or purposeful human activity *holon* (Eijnatten, 1993). In later studies Long (2016), suggested that the social technical systems approach enable to stimulate ideas about boundaries and how they differentiate systems from their environment. The STSD made it possible for people doing the same job to share experiences and develop explicit practices.

The capability to do things right first time and always is critical in highly competitive markets. The STSD focuses on the knowledge skills technology and the attitudes to get the job done first time and always. The approach compels organizations to identify external and internal customers, and proceed to categorize them in terms of their consumption patterns, and where they are located. It is a form of creating a customer-database. The second procedure is establish the needs of the customers and assessing the capability to meet the demand. This stage involves working with planners, suppliers, purchasing, and finance and quality departments to see how the job can be configured and implemented.

Continuous Training and Improvement

On-job training (OJT) is one of the best interventions for introducing and managing change in successful enterprises. OJT enables the novice to build their confidence in doing the job. Organizational capability is enhanced when the organization can work efficiently and effectively. The ideal situation is when each labor can be skillful and resourceful to warrant increased productivity (see figure 2). The conceptual framework provides an opportunity to envision the techniques and tools essential in developing the explicit practices required in effective organization. Following the work of Adam Smith in Mupepi (2014), structures are viewed as open systems molded and determined by values and norms. They also contain job descriptions job specifications and techniques needed for the structure to make meaning contribution in the value creation process. The pin-production open system provides an opportunity to understand the explicit knowledge needed to increase output (see figure 2). In the STSD approach the organizational structure is viewed as the pattern of interrelationships among key actors. It includes the value creation process and hierarchical chart, attitudes and perceptions, quality of products, ways in which decisions are made and how things are done. Systems dynamics demonstrate the interdependence of each position and task, and how they are all related to whole production department or *holon*. The art of sociotechnical systems thinking includes learning to recognize the ramifications and trade-offs of the actions members choose to follow.

Figure 2. The brashness to get the job done right all the time retains customers (Mupepi, 2017b)

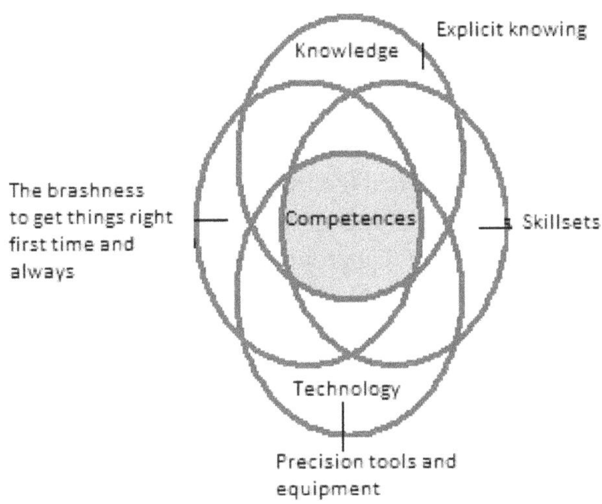

The historical development of sociotechnical systems design (STSD), can be argued to have roots in London's Tavistock Human Relations Institute before WW2. Trist & Bamforth (1951) attribute the first studies conducted by Fred Emery in the British coal fields in Yorkshire and Norwegian industries (Emery & Trist, 1981). These studies resulted in the development of effective STSD approach as a collaboration effort of many scholars including Lewin, Lippitt & White (1939), Bion (1949), Cummings (1978), and Eijnatten & Hoevenaars (1989), among many others. Sociotechnical systems thinking is espoused from STSD and the systems theory developed by von Bertalanffy (1969) and Lewin (1946) respectively (Eijnatten 1993). The current applications of the STSD in Long (2016) suggest that the technique is a viable tool useful to the OD practitioner and managers to reconfigure technology and human behavior.

Group Dynamics

Kurt Lewin (1943) is commonly identified as the founder of the movement to study groups scientifically. He coined the term *group dynamics* to describe the way groups and individuals act and react to changing circumstances. In Backstrom, Huttenlocher, Kleinberg & Lan (2006), group dynamics is a system of behaviors and psychological processes occurring within a social group (intragroup dynamics), or between social groups (intergroup dynamics). The study of group dynamics can be useful in understanding decision-making behavior, how the job is thought out and implemented and tracking the value chain to appreciate bottlenecks in efforts to increase productivity. In Bion (1949), alludes to idea that the software of a group's mind can be seen in thinking alike or systems thinking. Wilfred Bion's observations about the role of group processes in group dynamics are set out in a book entitled: *Experiences in Groups* first published in 1962. In this book Bion refers to recurrent emotional states of groups as basic assumptions. Bion suggested that the work group was interested in the aspect of group functioning which had to do with the primary task of the group—what the group has formed to accomplish. The primary group kept the organization anchored to a sophisticated and rational level of behavior. The secondary group was concerned with sustenance by the leader. The group was dependent on its leader for material and spiritual resources. In later research Salas & Diazgranandos et al (2008), posit that groups could focus on aligning around goals, building effective working relationships, reducing team members' role ambiguity and finding solutions to team problems. Salas & Diazgranandos add to the group dynamics discourse by adding performance factors: setting goals, role clarification, problem solving, and interpersonal relations to increase organizational effectiveness.

Transformative Small Groups

Many on-job training techniques have been adapted from the research conducted in many places including Tavistock Institute and T-Groups at National Training Laboratories at Bethel, Maine (Gallant & Rios, 2014). Team-based learning represents an even more intense use of small groups to craft the core capability of the organization. As team members become more willing to commit to very high level of effort in their learning they develop systemic way of seeing things, and techniques to solve the problems they encounter in progressing their tasks. In Gallant & Rios, a contention is made about building teams that can perform beyond the capability of even their most talented members. As groups think more about the task at end, the more innovative they can be (Lockheed, 2016).

The Sociotechnical Perspective

The historical background illustrates that the STSD can boast of a long tradition rooted in famous and successful intervention of the Tavistock Institute of Human Relations that solved what could have been a chronic productivity problem in the British pre-WW2 coal industries. The concept of structure was deployed with Adam Smith to define the organizational culture and the efficacies essential in making successful specialists (see figure 1). In Blau et al (1976), it is postulated that during the fifties and sixties Weber's distinction between the categories of *goal-oriented* behavior and *value-oriented* behavior were still regarded as being of fundamental importance. For example the learner had to develop his skills by observing and taking orders on what to do from the expert. It implied that the division of labor could be viewed as a structure whose rationality was to increase productivity by allowing key actors to become specialists. Blau et al argued that structure was related to behavior drawn from sociology and economics. The division of labor was the rationale to increase output and innovation became a reality as each divided labor thought about effective ways of doing the job as a means to earn better wages. In much later studies Occelli (2017), argued that the advancements in information communication technologies (ICTs), and mobile computing, has created an information-rich environment where new types of socio-technical systems (STS) can be established. Due to the pervasiveness of ICT in the value creation systems designing and implementing socio-technical systems continue to raise an increasing interest in organizations. They play a crucial role in the improvement of productivity. Occelli suggested that STS were essential in leveraging technology and talent management in competitive environments.

In Beal (2016), the ERP is short for enterprise resource planning. An ERP is a socio-technical system in the sense that it is a tool or know-how deployed to make the job easy in many aspects of organization including human resources or manufacturing management. The enterprise resource planning (ERP) is business process management software that allows an organization to use a system of integrated applications to manage the business and automate many back office functions related to technology, services and human resources. The ERP software integrates all facets of an operation — including product planning, development, manufacturing, sales and marketing — in a single database, application and user interface. It is a socio-technical system that engages management to effectively plan and implement human resources strategy pertaining to recruitment and selection, hiring, training and develop and compensate and retain talent in useful; organization. In Kasemsap (2015), the ERP has emerged as one of the major breakthrough information technologies that can re-shape the manufacturing industry. The ERP is the business application that weaves together all the data within an organization's business processes and associated functional areas. Kasemsap considered the advent of globalization and the appearance of new forms of organization based on networks of closely cooperating firms, it seems clear that successfully implementing sociotechnical systems such as ERP will take on an increased significance for the survival, growth, and competitiveness of many small and medium-sized enterprises (SMEs).

The Sociotechnical Systems Thinking Proposition

In Miller & Rice (1967), the argument that sociotechnical systems thinking was rooted in industrial democracy and the design of tasks compatible with generic human needs is made. In later research Davis Challenger Jayewardene & Clegg (2014), posited that sociotechnical systems thinking can be viewed as a subset of social theory and philosophy. This way of thinking is particularly relevant in domains such as organizational development which are closely related to knowledge management. Socio-technical systems thinking has predominantly been applied to the domains of new technology and work design in postwar industries. Whilst it has made an impact, Davis et al argue that they need to be valiant, encouraging the approach to evolve and extend its reach. In particular they suggested that the conceptualization of what constituted a system applied in the organization's thinking. To illustrate the claim, Davis et al provided examples of socio-technical perspectives on the management of change and how the approach can be applied to increase in productivity. They argued that there was a positive correlation between sociotechnical systems thinking and reduction in risk resulting in increased yields.

The participative view in sociotechnical systems thinking imply continuous learning and improvement and use of appropriate technology. An assumption can also be made that the key actors in the value chain must perfect their act to remain relevant to the job at hand. In Senge (1990), system thinking encompasses a large and fairly amorphous body of methods, tools, and principles all oriented to looking at the interrelatedness of forces and seeing them as part of a common process. In Daft (2013), a group of technocrats referred to as skunkworks can meet regularly to solve organizational problems. Their main asset is what they know, and how they coordinate their expertise to create organizational advantages. They examine interrelated forces and see them as part of a common process. Senge asserted that systems thinking follow certain common principles, the nature of which are being discovered and understood by all in the organization. In Mupepi (2017b), the ultimate success or failure of a business in modern society depends on a variety of factors across all levels of the organization. By utilizing dynamic human resource planning techniques and operational teams can lead organization more efficiently to reach desirable goals. Appreciating the configuration and combination necessary in socio-technical systems is pivotal to maintaining and increasing the competitive advantage. For example, the Skunkworks philosophy has been tested successfully at Lockheed Martin Aerospace industry (Lockheed, 2016) and its thesis can be applied to create diffuse and distribute the explicit knowledge required to differentiate the organization in competitive environments successfully. The Skunkworks has continued to be a combination of highly qualified and experienced aeronautical engineers who designed and built one of the most effective jetfighter plane in use today. Daft suggested that the competitive advantage can be created successfully by a people who share the same thinking and mindset. The Skunkworks were able to be innovative in all their deliberation top produce a product that continue to be in demand internationally.

Learning and Improving All the Time

Williams & Hummelbrunner (2010) explore the application of systems ideas to investigate, evaluate, and intervene in complex highly productive organizations. Their proposition serves as a field guide to how sociotechnical systems thinking can be implemented to take organizations to the next level. Williams & Hummelbrunner describe and analyze organizational learning, and how change can be designed and implemented successfully. Williams & Hummelbrunner places importance on how the sociotechnical systems concept can be put into useful practice that focus on developing system thinking and a shared mental model about how best to do the job at hand.

In Mupepi (2017a), a co-constructed vision of the future is made possible by an organization that can come together to strategize using the same heuristics to solve problems and enable continuous learning and improvement to happen in all facets of organization.

Organizations as Open Systems

In Soliman (2014), System theory provides a first perspective for critical and normative exploration. Systems theory has been deployed successfully to elucidate phenomenon in many fields including organization development cybernetics, and economics, among many others (von Bertalanffy 1969:2). Soliman (2014) posited that the centricity of systems thinking is to view a phenomenon holistically as a set of diverse interacting elements. Mingers & White (2010) suggested that the relationship between the components is more meaningfully than investigating each component in isolation. Vancouver (1996), suggested a hierarchical structure of a system enabled accountability and analysis of responsibility. Drawing on this early work Soliman (2014), considered that there were generic characteristics that applied to all open systems such as the importation of energy. In this acquisition all open systems are dependent on their environment for the resources they need to effectively function. Bertalanffy (1934) employs evolutionary biology to explain how the organism amoeba replicates itself to successfully thrive in marshy environments. The amoeba draws energy from the plants, water, sunlight, and air as through-put to replicate itself successfully. The absorbed energy will be transformed by the amoeba open system to continue to grow. Organization will transform the resources and materials into products or services. In the evolutionary cycle the output of the organisms will be exported back to the environment and thus the amoeba continues to replicate itself faster. Soliman argues that systems are cycles of events characterized by inputs and outputs. The offering of the products or services will generate new resources for organization in order to repeat its transformation process.

Open systems are bound to obtain negative entropy. Entropy as a universal law is the degree of disorder or uncertainty in a system. It states that all organizations will eventually result in disorganization or death. Thus, open systems tend to maximize their ratio of imported and consumed energy to maintain survival (von Bertalanffy 1969:3) Information input, negative feedback, and the coding process are some the characteristics of reproduction in organisms. Open systems not only absorb energy as input but also information. Negative information will provide feedback to the system about its operation and potential need of corrective action.

The Need for Homeostasis

Homoeostasis is the property of a system in which a variable is actively regulated to remain very nearly constant. This regulation occurs inside a defined environment. Open systems that are successful in importing energy to obtain negative entropy are epitomized by a steady state. Negative entropy has been used by biologists as the basis for purpose or direction in life, namely cooperative or moral instincts. However, as the environment of open system will change accordingly. Dynamics homeostasis predicts this process of adjustment (von Bertalanffy 1969:4)

Differentiation

In Barney (1991), firms are viewed as organizations that have different resource endowments that enable them to construct specific competitive advantages over competitors. Resource endowments allow firms to be different which reduces competition and makes it possible to reach new segments of the market. Thus, differentiation is the process of distinguishing the differences of a product or offering from others, to make it more attractive to a particular target market. Barney argued that differentiation is imperative in all open systems to allow specialization to occur and justify their existence and maximize efficiency.

Table 2. Hierarchy of systems

Level	Characteristics
Framework	Static descriptive (e.g. anatomy of the universe, gene; the patterns of electrons around a nucleus
Clockwork	Simple & predetermined motion; dynamic, stochastic, equilibria
Control	Self-regulation; Transmission & interpretation of information
Open system	Self-contained, reproduction, throughput of material (e.g. cell and river)
Genetic-Societal	Division of labor, differentiated and mutually dependent parts, Blue prints for growth
Animal	Increased mobility, teleological behavior, Self-awareness, specialized information-receptors
Human	Self-consciousness, self-reflexive quality, ability to produce, absorb, and interpret symbols
Social organization	Value system, Transcription of images
Inspiring	Ultimates, absolutes, and the inescapable unknowables

(Boulding, 1956)

Boulding (1956) provided a dual basis to treat organizations as open systems as well as social systems with the objective to attain a distinctive goal that sets it apart from other social systems. Human beings as open systems were superior among all organism for their capacity to think and reason.

Systems Thinking in Environmental Uncertainty

In Mingers & White (2010), perceived environmental uncertainty has long been employed to describe an objective state of an organization's environment or as a state of an individual's perception about the environment. Attributing certain characteristics to the environment enables organizations to explain and prepare for uncertainty. The adage: forewarned is forearmed makes organizational sense when risk can be planned and anticipated (Milliken 1987).

There are three types of uncertainty and these are: state uncertainty, effect uncertainty, and response uncertainty. State uncertainty is when an individual lacks information about the nature of the environment on how environmental events, changes, or set of changes will affect the particular organization. With response uncertainty an individual experiences an inability to predict accurately what the organization's response options are in accomplishing desired outcomes. Subsequently it is the type of information an individual lacks that determines which type of individual lacks that determines which type of perceived environmental uncertainty s/he experiences. State uncertainty is conceptually the closet to using the term environmental uncertainty to describe the state of an organization's environment (Milliken, 1987:121).

Feedback

Double-loop learning is an organizational development concept that involves engaging people in the entity to think more deeply about their own assumptions and beliefs. It was created by Chris Argyris, a founding member of the field of organizational behavior in the mid-1980's, and developed over the next decade into an effective tool. Argyris (1990) postulated about double loop learning and how organizations could improve productivity by giving each other constructive feedback. Argyris referred to this phenomenon about learning as the ladder of inference. Argyris suggested that the organization's ability to achieve desirable outcomes was truly eroded by feelings that generated ideas such as: our beliefs are the only truth, our beliefs are based on real data, or the data we select are the real data. Argyris & Schon (1978), suggested that double loop learning provided the learner with appropriate feedback which enabled the learner to draw useful lessons to perfect his act. Double-loop learning occurred when error an error was detected and corrected in ways that involved the modification of an organization's underlying norms, policies and objectives. In later studies Vliet (2012) argue that opinion of employees must be incorporated in the scheme of change. There is a need to communicate with employees on all matters pertaining to how the job will be done. This approach minimizes the resistance to change and increases productivity when all parties to change understand what is happening.

RECOMMENDATIONS

Learning to see the organization systematically is something intangible as deeply set attitudes found in many companies. There are four levels of a systems view. The first is made up of the organization's notable events such as success stories. How the team met the sales targets in a given period of time can be employed to remind current employees that targets can be achieved if there is teamwork (see Figure 3).

The second perspective concerns patterns of behavior (see Figure 2). Drawing lessons from trends of the system over time is important in charting the change discourse. Instead of listing isolated historical events forecasting can be deployed to chart the future with some degree of accuracy.

The third is about the systemic structure. This activity examines the interrelatedness of the events to the system and how the parts are connected to make the whole *holon.* The notion of a holon is derived from a self-reliant autonomous unit (Trist and Bamforth, 1951).The group can discuss the key interrelationships between these units and parts factors and events to understand if there are any causal relationships (see Figure 2).

Figure 3. Organizational interrelated factors impact the core competency (Mupepi, 2017a)

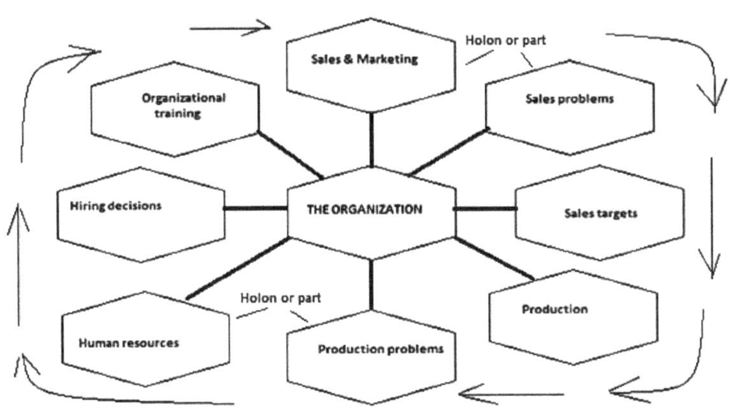

The fourth part is the mental model. The mental models are tacit, they relate to experience. Two people with different experiences can relate to the same object differently. Mental models shape how people behave. The core task of the fourth part is to talk about the job candidly. There are mental models that should not be sustained. For example managers may believe that poor quality is a sabotage by the hourly paid workers. What needs to be encouraged is the analysis of the system with its other parts to understand the causes of the problem of poor quality (see Figure 2). Mental models are also critical in designing and implementation of successful organizational training and development programs.

Sociotechnical Systems Thinking is Good for Business

In Beal (2016), the last couple of years have unleashed forces which are fundamentally shifting behavior in the use of sociotechnical systems such as the ERP. The industry has new and continuing trends such as the development of the following software:

Mobile ERP

The business community want real-time access to information, regardless of where they are. It is expected that businesses will embrace mobile ERP for the reports, dashboards and to conduct key business processes.

Cloud ERP

The cloud has been advancing steadily into the enterprise for some time, but many ERP users have been reluctant to place data cloud. Those reservations have gradually been evaporating, however, as the advantages of the cloud become apparent.

Social ERP

There has been much hype around social media and how important – or not -- it is to add to ERP systems. Certainly, vendors have been quick to seize the initiative, adding social media packages to their ERP systems with much fanfare. But some wonder if there is really much gain to be had by integrating social media with ERP.

Two-Tier ERP

Enterprises once attempted to build an all-encompassing ERP system to take care of every aspect of organizational systems. But some expensive failures have gradually brought about a change in strategy – adopting two tiers of ERP (Beal, 2016).

LIMITATION

Sociotechnical systems thinking approach in management can be limited to many aspects associated with teams. Creating a shared mindset among groups of workers may require building team work. In this process effectiveness can be enhanced when the group does the similar jobs where teamwork can become meaningful. Creating a shared mindset can require a lengthy period of time. People need time to reflect and build effective interpersonal communications among themselves. Failure to achieve a sociotechnical systems thinking can result in frustration among members of the organization.

FUTURE AREAS OF RESEACH

Future research should endeavor to study more contextual factors such organizational culture useful in socio-technical organization systems (see Mupepi 2017a). Surveys distributed to customers can be analyzed to produce performance metrics necessary in increasing output (see Mupepi (2017b). The same data can be analyzed to design and implement exploitable databases which be interpreted to understand the responsiveness of customers and behavior in competitive environments.

CONCLUSION

Organizational learning undergirds sociotechnical system thinking. Constructive feedback is essential in continuous learning and improvement. Feedback is a common mental pathway of increasing abstraction and can often mislead individuals to misguided beliefs such as the sabotage of quality by the hourly paid workers.

REFERENCES

Argyris, C. (1990). *Overcoming Organizational Defenses: Facilitating Organizational Learning*. Boston: Allyn and Bacon.

Argyris, C., & Schön, D. (1978). *Organizational learning: A theory of action perspective*. Reading, MA: Addison Wesley.

Backstrom, L., Huttenlocher, D., Kleinberg, J., & Lan, X. (2006). Group formation in large social networks. *Proceedings of the 12th ACM SIGKDD international conference on Knowledge discovery and data mining - KDD '06*. doi:10.1145/1150402.1150412

Barn, B. S., & Barn, R. (2016). An Exploration of Resilience and Values in the Co-Design of Sociotechnical Systems. *International Journal of Systems and Society, 3*(1), 1–17. doi:10.4018/IJSS.2016010101

Basemsap, K. (2015). Implementing Enterprise Resource Planning. In M. Khosrow-Pour (Ed.), *Encyclopedia of Information Science and Technology* (3rd ed.; pp. 798–807). Hershey, PA: IGI Global. doi:10.4018/978-1-4666-5888-2.ch076

Beal, V. (2016). *ERP - enterprise resource planning*. Accessed 11/14/16 http://www.webopedia.com/term/e/erp.html

Bertalanffy, L. v. (1969). *General System Theory*. New York: George Braziller Publishers.

Bion, W. R. (1949). Experience in groups, III. *Human Relations, 2*(1), 13–22. doi:10.1177/001872674900200102

Bion, W. R. (1962). A theory of thinking. *The International Journal of Psycho-Analysis*, 43.

Blau, P. M. (1976). *Approaches to the study of social structure*. London, UK: Open Book Publishing.

Boulding, K. E. (1956). General systems theory---the skeleton of science. *Management Science, 2*(3), 197–208. doi:10.1287/mnsc.2.3.197

Cummings, T. G. (1976). Sociotechnical systems: an intervention strategy. In W. W. Burke (Ed.), *Current issues and strategies in organization development* (pp. 187–213). New York: Human Science Press.

Daft, R. (2013). *Management*. London, UK: Cengage Learning.

Davis, M. C., Challenger, R., Dharshana, N. W. J., & Clegg, C. W. (2014). Advancing socio-technical systems thinking: A call for bravery. Applied Ergonomics, 45(2), 171-180.

Eijnatten, F.M. van & Hoevenaars, A.M. (1989). Modern sociotechnique in the Netherlands. *Gedrag en Organisatie, 2*(4/5), 289-304.

Eijnatten, F. M. van. (1993). *The Paradigm that Changed the work place.* Stockholm, Sweden: the Swedish Center for Working Life.

Emery, F. E., & Trist, E. L. (1981). The causal texture of organizational environments. In F. E. Emery (Ed.), *Systems Thinking* (Vol. 1). London, UK: Penguin Books.

Gallant, S., & Rios, D. (2014). The organization development consulting process. In B. B. Jones & M. Brazzel (Eds.), *The NTL handbook of organization development and change* (2nd ed.; pp. 153–174). San Francisco, CA: Wiley. doi:10.1002/9781118836170.ch8

Gharajedaghi, J. (2010). *Systems Thinking: Managing Chaos and Complexity a Platform for Designing Business Architecture* (3rd ed.). London, UK: Elsevier.

Juran, J. (1999). *Juran's Quality Handbook* (5th ed.). New York: McGraw-Hill.

Koeslag, J. H., Saunders, P. T., & Wessels, J. A. (1997). Glucose homeostasis with infinite gain: Further lessons from the Daisyworld parable? *The Journal of Endocrinology, 134*(2), 187–192. doi:10.1677/joe.0.1540187 PMID:9291828

Koestler, A. (1967). *The Ghost in the machine.* London, UK: Hutchinson.

Lewin, K. (1943). Defining the "Field at a Given Time." Psychological Review, 50, 292-310.

Lewin, K. (1946). Research on minority problems. *Technology Review, 48*(3).

Lewin, K., Lippitt, R., & White, R. K. (1939). Patterns of aggressive behavior in experimentally created 'social climates'. *The Journal of Social Psychology, 10*(2), 271–299. doi:10.1080/00224545.1939.9713366

Long, S. (2016). *Transforming experience in organization: A framework for organizational research and consultancy.* Melbourne, Australia: Karnac Books.

Miller, E. C., & Rice, A. K. (1967). *Systems of organization: the control of task and sentient boundaries.* London, UK: Tavistock Publications.

Milliken, F. J. (1989). Three types of perceived uncertainty about the environment: State, effect and response uncertainty. *Academy of Management Review, 12*(1), 133–143. doi:10.5465/amr.1987.4306502

Mingers, J., & White, L. (2010). A review of the recent contribution of systems thinking to operational research and management science. *European Journal of Operational Research*, *207*(3), 1147–1161. doi:10.1016/j.ejor.2009.12.019

Mupepi, M. (2014). Can the Division of Labor Be Re-Engineered to Advance Organizational Dynamism? *SAGE Open*, *4*(2). doi:10.1177/2158244014536404

Mupepi, M. (2017b). *Effective Talent Management Strategies for Organizational Success*. Hershey, PA: IGI Global; doi:10.4018/978-1-5225-1961-4

Mupepi, M. G. (2017a). Using Communities of Practice to Identify Competencies. In K. Rasmussen, P. Northrup, & R. Colson (Eds.), *Handbook of Research on Competency-Based Education in University Settings* (pp. 157–167). Hershey, PA: IGI Global; doi:10.4018/978-1-5225-0932-5.ch008

Salas, E., Diazgranandos, D., Klein, C., Burke, C. S., Stagl, K. C., Goodwin, G. F., & Halpin, S. M. (2008). Does Team Training Improve Team Performance? A Meta-Analysis. *Human Factors: the Journal of the Human Factors and Ergonomics Society.*, *50*(6), 903–933. doi:10.1518/001872008X375009 PMID:19292013

Senge, P. (1990). *The Fifth Discipline: The art and practice of the learning organization*. New York: Doubleday.

Skunkworks, L. (2016). *Lockheed SR-71 Blackbird*. Accessed 11/14/16 http://www.bing.com/images/search?q=skunk+works&view=

Stichweh, R. (2011). Systems Theory. In B. Badie & ... (Eds.), *International Encyclopedia of Political Science* (Vol. 8, pp. 2579–2582). New York: Sage. doi:10.4135/9781412959636.n597

Trist, E., & Bamforth, K. (1951). Some Social and Psychological Consequences of the Longwall Method of Coal-Getting. *Human Relations*, *4*(1), 1–38. doi:10.1177/001872675100400101

Vancouver, J. B. (1996). Living systems theory as a paradigm for organizational behavior: Understanding humans, organizations, and social processes. *Behavioral Science*, *41*(3), 165–204. doi:10.1002/bs.3830410301 PMID:8856949

Vliet, V. (2010). *Single and Double Loop learning model*. Retrieved 3/27/18 http://www.toolshero.com

Williams, B., & Hummelbrunner, R. (2010). *Systems concepts in action: A practitioner's toolkit*. New York: Stanford University Press.

KEY TERMS AND DEFINITIONS

Algorithm: An algorithm is a self-contained step-by-step set of procedures applied in solving mathematical or industrial problems.

Differentiation: The process of making products or organization different from others in competition.

Holon: Adapted from Hebrew, implying a self-containing part that is part of a larger system.

Skunkworks: A project typically developed by a small and loosely structured group of people who research and develop a project primarily for the sake of innovation.

Systems Thinking: Systems thinking involves the use of various techniques to study systems of many kinds.

Ubiquitous: Omnipresence or ubiquity is the property of being present everywhere.

Value Creation System: A value creation system is a production perspective that describes social and technical resources employed to produce goods and services demanded by customers.

Chapter 3
Improve Business Results by Learning From Experience in Proactive Reviews:
Find Solutions to Complex Problems

Ditte Kolbaek
Aalborg University, Denmark

ABSTRACT

This chapter aims to provide a theoretically based and proven educational design for lessons learned. Called a proactive review, this educational design is exemplified in a case study of a global information technology company classified as big business, where proactive reviews were developed and implemented in over 40 countries. This chapter explores how employees who solve a task together can learn from the experience and share this learning with relevant colleagues to improve work practices, services, and/or products. This chapter describes the format of proactive reviews, suggestions for starting points called PR triggers, and the four roles involved—the participant, sponsor, top management, and facilitator. The tangible and intangible results of proactive reviews are presented with their impacts on the participants, their teams, and the organization's products, services, and/or work practices. Finally, the chapter provides recommendations for implementing and maintaining proactive reviews in organizations.

DOI: 10.4018/978-1-5225-7390-6.ch003

INTRODUCTION

Value creation in the Western world has come to rely more heavily on intangible resources. This shift from an industry-based to an information-based economy demands new organizational capabilities and human skills (Qvortrup, 2000), which in turn depend on a systemic capacity to learn continuously (Easterby-Smith & Prieto, 2008). At the macro level, there is growing evidence that organizations produce superior results when they have the capability to facilitate the necessary interactions to support and advance knowledge creation and use (Akhtar & Khan, 2011; Holsapple & Wu, 2011; Chang, 2016). Enabling employees to learn in the context of work helps improve business results, competitive advantages, and revenues (Chang, 2016; Nonaka & Takeuchi, 1995) by upgrading work practices, services, and/or products (Elkjaer, 2003). At the micro level, this article seeks to answer the question "How can employees, who solve a task together, learn from the experience and share this learning with relevant colleagues to improve work practices, services, and/or products?"

This question stems from the top management of a global high-technology company. The top management had realized that mistakes and failures were repeated, whereas successes were not replicated to the same extent. Consequently, it asked for a process that enabled its employees at all hierarchical levels to learn from experience. The requirements for the process were that it should be easy to understand, communicate, and implement in most of the 60 countries across Europe, the Middle East, and Africa (EMEA) and should incur low costs. This article describes the theoretical background for the suggested solution called a Proactive Review. Finally, the article provides a real-life example of a Proactive Review, as well as recommendations for successful Proactive Reviews.

First, this article explores the term "learning" based on Bateson's (1972) theories, followed by considerations about learning from experience in the context of work. In this regard, the article draws on the work of Nonaka and Takeuchi (1995), who point out four ontological dimensions of learning, namely, individual, team, organizational, and inter-organizational learning; the term "knowledge conversations" is then discussed. Second, the article presents an educational design for lessons learned called a Proactive Review and discusses what should initiate the process and what roles are involved. Third, the theories are illustrated by an example of a Proactive Review, including the tangible and intangible results achieved. Finally, some recommendations for successful Proactive Reviews are offered.

This chapter is a slightly revised version of the article titled "Proactive Review - Learn from Experience to Improve Bottom Line" published in the International Journal of Organizational and Collective Intelligence, Volume 6, Issue 4, October-December 2016.

LEARNING IN THE CONTEXT OF WORK

This section explores the four dimensions of learning, starting with individual learning as described by Bateson (1972), whose viewpoint is drawn into considerations about learning in teams in the context of work and organizational learning (Elkjaer, 2013; Engeström, 2001; Engeström, Rantavuori & Kerosuo, 2013; Gherardi, 2001) including the lessons learned (East 1998). It becomes clear that the context is important for the process of learning, and this section ends by briefly describing the requirements for successful lessons learned.

Individual Learning

When an organization's top management decides that the employees should learn from their experiences in a structured way, the management needs to consider its own perception of learning, as well as the situations from which it wants the staff to learn (Elkjaer, 2013; Engeström, 2007; Nonaka and Takeuchi, 1995; Wenger, 1999). The global information technology (IT) company had many years of experience in training, online courses, and online certifications but realized that these were different from learning directly from individual or team experience (Rao, 2003). The top management lacked theoretical insights into "learning." To establish a common understanding and to leverage expectations, the term "learning" needed to be explored and explained. The top management perceived learning as a simple concept in which people would learn from classes and online courses, and such learning could be tested in exams with certifications. However, learning from experience is different, as evident in the work of Bateson (1972), who distinguished among the following four classes of learning:[1]

- **Sensing:** A stimulus is sensed but elicits no further response. The learners will change nothing in their behavior. For example, they feel cold but do not do anything about it. Because the stimulus does not cause a change, this is called zero learning (Bateson, 1972).
- **Realizing:** The learners receive a stimulus and choose a response from a set of alternatives. For example, they feel cold, so they put on jackets or go indoors. This is called class-one learning (Bateson, 1972).
- **Adapting:** The learners receive a stimulus and incorporate the context before they react. They are aware of repetitions and consider how to learn from repeated experiences. For example, they feel cold every winter, so they install fireplaces in their houses. This is called class-two learning (Bateson, 1972).
- **Changing:** They receive a stimulus and then change the context as part of their reaction. The double bind is a prerequisite for this class-three learning.

> For example, they feel cold every winter, so they put on jackets and warm up their houses. They are still bothered by the cold, so they decide to move far away to a new and warmer environment (Bateson, 1972).

The double-bind characteristics are as follows: a) An individual is involved in an intense relationship and thinks that it is crucial for the relationship that the communication be right. b) The other party in the relationship expresses contradictory messages. c) The first individual is unable to challenge the contradictions in meaning and therefore needs to change the framework of the relationship to overcome the problem (Gibney, 2006).

Bateson (1972, p. 208) gives the following example of a double bind:

You are my pupil and I hold a stick above your head. If you say the stick is real, I hit you. If you say the stick is unreal, I hit you. If you keep silent, I hit you.

The only way the pupil can avoid the pain is to take the stick from the teacher. The pupil needs to break the framework of the learning environment to avoid being hit. The pupil is used to respecting the teacher and doing what the teacher asks. Taking the stick from the teacher goes far beyond the tacit framework of the context (Bateson, 1972). Therefore, the double bind is very demanding for the pupil, who needs to be frustrated to the extent that he or she dares to break the framework of the learning environment. At the same time, the pupil has no idea about what an alternative framework is. And the pupil does not know what an alternative framework looks like. This poses a high risk, and according to Bateson (1972), it is rare for people to experience class-three learning.

Adapting or class-two learning includes considerations about how someone learns. This process is also called meta-reflection, which enables a person to learn more consciously (Bateson, 1972). It seems that Bateson views learning as an individual action affected by others. Bateson's classes of learning inspire a person to perceive learning as more than just what one gains from training courses. When behavioral changes or innovations are needed, a training course may be insufficient if Bateson's (1972) theories are taken into account. However, Bateson's theories do not imply learning in the specific context of work, so Nonaka and Takeuchi's (1995) work may serve as another reference in this regard.

Four Ontological Dimensions of Learning

Nonaka and Takeuchi (1995) claim that learning in the context of work is necessary to enhance competitive advantages because it enables employees to solve problems, thus upgrading work practices, services, or products. The content to be learned is related to an organization's vision and objectives, for example, the improvement of products, services, and work practices rather than learning to develop competencies (Brandi & Elkjaer, 2011).

According to Nonaka and Takeuchi (1995), knowledge creation occurs in different ontological dimensions—the individual employee, the team, the organization, and knowledge creation, which may also take place between organizations. Nonaka and Takeuchi claim that all employees within an organization can contribute to knowledge creation. *The individual and the team* create knowledge in collaboration and may involve employees at any level to develop products, services, systems, or work practices (Elkjaer, 2003; Nonaka & Takeuchi, 1995). Continuous learning is necessary for the execution of work duties throughout the practitioners' working life (Chang, 2016). Knowledge construction means that the individual or the group creates meaning by involving experiences, feelings, activities, and ideas (Nonaka, Toyama & Konno, 2000; Gherardi, 2001). Knowledge develops through engagement in an activity and is embodied in individuals and groups. The knowledge-creation process may be described as a spiral that begins with an employee who acquires tacit knowledge by socializing with colleagues, observing what they are doing and how they do it, and trying to do the same (Nonaka & Takeuchi, 1995; Nonaka et al., 2000). By doing so, the employee may construct technical skills and mental models. Colleagues try to create a common understanding (meaning) through dialogue and collective reflection. When a person combines different kinds of explicit knowledge, he or she discovers new structures, gaps, or insights. Over time, the new knowledge may be internalized, which means that the person "just knows it" without consciously thinking about it. In this case, the explicit knowledge has become tacit (Nonaka & Takeuchi, 1995, p. 71).

The key action in the knowledge-creation process entails "knowledge conversions" that change tacit to explicit knowledge. Knowledge conversions enable colleagues to create meaning by involving experiences, feelings, activities, and ideas (Nonaka & Takeuchi, 1995; Nonaka et al., 2000). Nonaka and Takeuchi (1995) stress the importance of mutual conversations, but they do not describe the requirements for how the conversation and collective reflection unfold. Consequently, it may be relevant to mention other theorists' work on this matter. Wegerif (2007) suggests that "dialogue" is a principle of learning conversations. The purpose of the dialogue is to create meaning, which does not exist before it is created during the dialogue (Wegerif, 2007). Meaning is not an artifact; rather, it is a common exploration by two or more people. Wegerif (2007) defines dialogue as "a verbal exchange between two parties, according to some kind of rules, conventions or expectations" (p. 147). When the dialogue is perceived in this way, it may be a method of conversation in groups (Bohm, 2014; Phillips, 2011; Wegerif, 2007). The important aspect of the dialogue lies in its rules. It is crucial for the dialogue to take place in an atmosphere of mutual trust that enables the participants to introduce or question any assertion; share their attitudes, desires, or needs; and feel accepted even when disagreements occur (Nonaka, Toyama & Konno, 2000; Phillips, 2011; Wegerif, 2007). The atmosphere has a huge impact on the dialogue, including its outcomes. If the participants are able to establish humor and trust, it allows them to explore more broadly as they dare to take the risk of "not knowing" (von Krogh, Ichijo, & Nonaka, 2000). Additionally, this builds a stronger relationship among the participants, which supports their ability to give time and space for more reflection (von Krogh, Ichijo, & Nonaka, 2000; Wegerif, 2007).

The organization creates knowledge when more groups or employees from more departments or divisions interact, and members from different teams externalize their tacit knowledge (Nonaka & Takeuchi, 1995; Nonaka et al., 2000). This exchange leads to the combination of knowledge across organizational boundaries; thus, new knowledge is developed. Nonetheless, how the knowledge is spread in the organization is rather vague. Shared goals and the problem-solving ways of communication are important means for learning across teams in an organization (Engeström, 2001; Engeström, 2013; von Krogh et al. 2000; Nickelsen & Elkjaer, 2014). Power structures may pose obstacles to cross-divisional collaboration if the top managers do not cooperate but try to keep the knowledge within their respective divisions (Nonaka & Takeuchi, 1995). If the top managers do not provide time for conversation or interaction, learning will slow down (Chang, 2016). If the employees are not used to interacting and talking with colleagues from other divisions and discussing contradictions, mistakes, or even conflicts, there is little chance of resolution, and any learning from the experience may be lost (Elkjaer, 2003; Engeström, Rantavuori, & Kerosuo, 2013; Nonaka & Takeuchi, 1995).

Nonaka and Takeuchi (1995) suggest that middle managers initiate knowledge creation because they possess the most insights into the organization's needs. The middle managers are the link between the top management developing the strategies and the employees performing their everyday jobs (Nonaka & Takeuchi, 1995, p. 128). This viewpoint excludes engaged employees from initiating the lessons learned, and it enables middle managers to stop the learning initiatives that they do not prefer although the lessons learned may be important for the organization as such. To define what initiates the learning process, the top management should create and communicate its knowledge vision, including who is supposed to be involved and what kinds of learning and knowledge are to be achieved (Kolbaek, 2014; Nonaka & Takeuchi, 1995). Nonaka and Takeuchi (1995) and Engeström (2001, 2013) suggest that a "problem" prompts the learning process. This statement is challenged by East (1998), who describes "Lessons Learned" as a format for learning from experience in the context of work, which is discussed in the next section.

Inter-organizational knowledge creation occurs when employees from an organization interact with colleagues from another organization. For example, by developing a new service together, the involved employees create new knowledge through exchanging explicit and tacit knowledge. This new knowledge may be shared within the employees' respective organizations, resulting in inter-organizational knowledge creation (Nonaka & Takeuchi, 1995; p. 73).

Lessons Learned

According to East:

A lesson learned is knowledge or understanding gained by experience. The experience may be positive, as in a successful test or mission, or negative, as in a mishap or failure. Successes are also considered sources of Lessons Learned. A lesson must be significant in that it has a real or assumed impact on operations; valid in that it is factually and technically correct; and applicable in that it identifies a specific design, process, or decision that reduces or eliminates the potential for failures and mishaps, or reinforces a positive result (1998, p. 14).

Lessons Learned critically analyze potential failures or mishaps to avoid them in the future by improving work processes or techniques. The starting point for learning from a work experience, a Lesson Learned is initiated when a company experiences a problem or challenge that causes either negative or positive emotions (East, 1998; Kolbaek 2012). In a business context, such an experience could be a successful deal or an IT implementation, or it could be something that did not turn out as expected. If Lessons Learned are mainly applied to negative cases, the participants may perceive joining Lessons Learned as a punishment, which may reduce the creativity of the solutions (Kolbaek, 2012). The response to Lessons Learned may be chosen from a set of alternatives or may be a new innovation. In any event, the outcome of a lesson learned must be an applicable solution to the problem or challenge (East, 1998; Kolbaek, 2015).

Maintaining a Learning Environment

Management support is vital for organizational learning. The top-level management must provide the appropriate physical space, time, and technology for organizational learning (Chang, 2016). It also needs to encourage and nurture learning initiatives such as Lessons Learned, not only for a few privileged employees but for all the staff at all levels (Chang, 2016; Kolbaek, 2015; von Krogh et al., 2000).

According to Bateson (1972), learning may be a demanding process. Vygotsky (1978) claims that human beings learn through problem solving under the guidance of or in collaboration with more capable peers. Consequently, an organization must create an environment suitable for problem solving. In traditional training courses, a framework is well known despite being rarely mentioned. When an organization wants to learn from experience, the learning environment may need to be described so that the management and learners have mutual expectations (Engeström, 2001; von Krogh et al., 2000).

Given that the lessons learned are based on dialogues among employees who have collaborated on a task, the learning environment includes requirements for dialogues (von Krogh et al., 2000; Vince, 2012). According to von Krogh and colleagues (2000), the ground rules of the dialogue include the parties' willingness to listen, ability to be patient, awareness of their own assumptions, and acceptance of conflicting viewpoints. Their patience allows others to speak and ask for more information to explore all perspectives. The participants share all relevant information; they discuss alternatives before making decisions, and everybody is encouraged to speak (von Krogh et al., 2000). It is important that the dialogue occurs in a caring atmosphere that allows each participant to speak his or her mind. Consequently, a facilitator is needed to initiate and maintain such a caring atmosphere (Kolbaek, 2015; Phillips, 2011; von Krogh et al., 2000). Utilizing the dialogue to learn from experiences in the workplace may lead to various results, such as more robust relationships and a stronger team spirit, creativity, critical thinking, and exploration of new possibilities (Kolbaek 2015, Wegerif, 2007).

Requirements for an Educational Design for Lessons Learned

An educational design for Lessons Learned should include both the possibility of individual reflection and collaborative learning activities (Bateson, 1972; Nonaka & Takeuchi, 1995). Lessons Learned may be initiated by all employees, and the starting point could be positive or negative experiences (East, 1998). Conversations should be the means of learning (Engeström, 2001, 2013; Nonaka & Takeuchi, 1995), including Lessons Learned; more specifically, these learning conversations may be described as dialogues (Defillippi, 2011; von Krogh et al., 2000; Wegerif, 2007). Certain behaviors support learning processes. Managers should provide a knowledge vision and appropriate resources, and the involved employees should participate in mutual dialogues (Nonaka, Toyama & Konno, 2000). The educational design should offer a caring atmosphere to initiate, maintain, and expand learning from experience in the context of work. However, an educational design for learning from the work experience is still missing (Abbariki, 2013; von Krogh et al., 2000).

PROACTIVE REVIEW: AN EDUCATIONAL DESIGN FOR LESSONS LEARNED

This section provides an educational design for Lessons Learned called a Proactive Review, which is developed according to the business requirements described in the introduction and the requirements condensed from the cited theories. First, the starting points for the Proactive Review are suggested, based on the experiences in the global IT company. Next, this section presents the educational design, which includes seven open questions and shows how each question is related to the overall requirements. Finally, the four roles involved in Proactive Reviews are explained.

Proactive Review Triggers

Any manager or employee may initiate a Proactive Review when a success or a failure has had an impact on operations (East, 1998; Nickelsen & Elkjaer, 2014). This means that the top management provides time for knowledge conversations on common experiences gained from important tasks (von Krogh et al., 2000; Nonaka & Takeuchi, 1995). A failure may be perceived as a problem to be avoided in the future, whereas a success may be regarded as a challenge to be repeated in the future (Kolbaek, 2015).

To meet the low-cost requirement, a Proactive Review typically lasts for three hours, and the management frames when Proactive Reviews are appropriate (Kolbaek, 2012). Such starting points for Proactive Reviews may be called PR Triggers, and they define who or what initiates a Proactive Review.

The top management of the global IT company decided on the following PR Triggers. When a case (a sale or an IT implementation) exceeded *x* million USD, and two or more divisions had been involved in the case, a Proactive Review should be performed. This PR Trigger would support cross-divisional problem solving and learning among individuals and teams in the organization. Furthermore, this PR Trigger would minimize the obstacles that power structures might impose on cross-divisional collaboration (Nickelsen & Elkjaer, 2014). The PR Trigger would enable cross-divisional exploration of contradictions, mistakes, or even conflicts and would increase the possibility of creating common resolutions (Engeström 2001).

Most divisional managers determined the PR Triggers for their specific divisions. For example, the marketing manager decided to conduct Proactive Reviews for campaigns that had been launched in more than four countries and exceeded the cost of *n* million USD or had underperformed with more than 30% of the expected result being revenue or customer feedback. The sales manager defined PR Triggers for sales, including strategic customers, new services, or markets that grew more than *y*% a year. The consulting manager defined PR Triggers as the "implementation of new products or services to strategic customers or new customers that impact[ed] the bottom line with more than *z*%." The HR manager defined PR Triggers for acquired employees exceeding a certain number in specific countries or global divisions.

Any employee could initiate a Proactive Review when he or she believed it was required. Most often, this situation occurred when a team encountered troubles in achieving the task they set out to do, and the issue indicated the need for a changed approach. The employee(s) would suggest a Proactive Review to his or her (their) manager, and the manager would offer the resources and receive the results of the Proactive Review (as explained further in the following section).

Now that the requirements for Proactive Reviews and what or who would start the process have been discussed, the seven open questions being the educational design of a Proactive Review are presented next.

Agenda of Proactive Reviews Related to Requirements for Educational Design

The requirements for Proactive Reviews were defined by the top management in the global IT company as follows. The process should incur low costs, as well as be easy to understand, communicate, and implement in most of the 60 countries across EMEA. It should allow all employees to be subjects for and contributors to the Lessons Learned.

According to the previously described theories, the educational design should meet the following criteria:

- Be based on dialogues and collaborative reflections (Bohm, 2014; von Krogh et al. 2000; Phillips, 2011; Wegerif, 2007).
- Define who or what initiates the Proactive Review (Engeström, 2001; Kolbaek 2014; Nonaka & Takeuchi 1995).
- Lead to the "adapting" class of learning and improvement of work practices, services, and/or products (Bateson, 1972; Elkjaer, 2003; Nonaka & Takeuchi, 1995).
- Have the ability to address frustrations with the "changing" class of learning (Bateson, 1972; Engeström 2001, 2013; Vince & Gabriel, 2011).
- Include meta-reflection (Bateson, 1972).
- Include a process for disseminating the new insights to relevant employees and managers throughout the organization (Nonaka & Takeuchi, 1995).
- Include the four ontological dimensions of learning (Nonaka & Takeuchi, 1995).

These requirements were considered when a tentative educational design for the Lessons Learned was tested in a pilot project in the global IT company. The feedback from the participants and managers at various levels and further experience led to the final educational design of the Proactive Review, which is described below. The Proactive Review turned out to comprise seven open questions to be asked in a specific sequence (Kolbaek, 2014).

The participants are employees who have solved a task together. In other words, they have engaged in a common activity, and the Proactive Review is an opportunity for collaborative reflection, maintained by the mutual dialogue as the basis for knowledge conversations (Engeström, 2001, 2013; von Krogh et al., 2000; Nonaka & Takeuchi, 1995; Wegerif, 2007). The dialogue itself is kept confidential so the participants can openly admit doubts, uncertainties, and "not knowing" certain matters (Kolbaek, 2014). A Proactive Review enables the individual and the team to create meaning by expressing experiences, feelings, activities, and ideas (Kolbaek, 2014; Vince & Gabriel, 2011).

Table 1. Seven questions in a proactive review

Sequence	Questions	Meeting the Requirement of
1	What is the purpose of this Proactive Review?	Setting a common direction for the dialogue
2	What was our goal?	Repeating the shared goal of the case on which the participants worked cooperatively
3	What happened and why? • Enablers • Obstacles	Leading to the "sensing" and "realizing" classes of learning
4	What should we do next time? • Continue • Stop • Start	Leading to the "adapting" class of learning and improvement of work practices, services, and/or products
5	What should we report, to whom, when, and how?	Ensuring the process for spreading the new insights to relevant employees and managers throughout the organization
6	What management challenge might be addressed from this Proactive Review?	Leading to addressing the frustration with the "changing" class of learning
7	What was your personal highlight from this Proactive Review?	Enabling meta-reflection

The question "What is the purpose of this Proactive Review?" sets a common direction for the conversation. Anyone in the organization may initiate a Proactive Review by suggesting it to their direct manager, who then takes on the responsibility and defines the purpose. The invitation to join the Proactive review informs the participants of this purpose. Typically, the purpose itself is formulated as a question (Kolbaek, 2014). For example, the HR manager could ask, "How do we decrease the attrition rate of the employees hired in the UK, France, and Sweden?"

To create common ground among the participants, they start by collaborative reflections on the past. Shared goals are important means for learning across teams in an organization (Nickelsen & Elkjaer, 2014). The question "What was our goal?" reiterates the shared goal that the participants should have worked to achieve. However, this shared goal may evolve over time because different divisions have varied goals that sometimes change or contradict the shared goal of a certain task (Kolbaek, 2014).

The question "*What happened and why?*" allows the participants to remember the occurrences to which they failed to react although they realize now that their reaction might have been beneficial. Additionally, the participants evaluate the way they worked and the decisions they made while they solved the task. In other words, they explore the "sensing" and "realizing" classes of learning (Bateson, 1972; Kolbaek, 2015).

The question "*What should we do next time?*" invites the participants to learn by repeated experiences, that is, applying the "adapting" class of learning (Bateson, 1972). The question makes the participants consider what went so well that it ought to be repeated in future work situations of the same kind, as well as what turned out to be obstacles to success. In the latter case, the participants create solutions for avoiding or overcoming these barriers; in the case of success, the participants define how to replicate similar accomplishments in the future (Kolbaek, 2014). By doing so, they create solutions to challenges that improve work processes, services, and products (Elkjaer, 2003, Nonaka & Takeuchi, 1995).

The question "*What should we report, to whom, when, and how?*" results in an action and communication plan, including concrete solutions to obstacles and enablers for success (Kolbaek, 2014). The action and communication plan ensures that the learning process is disseminated to those for whom it is relevant in the organization. Each participant takes responsibility for at least one action in the plan, and one or two participants deliver and explain the action and communication plan to the sponsor, who is responsible for implementing it (Kolbaek, 2014). This way, the new insights are spread to relevant employees and managers throughout the organization.

The question "*What management challenge might be addressed from this Proactive Review?*" directs the participants to consider if they have met obstacles that they are unable to solve because the solutions would have demanded more organizational power (Kolbaek, 2014). This kind of hindrance very often leads to frustrations, and this question allows the employees to present their dissatisfactions to the highest hierarchical level—the top management that is capable of changing the context of the organization if it is necessary for solving the problem (Kolbaek, 2014). Additionally, this question provides a process for addressing issues from any hierarchical level in the organization directly to the top management without being stopped by middle managers, who may not like the insights although they may be important for the organization as such (Vince, 2012).

The question *"What was your personal highlight from this Proactive Review?"* opens up for consideration how the individual participants and the team learned from the Proactive Review. This dialogue enables the participants to make the meta-reflection explicit (Bateson, 1972, Nonaka & Takeuchi, 1995).

Roles in a Proactive Review

A Proactive Review includes the following four roles that are described in more detail below: a) The sponsor invites to the Lesson Learned. b) The participants develop a shared meaning of the past and solutions to the identified issues. c) The facilitators manage the meeting, during which the participants and the sponsor have certain obligations. d) The top management initiates organizational changes as a consequence of the outcomes of the Proactive Review (Kolbaek, 2014).

The sponsor is the manager who invites to the Proactive Review and provides visible support and encouragement for participation (Kolbaek, 2014, von Krogh et al. 2000). The sponsor ensures the commitment of the participants and informs colleagues and subordinates about the educational design within their team or line of business. After the Proactive Review, the sponsor receives the action and communication plan and decides whether any of the proposals will not be developed or implemented; if this is the case, the sponsor informs the participants. Furthermore, the sponsor provides the resources, including travel and accommodation allowances, as well as the time for the participants to work on the actions in the plan. The sponsor may or may not participate in the Proactive Review (Kolbaek, 2012). Most often, the sponsor is a middle manager (Kolbaek, 2014; Nonaka & Takeuchi, 1995).

The participants could be employees at any level in the organization (Brandi & Elkjaer, 2011; Nonaka & Takeuchi, 1995). They prepare for the Proactive Review by considering the enablers for and obstacles to achieving the goal of the case (Kolbaek, 2014). During the Proactive Review, they take part in a mutual dialogue to develop a common understanding of the past and create solutions to the problems or challenges to be addressed (Engeström, 2003; Kolbaek, 2014, Wegerif, 2007). This may broaden the scope and/or enable the participants to think outside the box when developing solutions to the issues that they identify. In the Proactive Review, they voluntarily take responsibility for one or more of the actions that are listed in the action and communication plan. They contribute to the dialogue and maintain a caring atmosphere by respecting others' viewpoints and disagreements (Kolbaek, 2014).

The facilitator manages the Proactive Review and ensures that the participants go through all seven questions within the allotted time. More specifically, the facilitator ensures that an appropriate amount of time is spent on each question (Kolbaek, 2015). The facilitator is neutral about the case and is not supposed to offer any suggestions or exhibit any preferences. To achieve neutrality, the facilitator is normally not a member of the team of participants. A caring atmosphere is crucial for the dialogue in the Proactive Review (Bohm, 2014; von Krogh et al., 2000; Wegerif, 2007). During the Proactive Review, the facilitator prevents anyone from either dominating or not participating in the meeting. In other words, the facilitator invites everybody to contribute equally (von Krogh et al. 2000; Phillips 2011). The facilitator grasps the participants' ideas and helps them select which ones they should keep or disregard. The facilitator concludes each question by summarizing what was expressed by the participants (Kolbaek, 2014). At the end, the facilitator ensures that the results of the Proactive Review are given to the managers in charge—the action and communication plan is delivered to the sponsor, and the management challenge is addressed to the top-level executive who is responsible for the specific area of the challenge (Kolbaek, 2012).

The top management develops a vision for knowledge creation in the organization (Nonaka & Takeuchi, 1995; von Krogh et al. 2000). This vision should improve the organization's ability to acquire, create, exploit, and share knowledge. The top management changes the perception from "learning from failures" to "learning from experience," which is a much more positive approach to learning in the work context (Kolbaek, 2014; Nonaka & Takeuchi, 1995). If the vision includes Proactive Reviews, relevant results, such as management challenges, are communicated to the top management (Kolbaek, 2014).

To sum up, in the Proactive Review, the seven open questions asked in sequence address the theoretical and practical requirements for the Lessons Learned, which may be initiated by any employee at any level in the organization. The Proactive Review involves four roles with different obligations, which are dependent on each other to achieve and implement the results of the Proactive Review. The next section presents the tangible and intangible results attained by conducting Proactive Reviews.

RESULTS OF PROACTIVE REVIEWS

This section explains the tangible and intangible results of Proactive Reviews. The tangible results include a plan for further action and communication, as well as a management challenge. The plan and the challenge lead to improved products, services, or work practices. An important intangible result is the ripple effect of a Proactive Review, which involves individual, team, and organizational learning, and sometimes, inter-organizational learning, which comprise the four ontological dimensions of learning described by Nonaka and Takeuchi (1995).

Tangible Results

A Proactive Review develops at least three tangible results—first, the action and communication plan; second, the management challenge; and third, new inventions, for example, improved work practices, new services, or new products (Elkjaer, 2003; Kolbaek, 2014; Nonaka & Takeuchi, 1995).

During the Proactive Review, the participants recommend changes in the ways that they work, services are delivered, or products operate that would improve the work practices, services, or products (East, 1998; Elkjaer, 2003; Nonaka & Takeuchi, 1995). These recommendations are listed in the action and communication plan, and the participants decide who will be involved in the further investigation or development of the change and who will be informed about this work (Kolbaek, 2014; von Krogh, 2012). Furthermore, the participants decide the media they intend to use for this information and when they plan to deliver it. Each participant is expected to take responsibility for at least one action in the action and communication plan (Kolbaek, 2012). The action and communication plan is the only form of minutes from the Proactive Review since the dialogue itself is kept confidential (Kolbaek, 2014). After the Proactive Review, one or two participants deliver and explain the action and communication plan to the sponsor, who takes the responsibility for implementing the plan by following up on the changes (Kolbaek, 2014). *The action and communication plan is a tangible result of the Proactive Review.*

Sometimes, the participants in the Proactive Review identify the requirements for the changes for which they and their direct manager cannot be responsible since the requirements need more organizational power than they can provide (Kolbaek, 2014; Vince, 2012). Hence, a management challenge is pushed up in the organizational hierarchy, which enables the top management to gain insights into the problems and issues at the grassroots level. The participants describe the management challenge as detailed as possible, including its background and their limitations in solving the problem (Kolbaek, 2014). The facilitator has the responsibility for bringing up the management challenge with the relevant top manager. *The management challenge is a tangible result of the Proactive Review.*

Intangible Results

A Proactive Review invites participants to engage in a mutual dialogue for the purpose of "learning from their experience." The participants have sensed an issue (Bateson, 1972), and the Proactive Review enables them to express, share, and react to it by suggesting a set of alternative solutions (Brandi & Elkjaer, 2011; Engeström, 2001). According to Bateson (1972), the participants learn when they go through this process. The mutual dialogue allows them to share a problem or a challenge explicitly (Bohm, 2014; Nonaka & Takeuchi, 1995). The participants share what they already know and create solutions collaboratively. The learning takes its departure from what they already know, and by sharing both this knowledge and suggestions for solutions, the participants gain more insights (Engeström, 2001; 2013). According to Vygotsky (1978), the participants learn by building on the zone of proximal development. *The intangible result is that the participants learn.*

In the beginning of the Proactive Review, the participants agree on what they want to achieve, such as improved services, products, or working processes that lead to better business results (Nonaka & Takeuchi, 1995). The Proactive Review enables the participants to ask for second opinions. They create a common understanding of the past and collaboratively create a preferred present by answering the question "What should we do next time?" (Kolbaek, 2014) This journey from the well-known past to the unknown future solidifies their sense of belonging to the group (Engeström 2003; von Krogh, 2012). *The intangible result is that the participants create an informal learning network.*

The Proactive Review gives time and space for reflection. The participants face and formulate issues that they cannot solve; by doing so, they allow themselves to dare take the risk of "not knowing" (Wegerif, 2007) They need to listen to one another and occasionally change their points of view because they gain new insights. *The intangible result is that the participants build robust relationships and strengthen the team spirit.*

Ripple Effect Includes Three or Four Ontological Dimensions

A Proactive Review can be visualized as throwing a stone into the water; it starts a ripple effect that globalizes local learning, as illustrated in Figure 1 (van Winkelen & McKenzie, 2011). The starting point is the individual reflection initiated by the invitation and made explicit while shared with the other participants during the

Figure 1. The ripple effect of proactive reviews
(Inspired by van Winkelen & McKenzie, 2011).

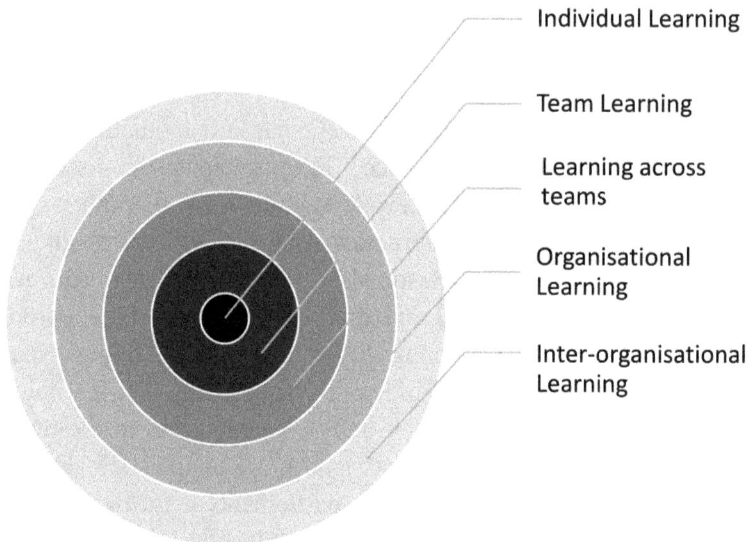

Proactive Review. Engagement in the Proactive review creates individual learning (Kolbaek, 2014)

The second circle is initiated by the question "What happened and why?"—during which the participants establish common ground about the past by exchanging experiences. Next, they answer the question "What should we do next time?"—during which they collaboratively create the preferred present. During the Proactive Review, they exchange and try to understand their peers' viewpoints, enabling them to create solutions to the issues they have identified (Kolbaek, 2014; von Krogh, 2012; Wegerif, 2007), and by doing so the participants develop team learning.

The third circle is initiated by the question "What should we report?" - resulting in the action and communication plan that may involve colleagues from other teams (Kolbaek, 2014, Nonaka & Takeuchi, 1995). This way, colleagues will learn from the Proactive Review which then initiates learning across teams, and organizational learning is completed.

The fourth circle begins by asking "What management challenge might be addressed?"—which enables the top management to learn from the Proactive Review and to respond to the issues identified by the participants (Bohm, 2014; von Krogh et al.,2000). The top management may initiate changes accordingly. When these changes are implemented, other parts of the organization learn from the Proactive Review (Kolbaek, 2014).

The fifth circle starts when team members interact with the outside world. According to Nonaka and Takeuchi (1995), the more mature the market, the more important it is to exchange information with the outside world. If external parties, such as customers or partners, participate in the Proactive Review, they may bring learning back to their organizations, in which case, the Proactive Review includes inter-organizational learning (Nonaka & Takeuchi, 1995).

To reiterate, the ripple effect illustrates the four ontological dimensions of individual, team, organizational, and inter-organizational learning (Nonaka & Takeuchi, 1995). Furthermore, the ripple effect shows two ways of vertical organizational learning, as follows: first, the bottom-up type when participants present management challenges to the top management, and second, the top-down type when the top management solves the management challenge and implements changes in the organization (Nonaka & Takeuchi, 1995). The action and communication plan also ensures horizontal organizational learning.

Summary

The purpose of the Proactive Review is learning, and the participants learn in the process of social engagement in their work context. The tangible results are the action and communication plan and the management challenge that lead to improved or new products, services, or work practices. The intangible results constitute learning, as follows: the creation of an informal peer network, more robust relationships, and a stronger team spirit among the participants. The ripple effect illustrates learning at four ontological dimensions, as well as horizontal and vertical organizational learning.

REQUIREMENTS FOR SUCCESSFUL PROACTIVE REVIEWS

This section discusses the framework around Proactive Reviews. First, important enablers and obstacles for successful Proactive Reviews are presented. Second, the section describes important prerequisites for implementing Proactive Reviews in an organization; which is followed up by a more detailed explanation of the four roles involved in a Proactive Review.

Enablers for and Obstacles to Successful Proactive Reviews

Based on the discussed theoretical considerations and the case study of a global IT company, Table 2 provides an overview of the important elements of successful Proactive Reviews, as well as the enablers for and obstacles to conducting Proactive

Reviews with beneficial results. The enablers in Table 2 should be perceived as recommendations for successful Proactive Reviews.

Recommendations for Successful Proactive Reviews

This section describes what is needed to initiate and maintain successful Proactive Reviews, including a few prerequisites and the different requirements for the four roles involved in Proactive Reviews.

Prerequisites

The top management should create and communicate its *knowledge vision* (Nonaka & Takeuchi, 1995; von Krogh et al. 2000), including what kinds of learning and knowledge should be achieved. Employees at all levels may participate in Proactive Reviews (Engeström, 2013; von Krogh, 2012) under the terms of "we are here to learn," which should be the participants' mindset (Kolbaek, 2012).

PR Triggers should be defined for the organization as such and for the different parts of the organization.

Appropriate physical settings frame Proactive Reviews and include a room that provides privacy for the participants. The size of the room should enable the participants to work in one large group or in several smaller groups (Kolbaek, 2012). The room layout should allow them to engage in mutual dialogues by facing one another and making eye contact (Wegerif, 2007). The agenda, including its schedule, should be visible at all times. The physical surroundings may be an internal location that offers privacy. Sometimes, this may not provide a relaxed atmosphere, but it saves travel time and other costs. An external site may be arranged as well. Meeting outside the office also indicates that the session is special and may support a more comfortable environment (Kolbaek, 2012).

Requirements for the Four Roles Involved in Proactive Reviews

The top management decides to implement Proactive Reviews; consequently, it articulates that learning is important for business survival. The top management should develop its vision of knowledge creation that includes a description of the world where the organization belongs today, where it wants to be in the future, and what knowledge is needed to arrive there (von Krogh et al. 2000; Nonaka & Takeuchi, 1995). The top management defines the learning objectives, which may include a number of annual action and communication plans, as well as several annual management challenges (Kolbaek, 2014). It should provide trained facilitators and suitable venues for conducting Proactive Reviews (von Krogh et al. 2000). To

Table 2. Enablers for and obstacles to successful proactive reviews

Elements of Successful Proactive Reviews	Enablers	Obstacles
Initiating Proactive Reviews	Employees at any hierarchical level may initiate Proactive Reviews.	Lack of defined roles—top management, sponsor, participant, and facilitator.
	Top management and division managers define PR Triggers that describe appropriate situations for Proactive Reviews.	Lack of PR Triggers.
	Most Proactive Reviews are conducted for positive cases to avoid being perceived as a punishment.	Proactive Reviews are only conducted for negative cases as failures and mistakes.
Learning environment	Appropriate physical setting, technology, and trained facilitators.	Lack of privacy in the physical setting.
	Employees from all hierarchical levels and divisions in the organization are welcome as participants.	Inviting participants who are not involved in solving the task.
Top management support	Top management should provide a knowledge vision and approve necessary resources.	Lack of appropriate resources, such as time, trained facilitators, or physical setting.
	Top managers welcome the management challenges, implement relevant organizational changes, and communicate the change process and the results.	The top management ignores the management challenges addressed to it or forgets to communicate the process and results of the changes caused by Proactive Reviews.
Other management support	Managers should provide appropriate resources and implement the action and communication plan.	Sponsors carry out Proactive Reviews mainly for negative cases. Sponsors do not define the purpose of the Proactive Review. Sponsors ignore the action and communication plan.
Participants' behavior	Bearing in mind that "we are here to learn". Sharing the problem or challenge, working collaboratively on the solution Keeping the dialogue confidential—the only communication from the Proactive Review is the action and communication plan and the management challenge Daring "not to know" Participating in the mutual dialogue Daring to bring up the management challenges with top management	Lack of mutual participation in the dialogue Gossiping about the dialogue in the Proactive Review Not contributing intensively Fear of sponsor and/or top management
Participants build a robust relationship	Participants face and formulate management challenges. Participants are brave enough to change viewpoints when they gain new insights.	Lack of constructive contributions to the dialogue Stubbornness
The facilitator creates a caring atmosphere	The facilitator creates a space for humor, trust, equality, and daring "not to know."	The facilitator's failure to stop hostile behavior
Ripple effect—learning in four ontological dimensions, namely, individual, team, organizational, and inter-organizational learning	Individual learning is constructed when the participant reflects on obstacles and enablers that led to the outcome of the task. Team learning occurs in the collective reflection among the participants.	If the participants do not contribute to the dialogue, they reduce both the individual and the team learning.
	Horizontal organizational learning is initiated by the implementation of the action and communication plan. Vertical organizational learning occurs when the management challenge is presented to the top management, and the top management creates and implements changes accordingly.	The organizational learning will drop or stop if the participants do not deliver the action and communication plan to the sponsor, the sponsor does not implement the plan, or the top management ignores the management challenge addressed to it.
	Inter-organizational learning is initiated when customers or partners are invited to Proactive Reviews.	Inter-organizational learning will only take place when other organizations participate in the Proactive Review.
Valuable results	New or improved products, services, and work practices should be provided quickly to customers or implemented in the organization.	Delays in the implementation of new work practices and in the delivery of new services or products to customers

support the Proactive Reviews, the top management should welcome the management challenges (von Krogh, 2012), and then communicate the process and results of solving these challenges (Kolbaek, 2014).

The middle managers should initiate Proactive Reviews (Nonaka & Takeuchi, 1995) according to the PR Triggers and ensure that most Proactive Reviews are performed for positive cases to avoid the participants' perception of Proactive Reviews as a punishment (Kolbaek, 2014). The middle managers implement the action and communication plan. They should also communicate the results of the Proactive Reviews to colleagues and subordinates.

The facilitators have the obligation of maintaining a caring atmosphere (von Krogh et al. 2000; Nonaka et al. 2000; Wegerif, 2007) and leading the participants through the seven questions while respecting the time constraints (Kolbaek, 2014). The facilitators remain neutral and ensure that the middle managers receive the action and communication plan and that the top management receives the management challenges (Kolbaek, 2014).

The participants should prepare for the Proactive Review by considering the obstacles and enablers that led to the outcome they experienced. The participants engage in the Proactive Review with the mindset, "We are here to learn" (Kolbaek, 2012). They remain involved in the Proactive Review all the way through the seven questions to welcome the other participants' contributions and to maintain the group's intimacy (Wegerif, 2007). They reflect collaboratively, listen to the other participants' viewpoints, accept conflicting perspectives, and should be brave enough to admit "not knowing" certain matters (von Krogh et al. 2000; Wegerif, 2007). They create an action and communication plan that ensures sharing the results of the Proactive Review with relevant peers. Each participant takes responsibility for at least one action in the plan, which one or two participants deliver and explain to the sponsor (Kolbaek, 2014). The participants define the management challenges to bring up with the top management these complex obstacles to success (Kolbaek, 2014; von Krogh, 2012). After the Proactive Review, the participants keep the dialogue confidential and only communicate according to the action and communication plan.

CONCLUSION

This article has addressed the question "How can employees, who solve a task together, learn from the experience and share this learning with relevant colleagues to improve work practices, services, and/or products?"

The seven questions in the Proactive Review provide a new and improved structure for the Lessons Learned, one that increases productivity. These seven open questions support mutual dialogues among the participants. The questions allow learning in the four classes described by Bateson (1972)—"sensing," "realizing," "adapting," and "changing"—and the last question allows the participants to make their meta-reflection explicit.

Any employee or manager may initiate a Proactive Review. To save costs, the top management and division managers define the PR Triggers for the cases appropriate for Proactive Reviews. Proactive Reviews may be conducted for positive or negative cases. More Proactive Reviews are preferably performed on successes than failures to avoid the participants' perception of Proactive Reviews as a punishment, which may reduce the creativity of the solutions. Any employee from any hierarchical level or division in the organization may participate in a Proactive Review on a task in which he or she has been involved.

A Proactive Review initiates a ripple effect of learning in three or four ontological dimensions. The individual learns when he or she prepares for and participates in the dialogue in the Proactive Review. In turn, it makes the other participants listen, think, and occasionally change their perspective, which constitute a team-learning process that leads to the creation of solutions to the identified issues and challenges. The participants involve colleagues in the new insights by creating an action and communication plan, which is implemented by the sponsor. The action and communication plan ensures horizontal organizational learning. The top management implements changes as a result of the management challenges brought to their attention. The implementation of these changes starts the vertical organizational learning. Inter-organizational learning is achieved when customers or partners are invited as participants in Proactive Reviews.

Proactive Reviews support the organization in finding solutions to complex issues. This way of learning from work experiences has proven beneficial in a world-class IT company that operates in a very competitive environment. The participants produce abstractions, tools, symbols, stories, and solutions leading to improved services, better products, increased sales, upgraded delivery, or innovative work practices, meaning that Proactive Reviews contribute positively to the bottom line.

Implementing Proactive Reviews in an organization may be regarded as similar to growing a tree. When more Proactive Reviews are conducted, the tree grows larger, and the corporate value increases. The Proactive Reviews improve the team spirit and foster robust relationships internally, as well as externally with customers and partners. The tree's shadow and the comfort it supplies grow as well. When an organization deliberately learns from experience, it not only enhances its value, but an integrated part of this value creation also encompasses the development and maintenance of the corporate values.

If the organization does not create value, it will soon be out of business. The organization thus perceives Proactive Reviews as an important tool for survival in a competitive environment. The rationale is that Proactive Reviews enable employees who collaboratively solve a task to learn from the experience and share it with relevant colleagues being peers or various management levels. This process leads to improved or innovative work practices, services, and/or products that improve business results.

REFERENCES

Abbariki, M. (2013). Knowledge sharing and work identity. *Knowledge Management: An International Journal, 12*(2), 45–60.

Akhtar, N., & Khan, R. A. (2011). Exploring the paradox of organizational learning and learning organization. *Interdisciplinary Journal of Contemporary Research in Business, 2*(9), 257–270.

Bateson, G. (1972). *Steps to an ecology of mind*. New York, NY: Chandler Publishing Co.

Bohm, D. (2014). *On dialogue*. London: Routledge.

Brandi, U., & Elkjaer, B. (2011). Tidsskrift for arbejdsliv. *Organisatorisk læring i organisatorisk forandring, 13*(2), 73- 89.

Chang, V. (2016). Review and discussion: E-learning for academia and industry. *International Journal of Information Management, 36*(3), 476–485. doi:10.1016/j.ijinfomgt.2015.12.007

Defillippi, R. (2011). *Psychological perspectives in organizational learning a four-quadrant approach* (H. Shipton, Ed.). West Sussex, UK: Wiley.

East, W. E. (1998). *Web-enabled design review and lessons learned*. USACERL Technical Report (ADA344693) CERL-TR-98/31.

Easterby-Smith, M., & Prieto, I. M. (2008). Dynamic capabilities and knowledge management: An integrative role for learning? *British Journal of Management, 19*(3), 235–249. doi:10.1111/j.1467-8551.2007.00543.x

Elkjaer, B. (2003). Organizational learning with a pragmatic slant. *International Journal of Lifelong Education, 22*(5), 481–494. doi:10.1080/02601370320000102841

Elkjaer, B. (2013). Organisational Learning as Movements in Practice. *Pedagogy and Teacher Education, Scientific Papers. University of Latvia, 790*, 22–33.

Engeström, Y. (2001). Expansive learning at work: Toward an activity theoretical reconceptualization. *Journal of Education and Work, 14*(1), 133–156. doi:10.1080/13639080020028747

Engeström, Y., & Kerosuo, H. (2007). From workplace learning to inter-organizational learning and back: The contribution of activity theory. *Journal of Workplace Learning, 19*(6), 336–342. doi:10.1108/13665620710777084

Engeström, Y., Rantavuori, J., & Kerosuo, H. (2013). Expansive learning in a library: Actions, cycles and deviations from instructional intentions. *Vocations and Learning, 6*(1), 81–106. doi:10.100712186-012-9089-6

Gherardi, S. (2001). From organizational learning to practicebased knowing. *Human Relations, 54*(1), 131–139. doi:10.1177/0018726701541016

Gibney, P. (2006). The double bind theory: Still crazy-making after all these years. *Psychotherapy in Australia, 12*(3), 48–55.

Holsapple, C. W., & Wu, J. (2011). An elusive antecedent of superior firm performance: The knowledge management factor. *Decision Support Systems, 52*(1), 271–283. doi:10.1016/j.dss.2011.08.003

Kolbaek, D. (2012). *Proactive reviews.* Copenhagen: Book on Demand.

Kolbaek, D. (2014). *Learning from experience in the context of work.* Aalborg, Denmark: Aalborg University Press.

Kolbaek, D. (2015). *Proactive Review. In Utilizing Evidence-Based Lessons Learned for Enhanced Organizational Innovation and Change.* Hershey, PA: IGI Global.

Nickelsen, N. C. M., & Elkjaer, B. (2014, April). *Performing task integration – the dilemmas of relational coordination and knowledge sharing.* Paper presented at the Organizational Learning and Knowledge Capabilities Conference, Oslo, Norway.

Nonaka, I., & Takeuchi, H. (1995). *The knowledge-creating company.* New York, NY: Oxford University Press.

Nonaka, I., Toyama, R., & Konno, N. (2000). SECI, *Ba* and leadership: A unified model of dynamic knowledge creation. *Long Range Planning, 33*(1), 5–34. doi:10.1016/S0024-6301(99)00115-6

Phillips, L. (2011). *The promise of dialogue: The dialogic turn in the production and communication of knowledge.* Amsterdam: John Benjamins Pub. Co. doi:10.1075/ds.12

Qvortrup, L. (2000). *Det hyperkomplekse samfund: 14 fortællinger om informationssamfundet* (2nd ed.). København: Gyldendal.

Rao, M. (2003). *Leading with knowledge.* New Delhi: TATA McGraw-Hill.

van Winkelen, C., & McKenzie, J. (2011). *Knowledge works*. Chichester, UK: Wiley.

Vince, R. (2012). The Contradictions of Impact: Action Learning and Power in Organizations. *Action Learning Research and Practice*, *9*(3), 209–218. doi:10.1080/14767333.2012.722356

Vince, R., & Gabriel, Y. (2011). *Organizations, Learning and Emotion* (H. Shipton, Ed.). West Sussex, UK: Wiley.

von Krogh, G. (2012). How Does Social Software Change Kopwledge Management Toward a Strategic Research Agenda? *The Journal of Strategic Information Systems*, *21*(2), 154–164. doi:10.1016/j.jsis.2012.04.003

von Krogh, G., Ichijo, K., & Nonaka, I. (2000). *Enabling knowledge creation*. New York, NY: Oxford University Press. doi:10.1007/978-1-349-62753-0

Vygotsky, L. S. (1978). *Mind and society: The development of higher psychological processes*. Cambridge, MA: Harvard University Press.

Wegerif, R. (2007). *Dialogic education and technology. Expanding the space of learning*. New York, NY: Springer. doi:10.1007/978-0-387-71142-3

KEY TERMS AND DEFINITIONS

Action and Communication Plan: A tangible result of a proactive review, including actions for further development of the findings and decisions regarding whom to involve and inform.

Enablers for a Proactive Review: Actions or behaviors supporting the participation in the proactive review or the implementation of the results.

Lessons Learned: Working processes or techniques that diminish or avoid potential failures or mishaps.

Management Challenge: An issue that cannot be solved by the participants and needs the attention of the top management.

Obstacles to a Proactive Review: Actions or behaviors opposing the participation in the proactive review or the implementation of the results.

Proactive Review: An educational design for lessons learned, consisting of seven questions asked in a specific sequence. The dialogue is the backbone of proactive reviews.

Ripple Effect of a Proactive Review: Refers to how the learning from a proactive review spreads to colleagues throughout the organization.

Roles in a Proactive Review: The four roles involved in this educational design for lessons learned are the participants in the proactive review, the facilitator, the sponsor, and the top management.

ENDNOTE

1 The titles of the learning classes and the examples are those of me.

Chapter 4
Modeling the Skunkworks Technology:
Sharing Experience to Make the Difference

Sylvia C. Mupepi
Grand Valley State University, USA

Kuda B. Mupepi
St. James College of Medicine, USA

Tatenda Mupepi
St. James College of Medicine, USA

ABSTRACT

Management view the skunkworks approach as an enriched environment composed of individuals possessing the required experience critical in the formulation of strategy to advance efficiency and effectiveness in the firm. It is a purpose-built forum where learning happens by sharing experiences to design and implement new products in at least four modalities. The first is its capability to ignite the company's mission by co-construction a shared vision. Organizations need to appreciate what the future may look like. The second is the collective experience of its membership where new ideas can lead to the design and implementation of the technology to progress the job. A company must do all it can to differentiate itself to compete successfully. The third is its ability to create diffuse and distribute knowledge to cognitive areas where it will be put into organizational context. The fourth is the need to sustain change by continuing to learn and improve. This chapter models the skunkworks technology.

DOI: 10.4018/978-1-5225-7390-6.ch004

INTRODUCTION

The skunkworks technology developed by a small team of individuals at Lockheed Martin Aeronautics Engineering Company to design and implement the most lethal fling combat machine in existence. Ben Rich and Leo Janos were part of what became the Skunkworks team that made America's quest to dominate the skies a reality. The skunkworks technology can be adapted in peacetime to recruit and select a team possessing the knowledge skills technology and the brashness to design and implement new products and re-examine existing tools to make new equipment to enhance the dexterity necessary to increase productivity (Rich and Janos, 2015).

Lev Vygotsky was a Russian neuropsychologist who wrote many theories about learning and cognitive development. When he developed the Zone of Proximal Development (ZPD) theory, he had no business organization in mind. Vygotsky was influenced by the systemic thinking of the scholars associated with German-American Gestalt psychology movement such as Kurt Lewin and Chris Argyris, among others, whose postulations were directly related to organizational development (Wertsch, 1984).

On-job training has been in use as a skills development strategy since time immemorial. It is one-on-one training located at site or office. It implies that people are taught how to complete the task while they are doing the job. Many scholars such as Senge (1990) and Mupepi and Mupepi (2016), have built upon OJT as strategy to create the competitive edge in successful organization.

This chapter juxtaposes the Skunkworks, ZPD, and OJT to advance shared meaning in system-wide organization aimed at increasing productivity.

BACKGROUND INFORMATION

In their audio book, Ben Rich and Leo Janos tell the story of how their company Lockheed Martin developed new products such as the Stealth Fighter jet which answered America's quest to dominate the skies. The team's mission was characterized by the notion that failure was not an option. The Skunkworks team was selected from military personnel who had aeronautical, electrical, ballistic, information systems, mechanical, and logistics engineering backgrounds. The Skunkworks team was located in an abandoned barn where real skunks and raccoons and the occasional owl thrived. The team got its name from that habitat. It had to clear the barn to make room for their meeting place, offices, computer simulation, and break rooms. When the Skunkworks finally got to work, their end products were numerous classified military technology resulting in products such as the U2 reconnaissance aircraft and Stealth Fighter Jet. The gregariousness of the Skunkworks team was characterized by deep mental involvement to create possible end products and where algorithms had to be perfect in finding answers to known problems. Ng (2012) suggested that deep learning was a subfield of machine learning concerned with algorithms inspired by the structure and function of the brain called artificial neural networks. The argument progressed by Ng is that machine learning could be utilized to enhance product improvement and development. Ng is a founding entrepreneur credited with products and services such as Coursera and Google Brain. Ng is at the leading edge of artificial intelligence, the application of computers to areas normally regarded as requiring human intelligence.

Deep mental involvement entails applying Gestalt probing techniques such as: *What is the most spontaneous thing you have ever done?* In Haggbloom and Warnick et al (2003), Kurt Koffka Wolfgang Kohler and Kurt Lewin, among others, argued about Gestalt psychology as a unique field of study in which the subjective experience of visual perception was of a world composed of solid volumes, bounded by the belief that the mind made the global whole with self-organizing tendencies. In Haggbloom et al (2003), Kurt Koffka coined the phrase that the whole was something else than the sum of its parts incorrectly understood. The Gestalt school of thought attempted to articulate perception in a chaotic world. In Carlson and Heth (2010) Kurt Kokka and Wolfgang Kohler attempted to comprehend the organization of cognitive processes in the study of perception. The centricity of Gestalt school of thought was its capability in deconstructing the whole units into its elements. Deep mental involvement enables structuralism to develop different perspectives of a whole. The Skunkworks approach developed different perspectives to a problem and as well as algorithms to solve each difficult situation. Kurt Lewin was a Gestalt psychologist who developed the field theory which was the foundation of social psychology. Marrow (1977) propounded that the thesis has remained influential in the study of dynamics and manipulation of human behavior. Lewin contested that human behavior was largely influenced by the environment.

The Skunkworks team had to fashion an environment conducive to creativity. They had to create a culture that enabled deep mental involvement happen and appreciate each team player's perspectives to advance new product development and perfect existing technology to make the job easier.

Shifting the Mindset to Create a Shared Vision

The Skunkworks could apply organization development techniques to shift the mindset from past-focused to future-focused. Many of the answers the Skunkworks wanted could not be found in the past since the issues never existed before. There are at least six performance areas where the mindset had to be changed:

There were no airplanes that exceeded the speed of a Mach and no standards to go by. The jetfighters that existed during WW2 include Spitfires or Gloster Meteor, among others whose top speeds were not what the Skunkworks was looking for.

From discipline-focused to having an organization focused mindset, was the second challenge the Skunkworks had to face. Theirs was a team focused on different engineering disciplines. The team members had to focus on the needs of the US military to design the technology the US military needed to conquer the skies at a time the Cold war was a reality.

From authoritative to consultative partnership. The Skunkworks had to work with Lockheed Martin as a partnership. This changed expectations from condition of service and time management to increased expectations such as profit sharing (Jamieson and Vogelsang, 2013).

From being engineering professionals to being an entrepreneur who specializes in the design and implementation of jet fighter planes.

The change required in all six performance areas enabled cutting edge research and the development of winning products to happen. The new entrepreneurs were successful in their efforts.

Knowledge Creation

In Mupepi and Mupepi (2018), Tenkasi and Mohrman (1999), and Beaulieu Carriere and Schoch (2013), knowledge creation is viewed as a collaborative activity where a group of people from the same company who meet all the time on-line or in designated places to make the technology and logistics to fulfill the needs of customers. Beaulieu et al suggested that interactive collaborative designs were open systems enabling ambitious business plans to succeed through interactive collaborative designs (ICD). The ICD approach could have been applied by the Skunkworks to remove the traditional hierarchy which is top-down structure. There were no ranks recognition, they reduced themselves to just engineers with a passion in flying machines. Tenkasi and Mohrman (1999) propounded that the operative assumptions of the traditional models of knowledge transmission included three theses: the first was that knowledge could be objectively realized. The Skunkworks could co-construct the knowledge required in every step of the assignment at hand. The second thesis was that the type of knowledge they were pursuing was applicable across contexts. For example, technology about jet propulsion could be applied in the navy or marines. The third proposition was that the knowledge they hoped to create should be complete (see Figure 1).

The Skunkworks team had access to all the resources they needed to shoot for their goal of a lethal jet fighting machine (see Figure 1). The technology as well as the knowledge they needed to meet their goals could be objectively realized. The

Figure 1. Shooting for specific goals

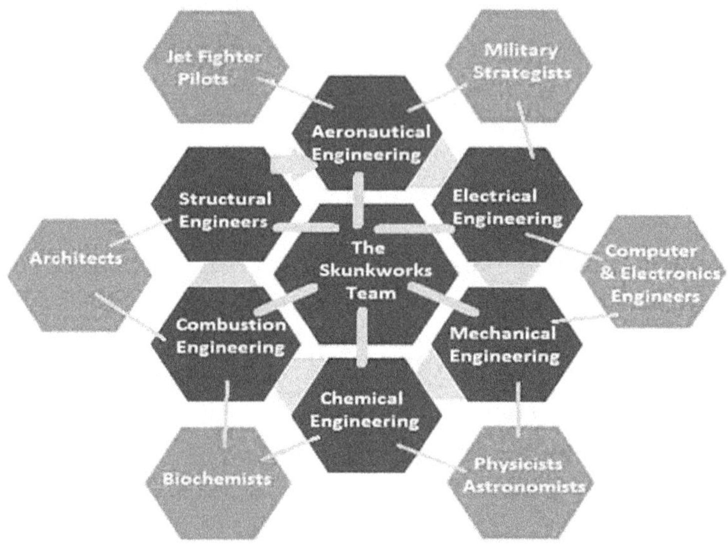

knowledge they were looking for could be applied across military contexts. Both the naval and ground forces deploy all types of aircraft to make ends meet (see Figure 1).

The Skunkworks team had specific goals to fulfill in a given period of time. In Mupepi Essila Opoku Mensah and Mupepi (2018), an alternative change management strategy hinged on pragmatic social construction ontology to champion productivity. All companies are designed and up-shoot specific goals. In those entities, talented individuals can be hired to play exact roles in the production of goods and services valued by customers. The customers of the Skunkworks team were the Lockheed Martin Company whose expectations were the success of the project. Data available show that corporations that prioritize activities by re-engineering the division of labor and comprehending emotional intelligence in organization yield increased outputs (Mupepi, 2014). The new specialists can define the explicitness critical to optimization of production and minimization of liabilities and typify that practice makes perfect in supporting extraordinary performance. The Skunkworks divided the work setting targets for themselves and going outside the normal box to envision possibilities. Mupepi et al assert that dividing work in the value-creation process enables innovative thinking to happen. The structure should be assessed and evaluated to match talents to tasks and to use the comparatives to advance team play necessary to win.

An Interdisciplinary Team

The Skunkworks team had a common denominator, the military. They shared a passion of flying military aircraft. They viewed the project as something that challenged their capabilities in various engineering fields. They developed a systemic way of perceiving the project and each other's field of specialization. The Skunkworks viewed the project as a whole whose elements hang together because they continuously affect each other over time and operate toward a common purpose (see figure 1). In Wilkinson (2006), systems theory is defined as an interdisciplinary study of systems in general, with the goal of discovering patterns and algorithms necessary in maintaining the value creation system to produce the goods and services demanded by the customers. Wilkinson elucidates the definition of systems theory as an understanding related to the General System Theory of biologist Ludwig von Bertalanffy (Bertalanffy, 1934), physiologists Walter B. Cannon, Walter Pitts, Warren McCulloch and cybernetics technologists Claude Shannon, Norbert Wiener, and William Ross Ashby. In Daft (2013) a group of technocrats from the same organization referred to as skunkworks meet regularly in defined physical places and in cyberspace to progress organizational goals. Daft argued that the skunkworks were a people who shared the same vision about their organization. They deliberated in designing new products and appropriate technology to make those new products a reality. Systems thinking can be applied as a strategy to search for solutions to the problems the organization faces such as competition. It is handy in creating innovation and in creating a shared vision of the future. Systems thinking can be applied to design and implement the competitive advantage.

Constructing High Performance Organization

The epistemology to effectively construct high performance organization is drawn from Giddens (1984), Berger and Luckmann (1966), Mupepi (2016, 2017a and 2017b), Porter (1985), Prahalad and Hamel (1990), and Sacab (2015), among others.

Structuration Proposition

The structuration theory was developed by Anthony Giddens in 1984 to explore the connection between individuals and social systems. This holistic view of modern societies has earned Giddens a reputation for restructuring fledgling organizations around the world. Falkheimer (2009) alluded to the demolition of apartheid in South Africa where racism and discrimination had been institutionalized. Since the ending of the apartheid regime the country implemented one of the most liberal constitutions in the world. In this consultation Falkheimer applied the structuration approach to understand race and ethnicity, discrimination and prejudice, and ethnic conflicts in South Africa. Race is a widely-used term, often used in everyday language to describe biological differences. Racism is often blind of talent or it jibs what talent is. However, there is no scientific basis for the concept to be used within the contexts of the military for many reasons. One of them is that rank in the military determine structure and effective communication channels (see Figure 2)

The Skunkworks team needed effective communications to successfully accomplish their goals. Communication skills are developed and may be enhanced or improved with increased knowledge and practice. During interpersonal communication, there is message sending and message receiving. This can be conducted using both direct and indirect methods (see Figure 2). The assumption that knowledge can be created implies existence of effective interpersonal communications. Highly cohesive teams increase gregariousness by using all formats of communication technologies. Email, WhatsApp, Mobile phones and other social media are just a few modalities enabling people teams or organizations keep in touch. Saha (2018) assert that sustaining a competitive edge in today's business world requires innovative approaches to effective communications, product, service, and management systems design and performance. Advances in computing technologies have presented managers with additional challenges as well as further opportunities to enhance their business models. Progress in data communications and networking for digital business transformation is a one of the ways an organization could deploy to keep abreast of competition

Learning Successfully

In any lesson plan or training project what must be learnt should be made clear to the learner. Learning objectives are imperative in skills development or knowledge acquisition lessons. The Skunkworks team had to interpret the orders they received

Figure 2. Effective interpersonal communications
(Mupepi, 2017).

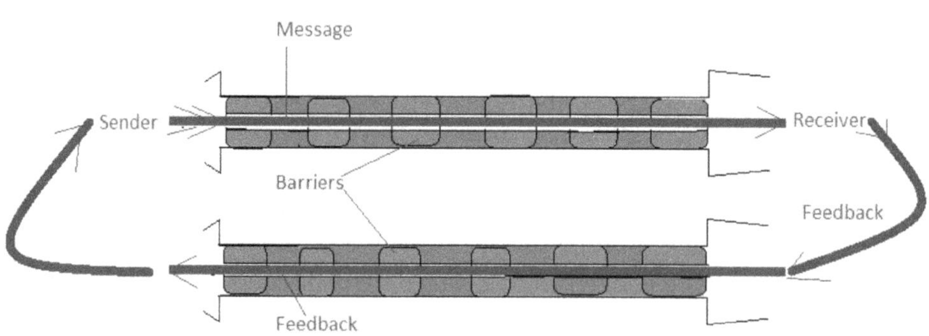

from their various clients into job specifications to create new products or improve upon existing ones. In Kaya (2008) professional development is viewed as an individual's lifelong learning process. Learning needs are defined based on personal learning gaps and career goals. As technology changes and work practice standards are renewed, professionals need to keep their knowledge and skills updated. For this, professionals continue to gain new knowledge and skills formally or informally through daily work practices and interactions in a community of practice and build a formal record of individuals' certificates, credits, and credentials. This learning process is lifelong journey, called continuing professional development. Accessing knowledge in a relatively unfamiliar domain (however necessary for professional development) can be limited and difficult in traditional higher education and training settings because they are expensive and time consuming for addressing their immediate needs for practice. Kaya suggested that active learners often sought new channels of information in order to fulfill learning needs.

For the Skunkworks team their zone of proximal learning was determined by what they wanted to accomplish. They were the experts in various engineering fields. They were given access to all types of resources to progress their quest. Through technological developments and the emergence of social network service platforms, an alternative learning phenomena could have been established which combined hybrid with traditional classroom teaching (Dickinson, 2015).

Learning Materials

In Garet and Porter et al (2001), oftentimes the acquisition of knowledge for professional development requires structural instructions on account of the sheer volume and complexity of the learning materials. This situation is a paradoxical one, as participants in the professional online community tend to have innovative online curriculum options. One example is the Massive Open Online Course Although such emergent learning phenomena underscore the importance of understanding how technology and open accessibility to digital content lead to changes in the learning context, particularly with respect to informal learning and communities of practice (COP) (Lave and Wenger 1991), there is a notable gap about this issue in the professional development literature.

The process of professional development using online learning could be facilitated successfully by responding to the following questions: (1) what is the current understanding of the literature on informal learning, on-line learning and communities of practice, and what are the relevance to professional development, (2) what are the factors to be considered to best utilize COP and online learning in professional development multiple levels of learning environments, (3) how are different case studies illuminating the effective use of online and COP within various learner-driven informal learning tool or as a process to accelerate their professional development practices and outcomes (Mupepi, 2017a).

Discourse of Learning

Learning and continuous improvement is the basis of successful operations in many organizations. Organizational talent can be viewed as a social assert that can be improved upon by continuous learning and improvement. The value creation system made up of technology knowledge skills and the brashness to effectively do the job is constantly changing. Technology as well skills are constantly changing. If organizations fail to articulate this change that could be their end. Talent can be deconstructed to progress the necessary efficacy in organization. A limited literature is drawn to understand the role of structures and technology in the value creation process. Value is created anytime an action is taken for which the benefits exceed the costs, or the moment an action can be prevented for which the costs exceed the benefits. A co-constructed competency model can be initiated to comprehend a systemic approach to enhancing performance and the design of strategy to retain talent and nurture the skillfulness and knowing necessary in boosting yields in diversified entities.

Action Learning

Lewin (1943) developed a method of change he referred to as Action Research. It is either research initiated to solve an immediate problem or a reflective process of progressive problem solving led by individuals working with others in teams such as Skunkworks as part of a strategy to introduce and manage change. Lewin argued that action learning could be applied to improve organizational performance.

Experiential Learning

In the early 1970s, Kolb and Ron Fry (now both at the Weatherhead School of Management) developed the Experiential Learning Model (ELM), composed of four elements:

1. Concrete experience,
2. Observation of and reflection on that experience,
3. Formation of abstract concepts based upon the reflection,
4. Testing the new concepts

These four elements are the essence of a spiral of learning that can begin with any one of the four elements, but typically begins with a concrete experience. Kolb and Fry popularized experiential learning with their books entitled: Organizational Psychology: A Book of Readings (1975), Toward an Applied Theory of Experiential Learning (1974) and Learning and the Kolby Learning Style Inventory 4.0 (2011).

In Mupepi (2017a) sharing experience is contested to be at the heart of successful organization leading to the creation of the competitive advantage. The notion that a problem shared is a problem solved could have been the thinking and practice at the Skunkworks. The team composed of engineers from different areas of specialization cohered to produce cutting-edge fighting machines successfully.

Systems Thinking

The idea of the learning organization developed from a body of work called systems thinking (Senge 1990). This is a conceptual framework that allows people to study businesses as bounded objects. Learning organizations use this method of thinking when assessing their company and have information systems that measure the performance of the organization as a whole and of its various components (Argyris, 1999). Systems thinking states that all the characteristics must be apparent at once in an organization for it to be a learning organization. If some of these characteristics

Figure 3. Building effective capability
Senge (1990)

are missing, then the organization will fall short of its goal. However, O'Keeffe (2002) argued that the characteristics of a learning organization were factors that are gradually acquired, rather than developed simultaneously.

Mental Models

Senge (1990) propounded that a mental model was an explanation of someone's thought process about how something works in the real world. It is a representation of the surrounding world, the relationships between its various parts and a person's intuitive perception about his or her own acts and their consequences. The assumptions held by individuals and organizations are called mental models. In organization mental models are important in shared work or producing the goods and services demanded by customers (Senge, 1990).

Team Learning

In O'Keeffe (2002) the accumulation of individual learning constitutes team learning. The benefit of team or shared learning is that staff grow more quickly and the problem solving capacity of the organization is improved through better access to knowledge and expertise. McHugh Groves and Alker (1998), suggested that the learning organizations have structures that facilitate team learning with features such as boundary crossing and openness. Senge (190) argued that team learning was critical for organizational success. It required individuals to engage in dialogue and discussion ab out the job at hand and how it should be done. Therefore, team members must develop open communication, shared meaning, and shared understanding. Wang and Ahmed (2003) posited that the learning organizations typically have excellent knowledge management structures, allowing system-wide creation, acquisition, dissemination, and implementation of explicit practices to increase productivity.

Personal Mastery

Senge (1990) suggested that the commitment by an individual to the process of learning was known as personal mastery. There is a competitive advantage for an organization whose workforce can learn more quickly than the workforce of other organizations. Individual learning was acquired through on-job training and staff training, development and continuous self-improvement. However, Senge (1990) propounded that learning could not be forced upon an individual who was not receptive to learning. Research shows that most learning in the workplace is incidental, rather than the product of formal training (Argyris, 1999), therefore it is important to develop a culture where personal mastery is practiced in daily life. A learning organization has been described as the sum of individual learning, but there must be mechanisms for individual learning to be transferred into organizational learning (Wang and Ahmed, 2003).

Hoffman (2013) suggested five factors that a manager should keep in mind when leading or managing personal mastery: Linkage, energy, focus, skills and anchor

- Linkages…strength in numbers
    - Is there a powerful guiding coalition?
    - Are relationships built and maintained among the informal leaders?
    - Are relationships built with key customers and other stakeholders?
- Energy…Motivation to get there
    - Is there a clear and compelling vision of the future state/goal?
    - Are people able to see themselves in this vision and the benefit to them?
    - Does the majority share a sense of urgency?
- Focus…Where are we headed?
    - What is the most leverage point for influencing the system?
    - Is there a clear and compelling vision of the future state/goal?
    - Is there a coherent and relevant metaphor?

Shared Vision

Senge (1990) asserted that the development of a shared vision was important in motivating the staff to learn, as it created a common identity that provided focus and energy for learning. The most successful visions are those built on the individual visions of the employees at all levels of the organization (McHugh Groves and Alker 1998). Thus the creation of a shared vision can be hindered by traditional structures where the company vision is imposed from above (Senge, 1990). Therefore, learning organizations tend to have flat, decentralized organizational structures. The shared vision is often to succeed against a competitor however, Senge states that these are transitory goals and suggests that there should also be long-term goals that are intrinsic within the company.

Mupepi (2017a) suggested that creating a shared vision meant that all stakeholders understood the need to progress organizational success. Creating a shared mission means:

- Seeking consensus: planning with partners to design a plan all can live with.
- Allow plenty of time to implement the plan
- Giving employees energy and focus
- People tend to learn more about the things that matter to them

BARRIERS TO LEARNING

The worksite for the Skunkworks was situated in the woods of a derelict farm barn where there was privacy and less noise. Barriers to learning include little or no motivation, distractions, unclear learning objectives, and the absence of feedback, among many others. Most of the problems to learning arise from an organization not fully embracing all the necessary facets about knowledge acquisition and skills development. Once the barriers to learning have been identified, work can begin on dismantling them. Senge (1990) urged management to embrace the learning organization as a tool enabling learning and change to happen successfully. Some organizations find it hard to embrace personal mastery because as a concept it is intangible and the benefits cannot be quantified personal mastery can even be seen as a threat to the organization. This threat can be real, as Senge points out, that to empower people in an unaligned organization can be counterproductive. In other words, if individuals do not engage with a shared vision, personal mastery could be used to advance their own personal visions. In some organizations a lack of a learning culture can be a barrier to learning. An environment must be created where individuals can share learning without it being devalued and ignored, so more people can benefit from their knowledge and the individuals becomes empowered.

Resistance to learning can occur within a learning organization if there is not sufficient buy-in at an individual level. This is often encountered with people who feel threatened by change or believe that they have the most to lose. They are likely to have closed mind sets, and are not willing to engage with mental models. Unless implemented coherently across the organization, learning can be viewed as elitist and restricted to senior levels. In that case, learning will not be viewed as a shared vision. If training and development is compulsory, it can be viewed as a form of control, rather than as personal development. Learning and the pursuit of personal mastery needs to be an individual choice, therefore enforced take-up will not work (Senge, and Kleiner et al 1999).

Problems Organizational Learning Addresses

Some of the issues that learning organizations were designed to address within institutions is fragmentation, competition and reactiveness. Fragmentation is described as breaking a problem into pieces. For example, each organization has an accounting department, finance, operations, IT and marketing. Competition occurs when employees are trying to do better or 'beat' others in an assignment instead of collaborating. Reactiveness occurs when an organization changes only in reaction to outside forces, rather than proactively initiating change (Chawla, Santa and Renesch, 1995).

Continuous Learning and Improvement

The first type of change begins with the study of what the organizational unit is presently doing to locate opportunities to learn and improve. It is assumed that everyone in the unit by now knows how to do their jobs with some margin of error. Stoner Wankel and Werner (1999) proposed that the Kaizan approach involved continuously improving existing operations in incremental steps. Imai (1986) suggested that innovation occurred as a result of large-scale changes in how the value creation process and how the company produced products demanded by customers.

SUMMARY

Organizations have a lot in common such as skills knowledge and the disposition to effectively do the job. These attributes can be improved upon through on-job training, staff development, and learning and continuous improvement. In any project, objectives are important in guiding how the job will be done, and how it will be evaluated. The Skunkworks team had to learn to work together and to appreciate the job at hand in terms of what was needed to be done using the skills technology and explicit practices possessed by the members of the team. The resistance to change is imminent in most organizations. Well-managed resistance enabled the Skunkworks team to design and implement new products successfully.

LIMITATION OF THE ARGUMENTS PRESENTED

The Skunkworks was an extraordinary project supported by the military and as such resources were not a constraint. The Skunkworks team was not a hierarchical structure but more or so of King Arthur's roundtable. Change and resistance go together, hand in glove. Each is natural pervasive and universal. Resistance is neither avoidable nor bad. It is a fact of organizational life. As such the Skunkworks team could have successfully managed the resistance. Resistance is feedback and feedback is information. Poorly managed resistance, like poorly managed information about productivity and markets can be costly.

Learning in organization is the most cost-effective strategy to progress the competitive advantage

THE WAY FORWARD

The Skunkworks team was very committed. There is need to:

- Be fluent in knowledge management to make the most of shared experiences
- Buy employee commitment
- Customize training for all employees
- Understand the resistance to change which is a group level construct. Groups can be selected to work on a project and as such, there should be minimal or no resistance to change
- Comprehend that learning objectives should be made clear to the learner
- Appreciate that the learning in organization can be applied to build desirable capability

CONCLUSION

Organizational learning on-job training and the zone of proximal learning can be applied to progress desirable goals successfully. Much depends on who owns the entity and whether they are willing to invest in intellectual capital or not. In experiential learning experts may not be willing to share what they know. The resistance to change is a construct of groups which implies that it is critical to organizational success to recruit and hire people possessing the right attitudes compatible with the interests of the business.

REFERENCES

Argyris, C. (1999). *On Organizational Learning* (2nd ed.). Oxford, UK: Blackwell Publishing.

Beaulieu, J.-P., Carriere, E. J., & Schoch, C. (2013). The Power of Interactive Collaborative Designs. In J. Vogelsang & M. Townsend (Eds.), Handbook for Strategic HR: Best Practices in Organization Development from OD Network. Academic Press.

Berger, P. L., & Luckman, T. (1966). *The social construction of reality*. New York: Anchor Books.

Carlson, N. R., & Heth, C. D. (2010). *Psychology the Science of Behavior*. Ontario, CA: Pearson Education Canada.

Chae, C., Suh, B., Han, S., Han, H., & Lim, D. H. (2018). Enhancing Learner-Driven Informal Learning in a Virtual Practice Community: The Massive Open Online Course (MOOC) as a Learning Solution for Professional Development. In J. Keengwe (Ed.), *Handbook of Research on Digital Content, Mobile Learning, and Technology Integration Models in Teacher Education* (pp. 207–226). Hershey, PA: IGI Global; doi:10.4018/978-1-5225-2953-8.ch011

Chawla, S., & Renesch, J. (1995). *Learning Organizations: Developing Cultures for Tomorrow's Workplace*. Portland, OR: Productivity Press.

Daft, R. (2013). *Management*. London, UK: Cengage Learning.

Dickinson, B. (2015). *Skunkworks Audio Tape*. Amazon Digital Services LLC.

Drack, M., Apfalter, W., & Pouvreau, D. (2017, March 11). On the Making of a System Theory of Life: Paul A Weiss and Ludwig von Bertalanffy's Conceptual Connection. *The Quarterly Review of Biology*, 349–373. PMID:18217527

Falkheimer, J. (2009). On Giddens: Interpreting public relations through Anthony Giddens' structuration and late modernity theory. In O. Ihlen, B. van Ruler, & M. Frederiksson (Eds.), *Public relations and social theory: Key figures and concepts* (pp. 103–119). New York, NY: Routledge.

Garet, M. S., Porter, A. C., Desimone, L., Birman, B. F., & Yoon, K. S. (2001, January 1). What Makes Professional Development Effective? Results From a National Sample of Teachers. *American Educational Research Journal, 38*(4), 915–945. doi:10.3102/00028312038004915

Giddens, A. (1984). *The constitution of society: Outline of the theory of structuration*. Cambridge, UK: Polity Press.

Haggbloom, S. J., Warnick, J. E., Jones, V. K., Yarbrough, G. L., Russell, T. M., Borecky, C. M., & …. (2002). The 100 most eminent psychologists of the 20th century. *Review of General Psychology*, *6*(2), 139–152. doi:10.1037/1089-2680.6.2.139

Hoffman, C. (2013). Change Mastery, Simplified. In J. Vogelsang & M. Townsend (Eds.), *Handbook for Strategic HR*. New York: Amacon.

Imai, M. (1986). *Kaizen: the key to Japan's competitive success*. New York: McGraw-Hill.

Jamieson, D., & Vogelsang, J. (2013). Changing world of human resources. In J. Vogelsang & M. Townsend (Eds.), *Handbook for Strategic HR*. New York: Amacon.

Kaya, Y. (2008). Constructivism: Its Theoretical Underpinnings, Variations, and Implications for Classroom Instruction. *Educational Horizons, 86*(3), 161-172.

Kolb, D. A., & Fry, R. (1975). Toward an applied theory of experiential learning. In C. Cooper (Ed.), *Theories of Group Process*. London, UK: John Wiley.

Kolb, D. A., & Kolb, A. Y. (2011). *The Kolb Learning Style Inventory 4.0*. Prentice-Hall.

Lave, J., & Wenger, E. (1991). *Situated Learning: Legitimate Peripheral Participation*. Cambridge, UK: Cambridge University Press. doi:10.1017/CBO9780511815355

Lewin, K. (1946). Action research and minority problems. *The Journal of Social Issues*, *2*(4), 34–46. doi:10.1111/j.1540-4560.1946.tb02295.x

Marrow, A. J. (1977). *The practical theorist; the life and work of Kurt Lewin*. New York: Teacher's College.

McHugh, D., Groves, D., & Alker, A. (1998). Managing learning: What do we learn from a learning organization? *The Learning Organization*, *5*(5), 209–220. doi:10.1108/09696479810238215

Mupepi, M. (2014, May 20). Can the division of labor be re-engineered to advance organizational dynamism? *SAGE Open*, *4*(2). doi:10.1177/2158244014536404

Mupepi, M. (2017a). *Effective Talent Management Strategies for Organizational Success*. Hershey, PA: IGI Global; doi:10.4018/978-1-5225-1961

Mupepi, M. (2017b). Deconstructing Talent: Understanding know-how in organization. In M. Mupepi (Ed.), *Effective Talent Management Strategies for Organizational Success* (pp. 83–100). Hershey, PA: IGI Global; doi:10.4018/978-1-5225-1961-4.ch007

Mupepi, M. G., Essila, J. C., Mensah, A. O., & Mupepi, S. C. (2018). Alternate Techniques to Chart Practicality in Organizations. In N. Baporikar (Ed.), *Knowledge Integration Strategies for Entrepreneurship and Sustainability* (pp. 334–352). Hershey, PA: IGI Global. doi:10.4018/978-1-5225-5115-7.ch016

Mupepi, M. G., & Mupepi, S. C. (2018). Amplifying the Significance of Systems Thinking in Organization. In M. Khosrow-Pour, D.B.A. (Ed.), Encyclopedia of Information Science and Technology, Fourth Edition (pp. 551-562). Hershey, PA: IGI Global. doi:10.4018/978-1-5225-2255-3.ch048

Mupepi, M. G., Tenkasi, R. V., Sorensen, P. F., & Mupepi, S. C. (2013). Creating High Impact Organization in the SADC: Adapting OD Methods and Practices. In J. Vogelsang & M. Townsend (Eds.), *Handbook for Strategic HR*. New York: Amacon.

Ng, A. Y. (2012). *Deep Learning of Invariant Features via Simulated Fixations in Video*. Accessed 05/10/18 http://papers.nips.cc/author/andrew-y-ng-1853

O'Keeffe, T. (2002). Organizational Learning: A new perspective. *Journal of European Industrial Training*, *26*(2), 130–141. doi:10.1108/03090590210422012

Prahalad, C., & Hamel, G. (1990). The core competence of the corporation. *Harvard Business Review*, *68*, 79–91.

Rich, B. R., & Janos, L. (2015). *A personal memoir of my years of Lockheed*. New York: Simon and Schuster Audio Books.

Rogers, E. M. (1983). *Diffusion of innovations*. New York: Free Press.

Saha, D. (2018). *Advances in Data Communications and Networking for Digital Business Transformation*. Hershey, PA: IGI Global; doi:10.4018/978-1-5225-5323-6

Senge, P., & Kleiner, A. (1999). The Dance of Change. New York: Currency Doubleday.

Senge, P. M. (1990). The art and practice of the learning organization. *The new paradigm in business: Emerging strategies for leadership and organizational change*, 126-138. Retrieved from http://www.giee.ntnu.edu.tw/files/archive/380_9e53918d

Stoner, J. A. F., Wankel, C. B., & Werner, F. M. (1999). The Need for continuous improvement. In Juran's Quality Handbook (5th ed.). New York: McGraw-Hill.

Tenkasi, R. V., & Mohrman, S. (1999). Global change as contextual collaborative knowledge creation. In D. L. Cooperrider & J. E. Dutton (Eds.), *Organizational Dimensions of Global Change: No limits to cooperation*. Thousand Oaks, CA: Sage. doi:10.4135/9781452231419.n5

von Bertalanffy, L. (1934). Untersuchungen über die Gesetzlichkeit des Wachstums. I. Allgemeine Grundlagen der Theorie; mathematische und physiologische Gesetzlichkeiten des Wachstums bei Wassertieren. *Arch. Entwicklungsmech.*, *131*, 613–652. PMID:28353935

Wang, C. L., & Ahmed, P. K. (2003). Organizational learning: A critical review. *The Learning Organization*, *10*(1), 8–17. doi:10.1108/09696470310457469

Wertsch, J. (1984). *Vygotsky the social formation of Mind*. London, UK: Wiley Ltd.

Wilkinson, D. M. (2006). *Fundamental Processes in Ecology: An Earth Systems Approach*. Oxford University Press. doi:10.1093/acprof:oso/9780198568469.001.0001

KEY TERMS AND DEFINITIONS

Continuous Learning and Improvement: Forming an unbroken learning and making corrections to errors, without interruption to perfect performance.

Deep Mental Involvement: The action of immersing someone or a team in problem solving or creating explicit practices to advance organization.

Experiential Learning: Experiential learning is the process of learning through experience and is more specifically defined as learning through reflection on doing.

Purpose-Built Forum: A purpose-built forum is one created to do a specific job. For example, a knowledge community is made to create diffuse and distribute knowledge throughout cognitive areas where it will be put into context to make the goods demanded by customers.

Resistance to Change: The degree to which a group or individual opposes change or new rules and procedures preferring the old regulations.

Skunkworks Project: A skunkworks project is a project developed by a small and loosely structured group of people who research and develop a project primarily for the sake of radical innovation. The terms originated with Lockheed's World War II Skunk Works project.

Chapter 5
Applying Theory to Inform Capability Development:
Bootstrapping the Community of Practice to Boost Productivity

Mambo G. Mupepi
Grand Valley State University, USA

Patience Taruwinga
Walla Walla University, USA

Sylvia C. Mupepi
Grand Valley State University, USA

ABSTRACT

This chapter describes the deliberate making of a community of practice to advance specialization in divided labor and structuring a successful enterprise. A knowledge network is characterized by mutual engagement in a joint enterprise that gives rise to a shared repertoire of knowledge, skillsets, and practices. The division of labor is identified to enable the novice to develop the proficiencies required for specialty to happen. Bootstrapping and other techniques are applied to replicate the performance required in making effective specialists. A conclusion is drawn taking the position that the centricity of an epistemic community is the locus of control of the job, individual, and team; additionally, it is the only organization that can authenticate the practices necessary to boost productivity.

DOI: 10.4018/978-1-5225-7390-6.ch005

INTRODUCTION

In many businesses, the function of management has been split as traditional transactional and administrative functions (e.g., purchasing, payroll, benefits, training) have been outsourced, reengineered, and automated, leaving management with more strategic responsibilities and roles. This change has left a lean structure of at most five-line managers reporting directly to the chief executive. In this article, we argue that line managers and their superiors can form a community of practice, a collaboration forum whose application can take the business to the next level. An analogy from the Adam Smith Pin-production factory is drawn to explain specialization and structuring efficient and effective organization. To advance the discourse, the following question will be asked: How can a community of practice inform competency development? The article is organized in four parts: the first part offers an introduction to the debate and proceeds to offer a description of some of the key terms used in the discussion. The second part provides a carefully selected literature to understand the practices in developing organizational competences. The third part makes a proposition how a community of practice (COP) can craft competences for similar companies in the same business which are difficult to imitate. In the fourth part, a conclusion is drawn mentioning the limitation in the arguments presented. In this discussion, a COP, an epistemic community (EC), or a knowledge community imply the same thing. The COP can be described as a group of people who meet regularly at defined places at agreed times or in cyberspace at any time to create, diffuse, and distribute explicit practices about the issues of which they are passionate. They can create self-sustaining processes and enable the divided novices to specialize to advance productivity.

BACKGROUND INFORMATION

A History of Competency Development

How can competences draw lessons from a community of practice? The historical origins of competences are varied and have been applied as the basis for building effective military, teachers and professors, and managers, among other professions. Allegedly, Spartans excelled militarily because they recruited their soldiers early in life and spent more time than did other armies on bringing all the recruits to the same level of military competency. The Romans adopted a comparable approach. For both the Romans and the Spartans, the attainment of competences was central to the organization to effective administration and structure of the army (Mupepi, 2010). By contrast, the history of competencies in higher education and in developing corporate organizations is relatively short. Competency-based management (CBM) was used as a strategy during both World Wars. In 1918, the US military found itself in need of more than 50,000 men and women qualified in different trades (Labor Review, 1918). The War Committee decided to train a few individuals who, in turn, trained others using the competency-based education and training methodology (Mupepi, 2010, p. 24). The origins of the CBM construct in higher education can be traced back to early American universities including Harvard, Columbia, or Eastern Michigan University (Westmeyer, 1985). Paradoxically, the construct benefited from both World Wars. Effectively deployed during both wars, it gained considerable credibility and popularity. After World War I, the methodology was used again in a military context to develop the professional competences the USA needed to participate usefully in the war effort (Liaropoulos, 2006). After the great wars, CBM was used in industry and commerce in human resources strategy and it is the theoretical underpinning of CMB in peacetime that forms part of strategy management the focus of this discussion. It can be argued that the theoretical framework that undergirds competency development is a combination of four constructs: social constructivism, appreciative inquiry, action research, and COP. In the latter construct, the collective experience of the members is combined and applied to make a difference in the organization. Polanyi (1966) argues that useful knowledge can be made from the collective experience of the organization. The tacit experience of the membership can be put into the context of the business to advance productivity. Tacit knowledge may be difficult to teach anyone. Mupepi (2014) propounds that the experts can transfer tacit knowing to the novice by means of writing down the job procedures, demonstrating how the job is done, or by the job processes.

Action Research

It can be contested that Action Research is one of the tools a community of practice can apply to solve problems in organization. Action research can be applied to improve the way a COP addresses issues and solve problems. There are two types of action research: participatory action research and practical action research. Kurt Lewin (1946), one of the founding fathers in the field of Organization Development, created Action Research (AR) as a tool that could be deployed to solve social problems. In much later research, Denscombe (2010) posits that the AR methodology can also be applied to produce guidelines for best practice. Lave and Wenger (1991) advance a discourse on work organization using a situated community of practice. Mupepi et al. (2013) build upon Lave and Wenger and suggest that knowledge creation entails a special discourse that puts words and images in ways that are useful to an organization. The Internet has become a standard tool that can be applied for a

COP to continue to cohere all the time in cyberspace and not needing to wait for scheduled meetings in defined places. Mupepi et al. (2013) asserts that a COP can deny objective knowledge created outside its sphere of influence because what they call explicit knowledge must be made with the linguistic and other meaning-making resources of their community. Lave and Wenger (1991) posit that a COP can be created as a group within a structure or organization. This membership can be possible because the group could have a common interest in a domain or area, or it can be created specifically with the goal of gaining knowledge related to their field. It is through the process of sharing information and experiences with the group that the members learn from each other, and have an opportunity to develop themselves personally and professionally. In Brown and Duguid (1991), a contestation that ethnographic studies of workplace practices show that the ways people work usually differ fundamentally from the ways organizations describe that work in manuals, training programs, organizational charts, and job descriptions. In later research, Mupepi et al. (2013) develop a premise that innovation can be made possible by a COP situated at the points of production. This assumption leads to a co-constructed situational knowledge. Situational analysis enables the COP to collect data which can be analyzed to understand the organization's capabilities in relation to the needs of customers and other stakeholders. Brown and Duguid (1991) propound that conceptual knowledge could be acquired in the context of specific situations. Thus, employers in recruitment of potential job candidates insist of experience to be relevant to the vacant job. Duguid (2005) suggests a useful community is one that learns to know what not to waste time on and what it must understand. Simply, it is a question of relevance in creating the practices that are necessary in the organization. Mupepi (2014) proposes that the novice can master all the relevant practices but must be assisted in defining useful knowledge and useless information. In learning to become a pin-production specialist under the guidance of an expert, the learner can end up acquiring even the habits of the expert such as breaking work for a cup of tea or smoking a cigarette a community of practice. In Polanyi (1966), the argument progressed is that tacit knowledge is difficult to impart to others because it is directly related to the experience of the person possessing it. The notion of a community of practice enables a business to share its experiences with stakeholders. In later research, Bratianu (2015) propounds that promoting organizational knowledge is an important consideration for any organization looking toward the future. The COP can make the understanding of the dynamics of knowledge as a crucial step in establishing a strong knowledge-base for the business. Bratianu suggests that a COP could borrow some of the concepts to create explicit practices deploying metaphors. Knowledge is not a concept with a clearly delineated structure. Whatever structure it possesses it obtains through metaphor. It is said that a picture is worth a thousand words, but with only a few words one can paint a permanent picture in the stakeholder's mind. Metaphors can be developed in the language the organization is familiar with to draw attention, convey facts and abstractions with clarity, and make the mission memorable.

The Adam Smith Division of Labor

The division of labor is akin to business organization and process management. It is one of the most emulated methodology applied in building the efficacies required in successful enterprise. Adam Smith did not only write about the structures of businesses during his time but envisioned enormous potential in future organizations that drew the division of labor for each man to understand his role to make more money. It was a win-win situation where the employer gained when output was increased while the worker received a better was because of improved performance (see Figure 1).

The Adam Smith Pin-production company has numerous clusters or groups that form because of the divided labor. The clusters can become independent firms or self-managed groups taking on additional work within the agglomeration. This experience enables the novice to acquire explicit knowledge and attitudes necessary to progress specialization. In Mupepi (2014), for a group to become specialized and operate effectively its leader and members must behave ethically. Ethics refer to the rules or standards for right conduct or practice. Agglomeration The term agglomeration is used in economics to describe the benefits that firms obtain by locating near each other (agglomerating). This concept relates to the idea of economies of scale and network effects. Agglomerations can expand the network of a community of practice. As more companies in related fields of business cluster together, their costs

Figure 1. The division of labor: Creating specialists

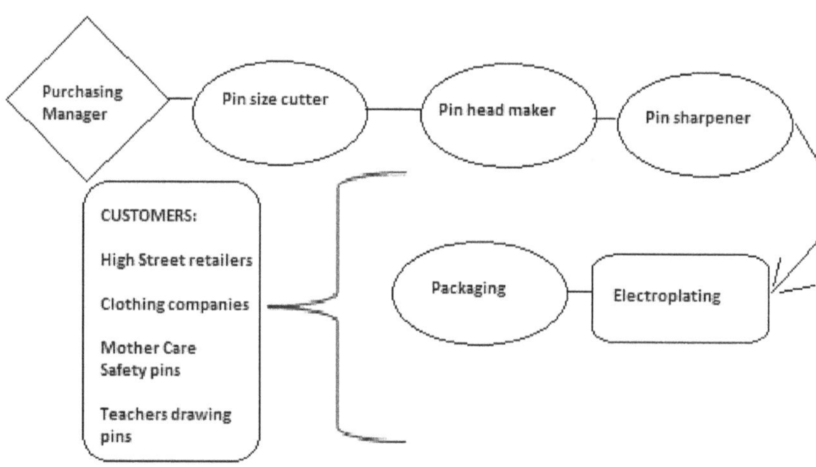

of production may decline significantly. This is because corporations compete for multiple scarce resources such as suppliers or specialist labor. Even when competing firms are in the same sector cluster, there may be advantages because the cluster attracts more suppliers and customers than a single firm could achieve alone. Cities form and grow to exploit economies of agglomeration.

Capability

A competency refers to the ability of a group or individual to do a job repeatedly successfully. In Figure 1, competency of the COP can be found where the attributes of knowledge, attitudes, skills, and technology meet. If one of these is missing or lacking, then one is not competent and if that implies many in the company are lacking one of the attributes, then it can be argued the organization might be misaligned (see Figure 1).

The Centricity of a Community of Practice

Community of Practice (COP) A COP is an autonomous group with a given area of freedom to manage its productive work within preset limits established by the organization. Lave and Wenger (1991) defined a COP as a self-organized or network of peers with diverse skills and experience in an area of practice or profession. Such groups are held together by the members' desire to help others and the need to advance their own knowledge (see Figure 2). A COP can solve problems in its

Figure 2. The strength of a COP is in knowledge creation and sharing (Mupepi, 2017).

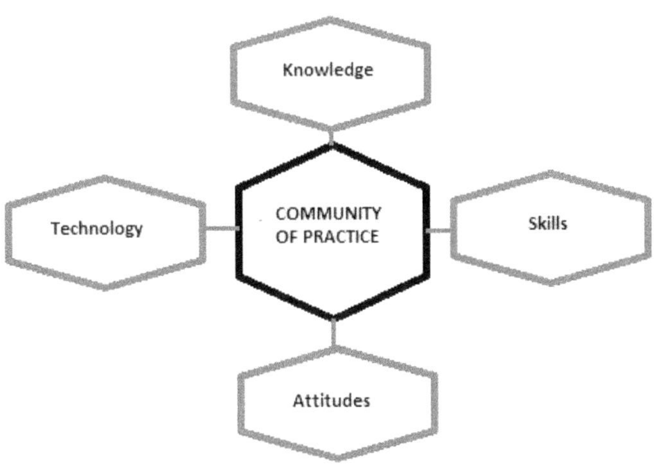

areas of expertise and learning and improvement is a continuous effort leading to the organization constantly embracing change. Since Lave and Wenger, many other scholars have built upon the notion of a community of practice to incorporate prevailing learning technologies. For example, in Mupepi (2017), specially built web-portals could be added to the e-commerce to mine human resource data. This data can be analyzed and interpreted to appreciate prevailing talents, expectations on conditions for service such as salaries, fringe benefits, and many others. Mupepi (2017) argue that data mining is an extension of e-commerce enabling the human resource department to maintain a useful presence on the internet. For example, their portals could contain all the competency development modules where the novice could login and continue to learn without waiting for the semester to begin to acquire the knowledge and skills needed to get the job done right first time and all the time.

Data available indicate that a COP is strategically placed to create diffuse and distribute the competency required to progress organization. Competency refers to the ability of a group or individual to do a job repeatedly successfully. The Knowledge, technology, brashness to do the job, and skills can be defined as the practices needed to make the difference in organization (see Figure 2).

Applying the Jig for Consistency

The Jig In production, a jig is a tool that can be applied to bootstrap the manufacture of parts or components or parts whose dimensions can be assembled in the end to make one whole unit. A jig makes the geometrical dimensioning of parts that need to be made from wood or doe molding stable. In the pin-production early days, there could have been jigs to produce all types of pins and innovative thinking in such processes could have led to additional products such as spoons or knife-blades. The guillotine or the brick mold could have been created to solve the problem of dimensions in engineering and construction industries (see Figure 3).

The forum of the COP can be bootstrapped to replicate desirable performance. Bootstrapping relies on drawing useful lessons from past performance. It can imply the starting of a self-sustaining process with the knowledge of right or unethical practices with no recourse to external input. The theory is that profits are the key to survival. The reality is that one pay bills with cash, so focus on cash flow. The past is useful to make meaningful projections…or bootstraps. Community of Practice (COP) A COP is an autonomous group with a given area of freedom to manage its productive work within preset limits established by the organization. Lave and Wenger (1991) defined a COP as a self-organized or network of peers with diverse skills and experience in an area of practice or profession. Such groups are held together by the members' desire to help others and the need to advance their own knowledge. A COP can solve problems in its areas of expertise and learning and

Figure 3. Bootstrapping a COP

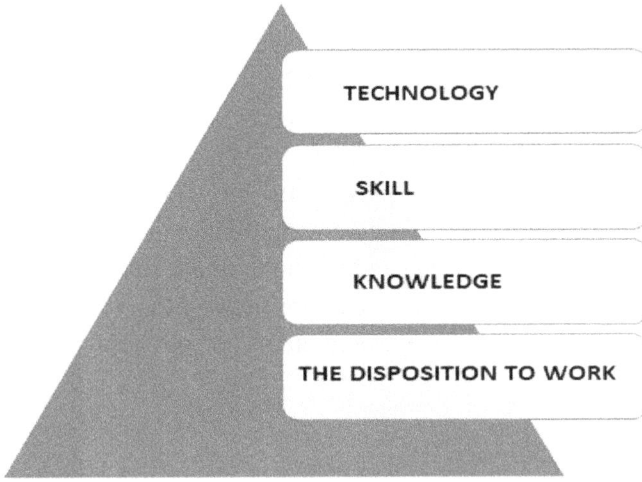

improvement is a continuous effort leading to the organization constantly embracing change. Since Lave and Wenger, many other scholars have built upon the notion of epistemic communities to incorporate prevailing learning technologies. For example, in Mupepi and Mupepi (2018), data collected from the many activities of the organization can be analyzed and interpreted to enhance productivity. This data can be appreciated to develop standards such as costing, production or sales. The COP is strategically placed to define the tools and equipment, skills, knowledge, and brashness to get the job done correctly all the time. Job specifications, job descriptions, and any other instruction pertaining to delivery become the modus operandi to work successfully (see Figure 3).

LOGO-CENTRIC ORGANIZATION

Metaphors and logos can be deployed as a learning strategy. Short, clear statements accompanied or unaccompanied with logo signs can be applied in developing a shared mindset in high performing organizations (Mupepi & Mupepi, 2015). The logotype is a graphic mark applied by organizations to aid instant recognition. For example, when one is driving on the freeway with kids in the car, one cannot miss the MacDonald Arch at night or day. The children will spot the sign before the driver is able to do so. Making excuses that "we have missed the exist" will not help because there will be similar signs in the next exists. Developing short phrases and signs which can be recognized and associated with the enterprise will be good for business. The signs and statements can be posted on the virtual websites, letterheads, and posters strategically posted along the corridors of the value creation process. This will serve as reminders to stakeholders to do the correct thing the first time all the time, and for them to remember for what the organization stands. In building construction zones, those who must work in these areas can be reminded to wear safety gear to eliminate down-times and ensure smooth flow of work (see Figure 4). Engel (2008) suggests that learning on the job allows introducing the novice to learn by seeing the job done and practicing doing the right things all the time. Posters can be developed to aid the learner the right positions to take when doing a job. The first responder to attend to one injured at work can be reminded by posters with the signs of the positions one should take when providing first aid.

ON THE NOTICEBOARDS

McDermott and Douglas (2010) propound those in-house networks of experts—or COP—were once entirely unofficial, and today they are integrated into companies' formal management structures. On the noticeboards, one can see invitations to attend meetings in both physical and cyberspace structures: "Members of the Mustang 2015 Team will meet today at 4:00PM. See email from Operations posted today for details". While metaphors may be applied in creating a shared mindset, like the logotype they can be useful in aiding learning and conveying messages…the Mustang car or thoroughbred horse can easily be identified with the appropriate logo. Many successful companies such as IBM or Apple have adapted the use of knowledge networks, logotypes, and metaphors to develop and implement winning strategy. McDermott and Douglas (2010) assert that triumphant organizations count on epistemic communities to deliver creative solutions to challenges that bridge functional gaps and development of customer-focused operations. The discourse indicates that explicit practices can be created and allow a business to compete on what its people know. Nonaka (1991) introduces standards of how organizational knowledge could be understood. The standards illustrate the dynamics of knowledge making processes. Nonaka posits that useful knowledge is comprised of a continuous repertoire between tacit and explicit knowing. The expert can show the novice how to make drawing pins and explain verbally the reason for action. The explanation could be: the drawing-pin is an assert in the classroom enabling the instructor to pin visual aids such as maps or pictures and as such the drawing pin must have an appropriate head and a sharp end making the job of hanging visual aids for the instructor easy. The novice can appreciate the uses of the products he/she is making and pays attention to such cues as pinhead or sharpness of the pins. Nonaka asserts that the dynamics of the knowledge creation process compel the experts to articulate the environmental needs in creating perspectives the learners must understand.

Competency as a Strategy

Competency-based education and training can be found historically in the military histories around the world. As mentioned earlier, the US military in World War I found itself in need of more than 50,000 artisans including boilermakers, welders, carpenters, tinsmiths, and aircraft technicians as soon as Congress declared war on Germany. The devastation of the Great War (as World War I was known at the time) had greatly destabilized Europe, and in many respects World War II grew out of issues left unresolved by that earlier conflict (Liaropoulos, 2006). Political and economic instability in Germany, and lingering resentment over the harsh terms imposed by the Versailles Treaty, fueled the rise to power of Adolf Hitler and his National Socialist (Nazi) Party (Howard, 2004). Project evaluation review technique (PERT) has its roots in the American naval forces during World War II (Gore, 1963). PERT is a sophisticated planning technique which has been adapted in management in industry and commerce as strategy development tool. One cannot accept new orders if the business has no capability to fulfill them. Gore (1963) argues that PERT and many other techniques and technology from the military have been adapted for use during peace time. For example, the heat resistant Teflon developed during the Cold War to build precision jet engines has also been adapted for the housewife's kitchen to craft non-sticky pots and pans.

A Positive Campos Mentis

In the field of Organization development, Group dynamics are viewed as critical to understanding competency development. The collective thinking of the organization has been argued by Lewin (1943), Bion (1943), Whyte (1943), and many others, as critical to performance. They are credited with the first research leading to the study of groups in efforts to expand productivity at work. Lewin (1943) is credited for coining the term group dynamics and is also commonly identified as the founder of the movement to study groups scientifically (Spears, et al., 2005). He coined the term group dynamics to describe the way groups and individuals act and react to changing circumstances. Group dynamics can be defined as a field of enquiry dedicated to the advancing knowledge about the nature of groups, the laws of their development and their interrelations with individuals, other groups and larger institutions (Spears, et al., 2005). Bion (1943) observed groups at work during his tenure as an army doctor during World War II. Bion observes the role of group processes set out in Experiences in Groups first published in 1943 in the Lancet, a British medical research journal. Group experiences were re-published in 1961 as a book on group dynamics drawing empirical evidence from the trenches in World War II. In this book, he refers to recurrent emotional states of groups as basic assumptions. Bion argues that in every group, two groups are present: the work group, and the basic assumption group. The work group is that aspect of group functioning which must do with the primary task of the group—what the group has formed to accomplish; it will keep the group anchored to a sophisticated and rational level of behavior. Rioch (1970) asserts that in the basic assumption a group can describe the tacit underlying assumptions on which the behavior of the group is based. Rioch argues that Bion specifically identified three basic assumptions: dependency, fight-flight, and pairing. When a group adopts any one of these basic assumptions, it interferes with the task the group is attempting to accomplish. Rioch posits that Bion believed that interpretation by the therapist of this aspect of group dynamics could result in insight regarding effective group work.

Productivity and Safety Are Synonymous

In Senge (1990), a system thinking approach is viewed as the positive campos mentis of the organization. A positive campos enable a people to think more about their jobs and to be safe all the time. Senge argues that it is possible to design and implement a modus operandi to keep everyone operating on the same page to increase output. Innovative ideas can lead to the creation of tools and equipment to make the job easier. The ideal situation is to continue to learn about the job and improve the dexterity required to operate safely (see Figure 4).

Figure 4. Safety is job number one

GROUPS CAN COHERE MUCH CLOSELY

The knowledge created by pioneers such as Kurt Lewin and Wilfred Bion, among many others, made it possible for organizations to apply group dynamics to grow useful businesses. More recently, researchers have applied the group dynamics theory and made it central to management practices. In Mupepi and Mupepi (2015), it is proposed that teams can be built to advance knowing and skillfulness in the business. The divided labor can be split into units, departments, sections, or teams that have positive dynamics where creativity can be central to cohesion. Team members must trust one another work towards the same goal and hold each other accountable for making the difference in organization. Mupepi and Mupepi (2015) argue that teamwork is critical to how the product will be made and how the customers will be served. The team can synthesize the activities in the value creation system resulting in positive performance and increased output. Teamwork is synonymous with safety and productivity.

ORGANIZATIONAL CAPACITY

In Mupepi and Mupepi (2015), a COP or knowledge communities (KC) are described as two collaboration forums which can be applied in useful organizations. They can be enacted to create diffuse and distribute explicit knowledge required in triumphant businesses. In this discussion, a KC, epistemic community, or COP implies the same structure comprised of a group of people preferably from the same company who are passionate about the same things. As stated earlier, Mupepi et al. (2015) assert the COP can meet regularly in designated places at structured times or in cyberspace at any time to advance the things about which they are passionate. The advancement of mobile telephony and other information communication technologies have made entire organizations to stay tuned to each other creating explicit practices to win in competitive environments.

Mupepi, Tenkasi, Sorensen, and Mupepi (2013) propound that another alternative change management technique referred to as the socially constructed competency model (SCCM) can be initiated within the forums of a community of practice to grow effective capability. It is a change management tool hinged on the COP platform, and the composition of the COP in any business is dependent upon how it is structured and controlled. The COP may exist and its mandate may be limited by management. In the design and implementation of the SCCM, an assumption is made of an empowered COP one that makes the best choices in the interest of the business and delivering value through its forum serving employees, line managers, customers, and investors. The SCCM contention is that organizational capacity can

Figure 5. A SCCM's properties are equal and equate to organizational capacity

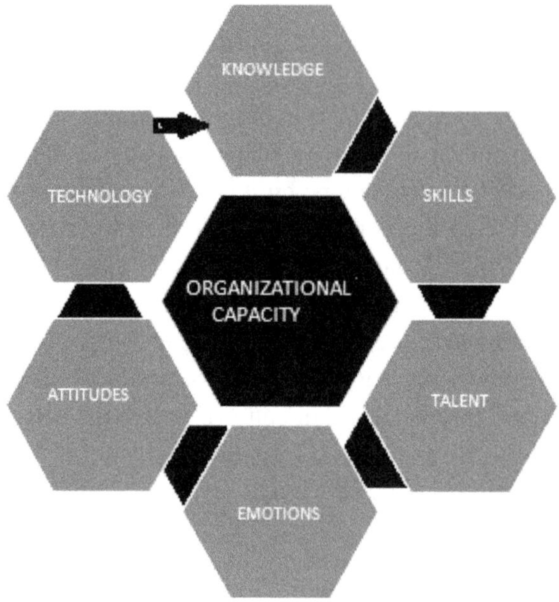

be socially constructed deploying the forums of the COP. The COP can be applied to design and implement individual competences and to grow an organization-wide competitive culture. The schemata for a desirable capacity can begin with the selection and recruitment of people possessing the right attributes necessary in organization. In Mupepi et al. (2013), the COP is understood to possess the ability to facilitate the process of change by creating a roadmap that leads from change to value creation and increase the speed with which the organization's systems adapt. They argue that the construction of the right capability in the divided labor can be made possible by appreciating the organization. The capacity to advance the organizational mission and is dependent upon what the people doing the work know and understand. The SCCM is a socio-technical systems approach to understand the value creation process in charting organizational efficiency and effectiveness, and progress innovation. The co-constructed competency model enables the design and implementation of tools and equipment to aid productivity. The unique feature of the SCCM is its capability to drive business strategy, delivering value in the divided experts, and amplifying the disposition of the people doing the work, their skillfulness talent and expertise and how all that impact business results.

Appreciative Inquiry (AI)

AI is a change management approach created by David Cooperrider and his associates at Case Western Reserve and Benedictine University. Many scholars such as Mupepi Tenkasi Sorensen& Mupepi (2013) have improved upon AI as a research management tool. Using AI's 4-Dimension assessment and evaluation technology, it will be possible for organization to pinpoint at the desirable change by shifting a deficit organizational mindset to a positive mindset which encourages to thinking positively about the future See Figure 6.

SUMMARY OF THE CHAPTER

The practices and knowledge required in successful organization can realized objectively. The arguments propounded by knowledge communities or communities of practice make organizational sense. A collaborative forum can be situated to construct the practices and tools required to prop the organization to perform better. Bootstrapping techniques can be applied to replicate the values and parameters for effective performance. Metaphorically the organization can pull itself up to increase productivity. A COP can appreciate the organization to pinpoint at prevailing

Figure 6. Appreciating what gives life to organization
(Mupepi Tenkasi Sorensen and Mupepi, 2013).

cultural conditions and pinpoint at the change required to advance efficiency and effectiveness in successful organization. AI can be applied to effectively engage employees to advance the efficacies necessary in highly productive businesses and to pin-point at the key elements of a systemic and strategic approach to foster organizational effectiveness.

WAY FORWARD

The interrelationship among social constructs in building useful competences has been expanded sufficiently to make a conclusion that people still make the difference in organization. A COP can be applied to build explicit knowledge and tools useful in the value creation process. There are two assumptions made. The first is that a COP can be composed of the people in the divided labor who can be experts after a given period of continuous learning and improvement. The COP in this situation can create situational knowledge and tools to advance pin-production output. Explicit knowledge can become an applied science juxtaposed with the right tooling and attitudes to increase output in the pin-production outfit. The cohesion of the COP can enable experiential learning and continuous improvement to occur in the development of the specialists. The second assumption is that social construction is the common denominator in collaborative forums. It is possible for a COP to study the situation and devise appropriate strategy to bootstrap sustainability in advancing productivity. Social construction enables the co-construction of jointly constructed competences. The arguments presented are limited in many ways. The concept of a COP is very noble and practical only with management that is prepared to accept that the design and implementation of cutting-edge practices is a social construct.

Appreciative Inquiry and Changing the Mindset

The essential mindset shifts include:

From past-focused to future-focused. Many of the answers to today's challenges cannot be found in the past since the issues never existed before. For example, if the company clings to a rule that an employee needs to be in a role for two years before being promoted, and if the employee is a top talent who feels ready for the next role, the organization may lose the employee.

From discipline-focused to having an organization focused. Business partners must focus on the organization's strategic needs and use more innovation, creativity, and problem solving to find unique solutions.

From problem-solving approach to appreciative inquiry: Appreciative inquiry approach has been proven to bring out the best in people. Creating the competitive advantage entail thinking outside the normal parameters. AI makes it possible for the entire organization to seat in one large group to determine what gives life to the business. All members of the organization will be able to significantly contribute during the dialogue stages in building desirable capability.

CONCLUSION

Management and ownership of the business may not agree with the notion of a strategy co-constructed by a KC or COP. A successful modus operandi is largely dependent upon the vision of those who have the largest say in organization. A critical stage of the change process is that of bringing the community together in one or several large-scale forums. In such collaboration all members of the organization or representatives of the different social components of the 'whole system' are invited to meet in real-time to collaborate the vision, the strategy and the change tactics. Resistance to change is always there in one way or another regardless whether individuals have been consulted or not. Sometimes old habits are hard to change.

REFERENCES

Appolloni, B., Malchiodi, D., & Gaito, S. (2003). *Algorithmic Inference in Machine Learning*. South Australia, Australia: Advanced Knowledge International.

Bion, W. R. (1961). *Experiences in Groups*. London, UK: Tavistock Institute; doi:10.4324/9780203359075

Bion, W. R., & Rickman, J. (1943). Intra-group tensions in therapy. *Lancet*, *2*(6274), 678–781. doi:10.1016/S0140-6736(00)88231-8

Bratianu, C. (2015). *Organizational Knowledge Dynamics: Managing Knowledge Creation, Acquisition, Sharing, and Transformation*. Hershey, PA: IGI Global. doi:10.4018/978-1-4666-8318-1

Brown, J. S., & Duguid, P. (1991). Organizational Learning and Communities-of-Practice: Toward a Unified View of Working, Learning, and Innovation. *Organization Science*, *2*(1), 40–57. doi:10.1287/orsc.2.1.40

Denscombe, M. (2010). *Good Research Guide: For small-scale social research projects* (4th ed.). Berkshire, UK: Open University Press.

Dubé, L., Bourhis, A., & Jacob, R. (2005). The impact of structuring characteristics on the launching of virtual communities of practice. *Journal of Organizational Change Management*, *18*(2), 145–166. doi:10.1108/09534810510589570

Duguid, P. (2005). The Art of Knowing: Social and Tacit Dimensions of Knowledge and the Limits of the Community of Practice. *The Information Society*, *21*(2), 109–118. doi:10.1080/01972240590925311

Engel, P. J. H. (2008). Tacit knowledge and Visual Expertise in Medical Diagnostic Reasoning: Implications for medical education. *Medical Teacher*, *30*(7), e184–e188. doi:10.1080/01421590802144260 PMID:18777417

Gore, W. J. (1963). Developments in Public Administration. *Public Administration Review*, *23*(1), 51–54. doi:10.2307/973389

Howard, J. H. (2004). *Workers at War: Labor in China's Arsenals, 1937–1953*. Stanford, CA: Stanford University Press.

Kimble, C. (2013). Knowledge management, codification and tacit knowledge. *Information Research, 18*(2).

Lave, J., & Wenger, E. (1991). *Situated Learning: Legitimate Peripheral Participation*. Cambridge, UK: Cambridge University Press; doi:10.1017/CBO9780511815355

Lewin, K. (1943). Defining the Field at a Given Time. *Psychological Review*, *50*(3), 292–310. doi:10.1037/h0062738

Lewin, K. (1946). Action research and minority problems. *The Journal of Social Issues, 2*(4), 34–46. doi:.1946.tb02295.x doi:10.1111/j.1540-4560

Liaropoulos, A. (2006). Revolutions in warfare: Paradigms and Historical evidence: the Napoleonic and First World War Revolutions in Military Affairs. *The Journal of Military History*, *70*(2), 363–384. doi:10.1353/jmh.2006.0106

McDermott, R., & Archibald, D. (2010). Harnessing Your Staff's Informal Networks. *Harvard Business Review*, *88*(3). PMID:20402051

McInerney, C. (2002). Knowledge Management and the Dynamic Nature of Knowledge. *Journal of the American Society for Information Science and Technology*, *53*(12), 1009–1018. doi:10.1002/asi.10109

Mupepi, G. M., Ram, V. T., Sorensen, P. F., & Mupepi, S. C. (2013). Creating high impact organization in the SADC: Adapting OD Methods and Practices. In J. Vogelsang, M. Townsend, & ... (Eds.), *Handbook for Strategic HR: Best Practices in Organization Development from OD Network*. New York: AMACOM.

Mupepi, M. (2014, April-June). Can the division of labor be re-engineered to advance organizational dynamism? *SAGE Open*, *1–5*. doi:10.1177/2158244014536404

Mupepi, M., & Mupepi, S. (2015a). Charting Highly Productive Organization: Wrapping it all in Social Constructs. *International Journal of Productivity Management and Assessment Technologies*, *3*(1), 13–30. doi:10.4018/IJPMAT.2015010102

Mupepi, M., & Mupepi, S. (2015b). *Inside social constructs: MBAA International Conference March 25-27.* Chicago: Palmer House Hilton.

Mupepi, M. G., & Mupepi, S. C. (2018). Amplifying the Significance of Systems Thinking in Organization. In M. Khosrow-Pour, D.B.A. (Ed.), Encyclopedia of Information Science and Technology, Fourth Edition (pp. 551-562). Hershey, PA: IGI Global. doi:10.4018/978-1-5225-2255-3.ch048

Nonaka, I. (1991, November-December). The knowledge creating company. *Harvard Business Review*, *69*, 96–104.

Nonaka, I., & Takeuchi, H. (1995). *The knowledge creating company: how Japanese companies create the dynamics of innovation*. New York: Oxford University Press.

Polanyi, M. (1966). *The Tacit Dimension*. Chicago: University of Chicago Press.

Rioch, M. J. (1970). The work of Wilfred Bion. Psychiatry, 33, 56–66. Smith, E. A. (2001). The role of tacit and explicit knowledge in the workplace. *Journal of Knowledge Management*, *5*(4), 311–321.

Spears, R., Ellemers, N., & Doosje, B. (2005). Let me count the ways in which I respect thee: Does competence compensate or compromise lack of liking from the group? *European Journal of Social Psychology*, *35*(2), 263–279. doi:10.1002/ejsp.248

The Entrepreneur. (2015). *Bootstrapping your start-up*. Retrieved from http://www.entrepreneur.com/article/55776

Whyte, F. W. (1943). *[1991]. Street Corner Society* (4th ed.). Chicago: University of Chicago Press.

Chapter 6
Workforce Diversity:
Gaining the Competitive Advantage

Kuda Mupepi
S. James School of Medicine, USA

Tatenda Mupepi
S. James School of Medicine, USA

Clara Mupepi
Grand Valley State University, USA

ABSTRACT

The growing acceptance of marrying across racial and ethnic lines (as reflected in US census statistics) together with the growth of demographic changes across workplaces is fueling fears among some who see their culture being threatened and react by engaging in overt discrimination. One concern regards employers having access to databases containing talented individuals who are ready to work. Their choices hinge on the abilities required to further their enterprise. Paradoxically, a business's culture's greatest strength could be its greatest weakness when not consistent with sound business strategies. Moreover, when such a culture prevents a firm from meeting competitive threats, this can lead to the firm's stagnation and ultimate demise. Diversity has never been thought of as a strategy until now. This chapter explores workforce diversity.

DOI: 10.4018/978-1-5225-7390-6.ch006

INTRODUCTION

Workplace diversity refers to the similarities and differences among people employed within an organization. Aspects of workplace diversity may include age, race, gender, personality, religion, sexual orientation, and education. When the coal mines closed; when the factory jobs disappeared; when Bessemer Road and Petticoat Lane and other high street businesses began taking down signs and logos; when the population started a steady decline; and when the healthcare industry was on the brink of bankruptcy; the residents of Tottenham, London, England or Hazelton, Pennsylvania, USA flocked downtown for their annual Funfest regardless of age, race, age, gender, religion, or education (Norris and Laub, 2018). The Tottenham, London festival brings together a diverse population ranging from African, Americans, Asiatic, Caribbean, European, Hispanic, and many other peoples who claim the British Isles as their home. In Hazelton, Pennsylvania, the festival attracts all those who are fascinated with aspects of American culture including beer, wine, music, and fancy attire (Norris and Laub, 2018).

BACKGROUND INFORMATION

Symbols of the Cities

Each week, in Tottenham City, the Hotspurs Stadium on White Hart Lane hosts live national and European football/soccer matches attended by more than 100,000 fans, with millions more watching the games on television. The crowds include Africans, Asians, Indians, Pakistanis, West Indians, and native Europeans. London demographic data show the presence of minorities in the workplace and in the school system. The demand for healthcare impacts children and adults from all races and ethnic groups.

Today's youth are of a different complexion than the youth of 50 years ago. Norris and Laub (2018) show that in America, the color of non-Hispanic whites is less than 50% of the youth population in 632 of America's 3,142 counties. Most of these are in southern and coastal states. It implies that employers have a wider selection of talent. Norris and Laub suggested that by 2020, 50.2% of American children will be from today's minority groups. By 2044.5, 50.3% of Americans of all ages will be from those same groups.

Organizational Culture

In Schein (1992), organizational culture encompasses values and behaviors that contribute to the unique social and psychological environment of an organization.

According to Needle (2004) organizational culture represents the collective values, beliefs and principles of organizational members and is a product of factors such as history, product, market, technology, strategy, type of employees, management style, and national culture; culture includes the organization's vision, values, norms, systems, symbols, language, assumptions, environment, location, beliefs and habits. In later research, Edgar (2013) asserted that a chronic issue in conceptualizing culture is whether to think of it as a static property of a given organization…its shared customs, beliefs norms and values and tacit assumptions or whether to think of principles as a dynamic human process of constructing shared meaning. Culture creation is one of the unique human characteristics of humans, being based on our capacity to be self-conscious and able to see ourselves and others from each other's points of view. It is this reflexive capacity of humans that makes culture possible. Schein suggested that given these human characteristics, it was then clear that culture was both a process and a state.

In Freiberg and Freiberg (2013), it is suggested that for many years companies have relied on employee surveys and gone are those days. The people doing the job need to be far more than satisfied. They essentially should be enthusiastic about the company. They must to continue to learn and improve their disposition to produce the goods demanded by the customers.

Flamholtz and Randle state that: A strong culture is that people clearly understand and can articulate. A weak culture is one that employees have difficulty defining, understanding, or explaining. Strong culture is said to exist where staff respond to stimulus because of their alignment to organizational values. Discrimination in the workplace can be viewed as signs of a weak culture where individuals possessing the brashness to effectively work are oppressed because of their race, ethnicity or gender. In such environments, strong cultures help firms to focus on integrating talent to increase productivity.

A Historical Perspective: Black Brown and White

In Conway (2005), most British people of West Indian origin were born in the United Kingdom as opposed to the West Indies themselves. Geographically Jamaica belongs to the group of islands known as the West Indies and include the Dominican Republic, Puerto Rico, Cuba and Haiti. The West Indies are a group of islands in the Caribbean called the Greater Antilles. Jamaica is the biggest of the islands and the United Kingdom Office for National Statistics estimates that in 2015, some 137,000-people born in Jamaica were resident in the UK. In Clark and Mezzofiore (2018), Jamaicans are said to have come to help rebuild Britain after the devastation of World War Two. They were invited by the UK government to lay roads, drive buses, clean hospitals and nurse the sick. Clark and Mezzofiore suggested that the

Jamaican immigrants were known then as the Windrush generation -- the first of their numbers came on the Empire Windrush passenger liner in June 1948 -- they were the first large group of Caribbean migrants to arrive in the UK. The *Windrush* was nicknamed the *Banana* boat because part of its payload were bananas and other fruits from the West Indies. The West Indians came to symbolize the seismic demographic changes that took place in post-war Britain, when hundreds of thousands of people came to the United Kingdom from former British colonies, known as the Commonwealth. According to the National Statistics Office (2018), the number of Jamaican nationals is estimated to be significantly lower, at 49,000 in 2015. Today they are part of the workforce in the United Kingdom and Europe.

In contrast to the US, Africans came as slaves who possessed no assets except their intellect. In Berlin (2004) slavery in the United States was the legal institution of human chattel enslavement, primarily of Africans and African Americans, that existed in the United States of America in the 18th and 19th centuries. Slavery had been practiced in British America from early colonial days, and was legal in all Thirteen Colonies at the time of the Declaration of Independence in 1776.

The Africans enter the new world in captivity. In colonization the institution of slavery was deployed as the workforce to build the colonies. After the Emancipation 1863, the Africans were freed and have been referred to as African -Americans or Blacks (Cromwell, 2014). However, many incidents of racial conflict have been experienced since the Civil Rights 1964 Act such as the Trayvon Benjamin Martin 2012. In Robles (2012), Martin was walking back alone to the house of his father's fiancée after purchasing candy and a soft drink at a nearby convenience store. The neighborhood had suffered several robberies that year. Zimmerman, a member of the community watch, saw Martin and reported him to the Sanford Police as suspicious. Moments later, an altercation between the two individuals took place and Zimmerman fatally shot Martin in the chest.

Robles suggested that Zimmerman who could have been injured during the encounter, claimed self-defense in the confrontation, and was not charged at the time. The police said there was no evidence to refute his claim of self-defense, and that Florida's stand your ground law prohibited law-enforcement officials from arresting or charging him (Robles, 2012).

WORKFORCE DIVERSITY

Talent Is Unevenly Distributed Within the Population

Sports talent, such as in basketball or football, is unevenly distributed – either in the US or anywhere else. Bell (2017) proposed that diversity in the workplace was increasingly being embraced among US businesses. Recognition that diversity is often a foundation for innovation is gaining momentum among businesses and leaders. Bell (2017) suggested that corporations were recruiting from varied talent pools to attract potential employees from various backgrounds. Advertising showcasing diversity is also on the rise; and employers have included induction and multicultural assimilation in their training and development offerings. These courses help the workforce to transition into a more diversified workplace. On-line courses are very handy and effective in developing the knowledge and skills required in effective organization. The people doing the work can continue to learn any time rather than waiting for classroom course offerings during a semester. Mupepi Sorensen and Tenkasi (2013) argue that different strategy to organizational learning could be focused on improving the workforce's brashness to produce goods to meet demand.

Equal Opportunities Regulations

In the European Union, human rights are protected by various laws. If one's employer is a European public authority, they must follow the principles of the Human Rights Act. The Human Rights Act is based on the European Convention on Human Rights and adds protection for workers' rights and freedoms. In the US, the Civil Rights Act of 1964 frames the workforce rights and the obligation of the employers to protect the interest of employees regardless of race, color, sexual orientation, or creed. In Wright (2005), the Civil Rights Act of 1964 was recognized for being a landmark civil rights and US labor law in the United States that outlaws, discrimination based on race, color, religion, sex, or national origin. It prohibited the application of unequal voter registration requirements; the practice of racial segregation in schools; and the provision of unequal access to employment opportunities and public accommodations.

Discrimination Based on Class Divisions

Fifty years ago, in Washington DC, a historically Black township called Shaw – ten blocks from the White House – was ablaze because of racial tension. As discussed in the *Economist* (April 7-13, 2018), the spark had been lit on April 4th, 1968, by the assassination of Martin Luther King in Memphis, Tennessee. After the murder of the civil rights leader Martin Luther King, riots gripped more than 100 cities throughout the nation. President Lyndon B. Johnson set up the Kerner Commission of Inquiry to investigate the race riots. The inquiry founded that the nation was moving towards two societies—one for the Blacks (in which there was endless poverty and unemployment, because of discrimination), and one for the Whites, an explanatory contrast. Blacks were discriminated against in all facets of life including employment, education, and business. Black women, too, faced their own unique challenges of being denied equal opportunities in the workplace. There are numerous forms of discrimination—and all are forbidden under the umbrella of civil rights legislation. For example, three methods of discrimination (with regards to money lending) are:

1. **Overt Evidence of Discrimination:** Occurring when a lender blatantly discriminates on a prohibited basis;
2. **Disparate Treatment:** Occurring when there is evidence that a lender treats applicants differently based on one of the prohibited facts; and
3. **Disparate Impact:** Occurring when there is evidence that a lender applies a practice uniformly to all applicants but the practice has a discriminatory effect on a prohibited basis and is not justified by business necessity (Title VII of the Civil Rights Act of 1964).

With respect to disparate treatment, the Policy Statement provides that disparate treatment ranges from overt discrimination to subtler disparities in treatment and, importantly, does not require any demonstration that such treatment was motivated by prejudice or a conscious intention to discriminate against a person beyond the actual difference in treatment itself (Comptroller of Banks, 2010).

Accommodating Diversity

The problems confronting workforces include racism sexism and ethnocentrism. These three are the most powerful forces impacting productivity in organizations. For example, White majority people dominate organizations in North America and Europe as being superior to minority races, women, and other ethnic groups solely because they are White. Culturally they were the first landlords which gave them ample time to create real wealth as compared to the African-Americans who were only freed as slaves in 1863 with no equality in society and employment until Civil Rights Act 1964. This law prohibits unequal application of voter registration requirements, racial segregation in employment or public accommodations. The basis for workforce diversity is language. Accepting diversity means much more than being able to look at another employee whose skin is an unusual color and feeling comfortable with that employee. It can mean accepting people who dress and eat differently. Change will be necessary to the food available in cafeteria.

In the US the workforce can include adherents of the African Traditional Religions, Christians, Muslims, and Jews, among many others. Changes will be needed in conditions of service to enable the Muslims to pray privately, allow the Seventh Day Adventists to work Sunday through Friday, and so forth. Introducing pluralism workshops could be helpful. Mupepi and Mupepi (2016) suggested that items such as job specifications and job descriptions could be used in diversity workshops to emphasize how the job should be done and explain the organizational structure to understand who is who.

Age Discrimination Amidst Shifting Demographics

The Age Discrimination in Employment Act (ADEA) forbids age discrimination against people who are age 40 or older. It does not protect workers under the age of 40; although some states have laws that protect younger workers from age discrimination. It is not illegal for an employer or other covered entity to favor an older worker over a younger one, even if both workers are age 40 or older. Discrimination can occur when the victim and the person who inflicted the discrimination are both over 40 (EUAFR, 2018).

Fernandez (1991) argues that in Europe there is tremendous bias against older workers and that there are few laws to protect them. The key factors influencing demographics in Europe are its aging population and its low birth rate. In 1990 the birth rate among EC countries on average was 1.58. Only Ireland had a rate slightly above 2.1. Fernandez argues that Europeans are aging at a very fast rate compared to North Americans or Australians. The US population is aging at a slower rate than other industrialized nations because immigrants gained are much younger. People have been retiring earlier for the past two decades; the average retirement age for men is 62 years. The percentage of workers retiring before age 65 rose from 62 percent in 1978 to 84 percent in 1986. The following are some of the demographics for the older population:

- In 1987, the median age of Americans was 32.7; in the year 2000, it was 36; by 2010, the median age was estimated at 39
- In 2010, 25 percent of the U.S. population was estimated at 55 years' old
- In 1890, only 2 percent of people lived to be 65 years of age; today 65 percent do.
- In 1900, 40 percent of the US population was 17 years of age and under, 3 percent was 65 years of age or older (Fernandez, 1991).

People have been retiring earlier for the past two decades; the average retirement age for men is 62 years. It implies that there will be elderly workers in the workplace in America.

Race/Color Discrimination

Race discrimination involves treating someone (an applicant or an employee) unfavorably because he/she is of a certain race or because of personal characteristics associated with race (such as hair texture, skin color, or certain facial features). Color discrimination involves treating someone unfavorably because of skin color/complexion. Race/color discrimination can also involve treating someone unfavorably because the person is married to (or is associated with) a person of a certain race or color. Discrimination can occur when the victim and the person who inflicted the discrimination are of the same race or color (EUAFR, 2018).

Discrimination and Harassment

In Spencer (2012), pluralism is a term used in philosophy, meaning doctrine of multiplicity, often used in opposition to Monism ("doctrine of unity") and Dualism ("doctrine of duality"). The term has different meanings in metaphysics, ontology, epistemology and logic. Pluralism exists in many workplaces to configure resources to minimize risk. For example, management policies are pluralistic in nature to accommodate the practices and procedures necessary to create the competitive advantage.

In the United States, the EEOC laws prohibit discrimination and harassment—practices which can include, for example, racial slurs, offensive or derogatory remarks about a person's race or color, or the display of racially-offensive symbols. Although the law doesn't prohibit simple teasing, offhand comments, or isolated incidents that are not very serious, harassment is illegal when it is so frequent or severe that it creates a hostile or offensive work environment or when it results in an adverse employment decision (such as the victim being fired or demoted). The harasser can be the victim's supervisor, a supervisor in another area, a co-worker, or someone who is not an employee of the employer (such as a client or customer).

Are Women Better Managers Than Men?

As reported in the *Department of Labor Report 2010*, Asian women and men earned more than their White, Black, and Hispanic counterparts did in 2009. Among women, Whites (with weekly earnings of $669) earned 86 percent as much as Asians did ($779); while Blacks ($582) and Hispanics ($509) earned 75 percent and 65 percent as much, respectively. By comparison, White men ($845) earned 89 percent as much as Asian men ($952); Black men ($621) earned 65 percent as much; and Hispanic men ($569), 60 percent as much.

The differences in earnings between that of women and men were widest for Whites and for Asians. White women earned 79 percent as much as their male counterparts did in 2009, while Asian women earned 82 percent as much. By comparison, Hispanic women had earnings that were 90 percent of those of their male counterparts, while Black women earned 94 percent as much as Black men did.

Across the major categories of Blacks Whites and Hispanic ethnicity, women's inflation-adjusted earnings grew significantly from 1979 to 2009. Growth in real earnings for White women, however, has outpaced that of their Black and Hispanic counterparts. Between 1979 and 2009, inflation-adjusted earnings for White women rose by 32 percent; while the growth of earnings among Black and Hispanic women was 25 percent and 18 percent, respectively. In contrast, real earnings for White men edged up by just 3 percent over the 30-year span; those for Black men showed no growth; and Hispanic men's earnings fell by 6 percent (US Department of Labor Report, 2010).

Gender and Jobs

Clancy (2018) conducted a longitudinal study in the harassment of women in selected science professions ranging from engineers to medical scientists and found that women accounted for half the United States' college-educated workforce in 2015 but only 29%of the workers in science and engineering occupations. There was rough gender parity in some science and engineering fields, but many remained disproportionately male. The study conducted by Clancy found that:

- Both sexual harassment and sexual assault were reported by more women than men---mirroring the situation in society at large.
- Women's experiences of sexual misconduct during scientific fieldwork were not just quantitatively higher but also qualitatively worse than men's. Women victims were more often targeted by perpetrators above them in the

Table 1. Distribution of women in selected science professions

Profession	Percentage of Women
Engineers	15
Physicists	18
Earth scientists	23
Chemists	32
Mathematicians	43
Biological medical scientists	53

hierarchy and felt they could not fight back or say so. Few individuals had any awareness of a sexual harassment policy or reporting mechanism; even fewer dared report their experiences.

- Scientists who are harassed face significant career consequences, ranging from having to make lateral career moves to not feeling safe enough to attend professional events…or even stay in the field.

The Story Is the Same

Clancy (2018) argued that too often the story was the same: a man sexually harasses a woman, the woman reports it, and she gets told that's just how it is. There are variations on this theme: women harassing women, people harassing those they don't think conform to their gender well enough, women of color receiving a toxic blend of racial and gender harassment. Clancy's research found that the following cases resulted in dismissal of the offenders:

Astronomer at the University of Berkeley California after investigations were concluded resigned in 2015. The astronomer for a decade was harassing women students. In another case, Paleoanthropologist resigned from the American Museum of Natural History in 2016 for admitting to sexual misconduct of women for many years.

The LGBT Community's Impact on Urban Business

Hofstede (1992) viewed gender differences as being cultural differences and argued that these impact roles in a group. Gender roles continue to change rapidly in most progressive countries around the world. In Raley and Lucas (2006), the LGBT activists and sociologists view LGBT community-building as a counterbalance to heterosexism, homophobia, biphobia, transphobia, sexualism, and conformist pressures that exist in the larger society. The issue of sexual orientation is an emotionally charged one; it arouses feelings like, yet very different from, those aroused by other diversity issues. Mupepi, Essila, Opoku, Mensah, and Mupepi (2018) consider sexual orientation as being a phenomenon present in all races and ethnic groups in the world, not just the United States. The discussion seeks to contrast the leadership of men, women, or those of a chosen sexual orientation, as an antecedent to the creation of situational management practices. An example of situational management is drawn from urban geography where astute leadership welcomes people of different sexual orientations bringing their intellectual capital and settling in multicultural populations such as those of San Francisco, US or London, England.

In Mupepi et al (2018), the out-of-closet practice and discussion of gender identity's underlying relation to sexual orientation is related to employers' appreciation of the paradigm shift towards embracing talent and recognizing the practicality of hiring talented people (regardless of their gender identity) in advancing organizational effectiveness and the 'bottom line' results in a successful enterprise. The practice of gender underlies sexual orientation. The discussion progresses the notion of accepting the sexual identity of men and women who choose to progress their careers. Emotional intelligence draws managerial appreciation of such inclusion's impact on managerial controls and performance. Mupepi et al. assert that top managerial positions in enterprises have been regarded as being male or female enclaves in many cultures around the globe. The trend towards reflect gender as a possible social construct continues to increase in enterprises that value diversity. Change management technology is examined to understand how entrepreneurship that is exercised by women (as compared to men) can impact profitability; and to comprehend whether there are any traits attributed to any specific gender. The perspectives are applied to model an organization acquiescent to the possibility of increasing productivity in a variety of settings.

Are Gay Business People Better Entrepreneurs?

When Joel Simkhai came out of the closet at age 18, he was worried about what kind of professional future he could have as an openly gay man. "One of my problems was I thought I couldn't be as successful," Simkhai says. "That's partially because I didn't have any gay role models who were very successful and in high-profile jobs" (Lapowsky, 2018). Now, as founder and CEO of the location-based gay social network, Grindr, which has more than 4 million users in 192 countries, Simkhai has become the very example of success that he says he never had. Maclean adds: "The fact is: Sexuality remains a sensitive subject in big corporate environments, especially among C-suite executives." Recently, the *Wall Street Journal* reported that there's not even a single openly gay CEO on the Fortune 1000 list. Even those who are widely reported to be gay, including Apple's CEO Tim Cook, have never publicly admitted it—a phenomenon often referred to as "the glass closet" (Lapowsky, 2018). Faced with so much secrecy, it comes as no surprise that promising gay business leaders are finding entrepreneurship a comparatively more attractive option. Additionally, some research indicates that openly gay people might even be better suited to the job (Lapowsky, 2018).

The Hofstede model highlights three elements of diversity:

1. The first element is the presence of a set of beliefs, values, and symbols which constitute cultural components shared by an identifiable group of people.
2. The second element is the presence of an individuated culture that values individual needs and goals more than group needs and goals.
3. The third element is the presence of a collectivist culture that values group needs and goals more than individual needs and goals

What Are the Characteristics of a Successful Diverse Enterprise?

Researchers such as Kohler (1929), Von Bertalanffy (1950), Lewin (1951), and – much later – Mupepi, Tenkasi, and Sorensen (2013), suggest that nothing has more impact on successful operations than a multi-talented diverse team. Kohler (1929) made it possible to examine diversity in a group and renamed it the "holistic system"—implying the deployment of talent, technology, and explicit practices to increase productivity. In today's modern production systems, a holistic technology is an approach to IT management that is concerned with viewing and treating a complex computer system as a single entity. It embraces the talent employed to play a significant part in increasing output. In Von Bertalanffy (1950), a feature common to all living systems, including diverse groups, is asserted to be the feature of complexity. Many factors combine to produce one outcome. For example, continuous learning, improvement, assessment, and evaluation can be combined to ascertain the configurations necessary to increase output. A related principle characteristic of groups is that there is usually more than one appropriate way to reach a goal.

Spencer (2012) argued that pluralism was the multiplicity of metaphysical models of the structure and content of reality, both as it appears and as socially constructed logic dictated that it might be.

In Mupepi, Tenkasi, and Sorensen (2013), systems such as diverse groups are viewed as being dynamic processes with inherent moments of stability and change. A living system's primary objective is survival; but at some point, stability can be impossible or difficult—leading to the system's demise. Mupepi, Tenkasi, and Sorensen (2013) propound that much of the work in corporate organizations is done by small, interlocking, diverse groups representing a series of interconnected ideas.

Mupepi, Tenkasi, and Sorensen (2013) argue that the links can also be viewed as sociograms linked by stakeholders whose safeties are associated with profit maximization. For example, the management is depicted as a self-management work team made up specialists from a diverse background intent on looking after the interests of stakeholders. Other teams, such as production or sales teams, ensure that the organization produces the goods and services demanded by customers.

Multiple Languages

The British Council (2018) is an international organization focused on promoting the many facets of British culture such as the language, sports, or democratic governance of the British Isles. It implies that multiculturalism in Britain means understanding English and other languages spoken in the British Isles (see Figure 4). A great deal of ethnocentrism is centered around language. Language issues are becoming a considerable source of conflict and inefficiency in the increasingly diverse workforce throughout the world. According to Mupepi and Mupepi (2015), language makes it easy to socially construct the existence of an enterprise. Language is at the heart of any business and it makes possible the abstractions that govern people's behavior and their beliefs values and attitudes and this makes business possible within a culture. To go global implies to be able to find mutual understanding of what those abstractions mean in other languages and other cultures. Mupepi and Mupepi (2015) asserted that the as the workforce grows it will mean more people will be speaking English as a second language.

The Gaelic and Welsh languages have radio and television channels of their own audiences and listeners throughout Europe. Sports such as cricket, rugby, soccer, and tennis are pervasive on television and radio and are broadcasted in many languages such as West Indian Australian, South African, or Zimbabwean versions of the English language. This demonstrates multiculturalism, as does the diversity of places where the 4'clock (BMT) tea represents a ritual where artefacts of teapots and kettles are used to boil Earl Grey Tanganda or Lipton tea leaves. The brew has specially associated cutlery comprising tea strainers, erns, cups, sauces, teaspoons, and sugar basins – and even knitted teapot covers to keep the brew hot. The inclusion of hot cross buns or scones with butter and marmalade spread characterizes the ritual. Quintessentially British culture is a unique culture shared by many in what constitutes a fluid British Empire. For example, manufacturers of marmalade jam have not shifted drastically away from the original Paddington recipes because the traditional recipes make sense in terms of sales. Likewise, beer, tea, and coffee beverage sales notably increase during winter and during sports games.

On its 2018 website, the British Council has a brochure in which it gives voice to its position that multiculturalism in the workplace involves more than just talking in different languages. It includes the need for managers to appreciate all their customers—people who are willing to buy goods and services produced by the business. Multiculturalism means that the companies must create databases that can be exploited to increase productivity. The databases can show consumers' location and race; and the company's share of the potential market.

The databases can be utilized in creating targeted adverts for television; or for creating huge billboards on the freeways or banners/posters for display during live sports games such as for soccer matches at White Hart Lane or for rugby in Arms Park Cardiff. Such advertisements can result in an upward surge in sales during a given period.

It is important to articulate that corporations rooted in the British Isles do business locally as well as globally—and that, as such, the leaders of these entities must embrace multiculturalism from all angles. Like culture itself, multiculturalism comes from many different people and can be practiced in many ways.

Metaphors for Multi-Vocal Populations Living Together

In Bell (2017), race and ethnicity are viewed as different voices representing individuals and groups in a diversified workforce –all of whom must be heard. Bell suggest that changing demographics and changing views compel organizations to appreciate diversity when making efforts to increase work output. Diversity has its roots from creation, as exemplified in the building of the Tower of Babel. The story of Babel has a common interpretation in our collective minds as being mankind's first defeat in attempting to cope with a plurality of languages. Ever since the building of this divine construction ended in a Babylonian confusion of tongues, polylingualism was viewed as being problematic and something to be prevented. In his book *La Recherche de la Langue Purfaite dans la Culture Europeenne*, Umberto Eco (1992) retraces the search for a universal language throughout European literature and tries to show the implications of this search for how Europe can cope today with its polyglot situation. In Eco's research, the story of the Tower of Babel plays a prominent part. Historically, it is the symbol of the *confusion linguarum*—a symbol of the transition from a universal language used by Adam and Eve to a melting pot of languages. After Babel, the world was doomed to live with linguistic confusion and misunderstanding. Eco questions this interpretation of the Babel story: *Pourquoi interpreter la confusion comme un Malheur?* (p. 24). He tries to show that the solution to this confusion is not to find a universal language but rather to recognize an original polylingualism. The multiplication of languages is socially positive instead of being destructive and conflictual.

An Advantage of Learning Another People's Culture

During WW2, Britain and its allied forces recruited women and men who could understand many languages, especially German and Japanese. The Mormon Church is one of the fastest-growing organizations because it sends thousands of missionaries throughout the world to propagate the Gospel. The missionaries, learning in a custom-built language school in Salt Lake City, are taught about the cultures of the places where they will be deployed. Imparting the knowledge and linguistic skills they need in the field has led to many people in distinct parts of the world embracing the Gospel and becoming baptized.

Barriers to Overcome

In Shafer (2013), barriers to diversity can include: policies and practices perceived as not valuing people over-reliance on technology and process change, under-investing in training and development, emphasizing only on cost and performance measures, restructuring without reasoning, and dragging on diversity. A company can have all the technology available but is people make the difference.

THE FOCUS OF THIS CHAPTER

The discourse presented here shows that human beings are highly gregarious animals that can reorganize themselves to suit the environment in which they draw the energy needed to grow. The problem of diversity in the workplace is primarily concerned with integration of the talent needed to progress organization. Diversity is a reality in the Western world—and certainly everywhere else. Games people play can be exploited to create customized products and services demanded locally and globally. Organizations must embrace multiculturalism to effectively increase productivity. They must create appropriate databases which can be exploited to increase market share. Multilingualism is an opportunity for different people to communicate effectively in their mother tongues. It is an advantage to learn another people's culture. It is critical to understand the problems confronting women, minorities in the workplace which include racism, sexism, and ethnocentrisms three of the most powerful forces affecting the ability of organizations to have efficient and effective enterprises.

LIMITATIONS

Life under different governments around the world is not necessarily as free as one might experience in the United Kingdom or the United States. In fluidly communist countries, freedom is a scarce commodity – even though the Cold War ended in the 1990 with the end of Michael Gorbachev's administration. In such a climate, not all organizations are ready to expand operations globally – while some are, others are quite satisfied with keeping their enterprise operating locally.

THE WAY FORWARD

High performance standards depend on having staff who are proud of the company. This is where the interests of the people doing the job comes in. In the end the long- term interests of the shareholders are damaged by giving them superficial short-term priority.

Building an Integrated Diversity Strategy Fit

Anderson and Anderson (2013) proposed that there were two important cornerstones for strategic change and these include understanding the executive's significant role in creating new business. However, announcing about a new business strategy is not enough to accomplish it. It must be executed in a way that delivers its intended business results. Anderson and Anderson posited that the creation of a fitting diversity strategy leaders must comprehend the type and scope of change their business strategy requires. The second point they make is that the mindset of the entire organization needs to be changed. The leadership must attend more thoroughly to the human dynamics at play. The organization's mindset must be shifted to perceive the talent needed to advance the enterprise. The mindset is causative. For example, it is the causal factor of behavior and more importantly business results.

An important and often avoided dimension of organizational life is the diversity of its members. Diversity includes many attributes, characteristics, and identity group memberships such as the following:

- Gender,
- Sexual orientation,
- Physical ability,
- Race,
- Age,
- Language,
- Nationality, and
- Ethnicity among other dimensions.

These identities add both potential complexity and richness to the organization's work. Ignoring these identities reduces a group's effectiveness—thus creating tensions in communications and reducing access to member resources.

Given their potential value to the organization, diversity awareness models should be explored and implemented to increase productivity. When worked effectively, differences among people 'in the room' can be the substantive basis for an opportunity for profound learning for all present. There are several theories of diversity, including the Dimensions of Diversity or Path to Competencies, which future research could explore.

Flamholtz and Randle (2014) state that: A strong culture is that people clearly understand and can articulate. A weak culture is one that employees have difficulty defining, understanding, or explaining. Strong culture is said to exist where staff respond to stimulus because of their alignment to organizational values. Discrimination in the workplace can be viewed as signs of a weak culture where individuals possessing the brashness to effectively are oppressed because of their race, ethnicity or gender. In such environments, strong cultures help firms to focus on increasing productivity.

The formulation and implementation how human practices and procedures and how a workforce can develop positive attitudes about their co-workers. Racism sexism and ethnocentrism can be nurtured by the entire organizations using the technology of positive scholarship to advance organizational culture.

CONCLUSION

According to population dynamics in the US and UK, future organizations will be more diverse than those of ten years ago. Cultural difference represents a major form of diversity in a group. Groups of the future will continue to be increasingly more multicultural than before. Organizations should view diversity as an opportunity to maximize output by producing goods and services needed by specific consumers in the market.

REFERENCES

Age Discrimination in Employment Act of 1967 (ADEA), which protects individuals who are 40 years of age or older. (n.d.). Accessed 04/28/18 https://www.eeoc.gov/laws/statutes/titlevii.cfm

Berlin, I. (2004). American Slavery in History and Memory and the Search for Social Justice. *The Journal of American History*, *90*(4), 1251–1268. doi:10.2307/3660347

British Council. (2018). *Equality, diversity and inclusion*. Accessed 04/28?18 https://www.britishcouncil.org/organisation/how-we-work/equality-diversity-inclusion

CCE. (2010). *Fair lending: Comptroller's handbook. Consumer Compliance Examination (CCE)*. Retrieved https://www.occ.treas.gov/publications/publications-by-type/comptrollers-handbook/fair-lending/pub-ch-fair-lending.pdf

Central Statistics Office. (2018). *Population Census and Survey United Kingdom*. Cardiff, UK: Central Statistics Office. Accessed 4/17/18 https://www.statisticsauthority.gov.uk/

Civil Rights Act of 1964. (n.d.). Retrieved from https://www.eeoc.gov/laws/statutes/titlevii.cfm

Clancy, K. (2018). Rid the sciences of Harassers. *National Geographic*, *233*(5), 15–18.

Clarke, H., & Mezzofiore, G. (2018). *Windrush' scandal forces UK government into U-turn*. Accessed 04/18/2018 https://www.msn.com/en-us/news/us/windrush-scandal-forces-uk-government-into-u-turn/ar-AAvWzLx

Conway, D. (2005). Transformationalism and return: Home as an enduring fixture and anchor. In *The experience of Return migration: Caribbean Experience*. Aldershort, UK: Ashgate.

Cromwell, J. (2014). More than Slaves and Sugar: Recent Historiography of the Trans-imperial Caribbean and Its Sinew Populations. *History Compass*, *12*(10), 770–783. doi:10.1111/hic3.12192

Department of Labor Report. (2010). *Employment situation summary*. Accessed 04/29/18 https://www.bls.gov/news.release/empsit.nr0.htm

Dimeo, P. (2001). Contemporary developments in Indian football. *Contemporary South Asia*, *10*(2), 251–264. doi:10.1080/09584930120083846

Economist. (2018). *Diversity and Development*. Accessed 04/28/18 https://www.economist.com/node/2926697

European Union Agency for Fundamental Rights. (2018). *European Convention on Human Rights.* Accessed 04/28/18 http://fra.europa.eu/en/publication/2018/handbook-european-law-non-discrimination

Fernandez, J. P. (1991). *Managing a Diverse Work Force: Regaining the Competitive Edge*. Toronto: Lexington Books.

Flamholtz, E., & Randle, Y. (2014). Implications of organizational Life Cycles for Corporate Culture and Climate. In B. Schneider & K. Barbera (Eds.), *The Oxford Handbook of organizational Climate and Culture* (pp. 235–265). OUP.

Freeman, Jo. (1991). How 'Sex' Got into Title VII: Persistent Opportunism as a Maker of Public Policy. *Law and Inequality: A Journal of Theory and Practice, 9*(2), 163–184.

Freiberg, K., & Frieberg, J. (2005). *Guts: Companies that blow the doors off business-as-usual.* New York: Random House.

Hofstede, G. (1993). Cultures and Organizations: Software of the Mind. *Administrative Science Quarterly, 38*(1), 132–134. doi:10.2307/2393257

Human Rights Act, C. 42. (1998). *An Act to give further effect to rights and freedoms guaranteed under the European Convention on Human Rights*. Westminster: House of Commons.

Kohler, W. (1929). *Gestalt psychology, an introduction to new concepts in modern psychology*. New York: Liveright.

Lapowsky, I. (2018). *Are Gay People Better Entrepreneurs?* Accessed 04/28/18 https://www.inc.com/issie-lapowsky/gay-people-make-better-entrepreneurs.html

Lewin, K. (1951). *Field theory in social science*. New York: Harper.

Mupepi, M. G., Essila, J. C., Mensah, A. O., & Mupepi, S. C. (2018). Alternate Techniques to Chart Practicality in Organizations. In N. Baporikar (Ed.), *Knowledge Integration Strategies for Entrepreneurship and Sustainability* (pp. 334–352). Hershey, PA: IGI Global. doi:10.4018/978-1-5225-5115-7.ch016

Mupepi, M. G., & Mupepi, S. C. (2017). The Structure of Talent: A Co-Constructed Competency Perspective. In M. Mupepi (Ed.), *Effective Talent Management Strategies for Organizational Success* (pp. 57–73). Hershey, PA: IGI Global. doi:10.4018/978-1-5225-1961-4.ch005

Mupepi, Tenkasi, & Sorensen. (2013). Creating High Impact Organizations in the SADC: Adapting OD Methods and Practices. In *Handbook for Strategic HR: Best Practices in Organization Development.* New York: Amacon.

Myrtle, P. (2017). *Diversity in Organization.* London, UK: Cengage.

National Statistics Office. (2018). *Population of the United Kingdom.* Accessed 04/29/18 https://www.bing.com/search?q=population+of+the+uk&form=EDGEAR&qs=AS&cvid=3d330c3445684ce08cb35d6070a58aea&cc=US&setlang=en-US&PC=HCTS

Norris, M., & Laub, G. (2018, April). As America changes, some anxious whites feel left behind. *National Geographic*. Retrieved from https://www.nationalgeographic.com/magazine/2018/04/race-rising-anxiety-white-america/

Norris & Laub. (2018). *As America Changes, Some Anxious Whites Feel Left Behind Demographic shifts rippling across the nation are fueling fears that their culture and standing are under threat*. Academic Press.

Platsis, G. (2018). The Human Factor: Cyber Security's Greatest Challenge. *International Journal of Public Administration in the Digital Age*, *5*(2), 23–39. doi:10.4018/IJPADA.2018040103

Raley & Lucas. (2006). Stereotype or Success? *Journal of Homosexuality, 51*(2), 19-38.

Robles, F. (2012). *A look at what happened the night Trayvon Martin died*. Accessed 04/29/18 http://www.tampabay.com/news/publicsafety/crime/a-look-at-what-happened-the-night-trayvon-martin-died/1223083

Schein, E. (2013). Corporate culture: How to think ab out and define culture. In E. Vogelsang & M. Townsend (Eds.), *Handbook for Strategic HR: Best practices in Organization Development*. New York: Amacon.

Spencer, J. (2012). Ways of being. *Philosophy Compass*, *7*(12), 910–918. doi:10.1111/j.1747-9991.2012.00527.x

Umberto, E. (1992). *Interpretation and Overinterpretation*. Cambridge, UK: Cambridge University Press.

Von Bertalanffy, L. (1950). An Outline of General System Theory. *The British Journal for the Philosophy of Science*, *1*, 114–129.

Wright, S. (2005). *The Civil Rights Act of 1964: Landmark Antidiscrimination Legislation*. The Rosen Publishing Group.

KEY TERMS AND DEFINITIONS

Change in Complexion: Change in complexion in humans is the changes in natural color, texture, and appearance of the skin, especially on the face.

Cultural Diversity: Cultural diversity is the quality of diverse or diverse cultures, as opposed to monoculture, the global monoculture, or a homogenization of cultures, akin to cultural decay.

Demographic Changes: Demographics are the quantifiable statistics of a given population. Changes such as the numbers of females or males categorized in age groups characterize the populations of any given geographic region.

Ethnicity: The state of belonging to a social group that has a common national or cultural tradition.

Ethnocentrisms: Cultural ideologies that characterize dominant race men and specific ethnic groups as being inherently superior to minority races, women, and other ethnic groups.

Multiculturalism: The presence of several distinct cultural or ethnic groups within a society or organization.

Polylingualism: Polylingual implies multiculturalism expressed in the ability to use several languages.

Windrush Generation: The West Indians who arrived in the United Kingdom in 1948 to reconstruct war-torn cities and work in the healthcare transportation and hotel and catering industries.

Workforce Diversity: The similarities and differences among people employed within an organization. Aspects of workplace diversity may include age, race, gender, personality, religion, sexual orientation, and education.

Chapter 7
Supporting the Needs of the Independent Learner Within Higher Education

Robert Costello
Newcastle College, UK

ABSTRACT

This chapter offers a case study in adaptive personalized learning for higher education learners. The chapter presents a postgraduate recommender system for educational pathway to aid with online support towards selecting suitable transferable skills depending on department and captures a current snapshot of the current trends that the university is facing.

DOI: 10.4018/978-1-5225-7390-6.ch007

INTRODUCTION TO TRANSFERABLE SKILLS

It is now widely recognised by employers, professional bodies and research funding agencies that specialist expertise alone is not sufficient preparation either for research or a subsequent career and that Higher Education (HE) institutions must still relate to the UK Quality Code "*Safeguarding academics; assuring the academic quality of learning opportunities; promoting continuous and systematic improvement (enhancement); and finally ensuring that information about programmes is fit for purpose, accessible and trustworthy*" (QAA, 2015, p1). It is still important that HE Researchers like Dennis, Smith, and Wadsworth (2012) Saiti and Prokopiadou (2008), Campbell et al., (2008), Hryciw, Tangalakis, and Best, (2017), Bolton, and Rosselli, (2017), Mawson, and Haworth, (2018) indicates that HE students require a balance between the skills needed within the labour market, adaptability, and transferable skills, ranging from literacy to highlighting the benefits working within a collaborative setting. Alpay and Walsh (2008) mentions that attitudes toward skills set of the students have shifted towards a positive outlook from not just postgraduates but also from employers and academia. Nägele, & Stalder (2017), has similar views to Alpay and Walsh (2008) and indicates that transferable skills play a pivotal role within practice, recruitment, selection process, and organisational entry when entering industry.

In this research, the author builds upon work carried out previous as indicated as indicated by (Costello, 2015), which was to present an approach tailored towards the requirements of Higher Educational Institutes by mapping educational pathways through the use of an Online-Recommender Systems (Drachsler et al., 2008; Wang and Wu 2011; Bridge and Dunleavy 2014) to provide pre-guidance transferable training skills for Higher Educational students within a variety of different disciplines. To support these different disciplines within Higher Education Institutions (HEIs) there are according to Chadha (2015) amount of pressure to develop learner's abilities to support skills that can tailor for everyone instead of "*one size fits all*" (Chadha, 2015, p3).

It is vital that that HEIs incorporate diversity to widen learning activities, to increase overall intake to Universities (Sherbin, and Rashid 2017; Chadha, 2015). This approach will address how academics will: lectur, build resources, provide tailored support, and develop new skills to give the learners the confidence they need before they go into industry through embedding "*knowledge, understanding, critical analysis and creativity*" (Chadha, 2015, p3).

Cryer, (1998), Gilbert et al., (2004) Craswell (2007) and Gokhale, V.A., (2018) all suggest that to enable Higher Educational students to build upon skills necessary for industry, supervisors are key to identifying any skills gaps that might exist, and in encouraging them to address these through empowerment and transformation.

As Gokhale (2018) points out this empowerment will lead learners to develop characteristics required to gain autonomy and can express well defined logical expression and ideas, which is needed within today's industries. Research from Andrews & Higson (2008) and Hinchliffe & Jolly (2011) would indicates that transferable skills of students can be synthesized to identify their key competencies to utilise and map their intrinsic links between what been learnt to what is needed within the industry. Hinchliffe & Jolly (2011) highlight four key areas that graduate needs to focus on when preparing students for the job market, these are value, intellect, social engagement, and performance through the use of transferable skills individuals can enhance and deliver what is expected from them within industry. It is important for HEI to measure what characteristics have enhanced or diminished within the industry to ensure that the correct approach to learning has been adopted, this is very similar to the thoughts suggested by (Carter, 2018).

Craswell (2007) has similar views to Linsay et al., (2002): if the supervisor can offer interest, relevance or utility, then the postgraduate student will, or might, want to learn more transferable skills, within or outside their own research area. According to Brodie (2007) supporting and developing employability skills for students will help to build and develop local and national economic infrastructures within society (Bao, Kehm, and Ma, 2018).

To support learners to grow within an ever changing, economically dynamic society, researchers like (Buchanan, Yu, Marginson, and Wheelahan, 2009; Bao, Kehm, and Ma, 2018) are trying to rectify the imbalance of transferable skills within the educational systems. These students are facing humiliation due to lack of knowledge, abilities, and transitional fluxes within the current employment markets. There should be a convergence of requirements relating to the needs of Higher Education ranging from the different challenges faces, opportunities, pathways, to acknowledgement which would allow for competency when processing the necessary skills required for the labour market.

As Buchanan et al. (2009) point outs, HEIs should be provides the higher levels of education and learning *"entails the acquisition of common knowledge, promotes skills transferability, and importantly enables workers to engage their intellectual capacities to adapt to work-process, organisational, technological and social changes"* (Buchanan et al., 2009, p16) that will support the learners before they go into the labour market. It is important to take into consideration other factors such as diversity and differentiation as mentioned by Chadha (2015) and features or tools that can support the basis for a supportive approach to autonomous, problem solving and self-directed learning. Through mapping the skills sets of the learners, this would enable a relationship to be created between a structure within education and the visions associated with competencies, that are required for work. These competencies will enable learners who gain and acquire new abilities to be able to form new motivation approaches to help them create a sense of identity, which makes the individual more specialized to all others.

According to Royal Society (2017) "*The UK's higher education and research system is undergoing extensive change. These changes include:*

- *The establishment of UK Research and Innovation (UKRI) and the Office for Students (OfS) on 1 April 2018;*
- *The bedding in of the Teaching Excellence Framework (TEF), the development of the Knowledge Exchange Framework (KEF);*
- *Reforms to the Research Excellence Framework (REF)" (Royal Society, 2017, p1).*

As indicated by the Royal Society (2017) this new approach from the government will assist with creating links with research and education, while HEIs can then have additional supportive capital to support the students to achieve employment. There are multiple approaches that HEIs can adopt from supporting personal development to online learning. It is up to the institution to pursue the appropriate course of action is towards offering them a more tailored educational setting. Whichever approach is adopted here, HEIs pay greater attention towards offering transferable skills before going into industry. One approach that can adopted to support the new recommendations from the Royal Society (2017) is that of "*The Postgraduate Pathway Model*" (Costello, 2015). The proposed model will use a Content-based Filtering mechanism, to shift through a result set belonging to students to offer the individual the opportunity to choose a variety of different learning pathways, to decide what transferable skill set to be studied. Once the student has selected a branch of required modules for training, the options are then simplified and then stored back into the management system.

The Content-based Filtering mechanism should be developed to facilitate online usage as this would provide a way of accessing materials whenever the students are required to go under their training. the desirable impact relating directly to employability, transferable skills etc. The aim of this study is to explore some of the challenges to developing support mechanisms for Higher Education Students and challenges. The research in this paper will explore some areas of adaptive and e-learning in the Cloud, and the importance they bring to this topic area, as these can influence the future trend of Higher Education.

RELATED WORK

Veitch, Strehlow, and Boyd (2018) suggested that there was a growing need for supporting higher educational students due to issues relating to barriers of technologies, diversity of learning preferences, quality of resources and provisions of services. This was once again highlighted by Higher Education Commission (2013) that supporting mechanism could be used to tackle this issue. There are a variety of different techniques that could be applied from personalization to academic development. Researchers like Blaschke, (2018) and Wu, Chan, Tan, and Wang, (2018). has used a variety of online learning techniques to improve online learning, this could be easily adapted to facility further development. There have been other notable improvements within this field belonging to the learners from integrating gamification to the education life cycle improving motivation techniques to encourage the learners to communicate more effectively, within an ever dynamic environment (Kyewski, and Krämer, 2018; Costello, 2018.).

Through the use of gamification online, learners within HEI can develop collaborative skills required for industry relating skills, which enables them to build upon a positive relationship by using collaborative/individual projects, tutorials, and training programmes, through gaming examples or gaming engines to harness the student's ability, with a variety of different types of intrinsic and extrinsic motivational techniques that enhance and empower the way they learn to maximize the results from the learning process. There are other types of other supportive mechanisms that HEIs can use from the likes of, Adaptive Technologies that use web-based technologies systems (Goyal, and Krishnamurthy, 2018) to E-learning Recommender Systems (Albatayneh, Ghauth, and Chua, 2018). This supportive mechanism approaches enables the learners to choose and select relevant educational pathways, programs, or options to assist with their learning. These techniques do effectively improve the students experience and overcome the traditional platforms issues that are found within modern academic institutions (Alves et al., 2008; Chang 2015; Ellis and Anderson, 2018).

Munawar, Toor, Aslam, and Hamid, (2018) and Chang & Wills (2013) indicates that with the ever changing needs of Higher Education, this will always bring new challenges. According to Chang & Wills (2013) the use of e-learning in the Cloud will enable the use of a blended learning approach to be used, through an integration of different learning resources while providing one-stop resource network and services to aid individual's learning experiences. The use of Cloud within e-learning can be seen as a way forward (Chang & Wills 2013), Chang (2013), Utpal & Majidul (2013), Munawar, Toor, Aslam, and Hamid, (2018), Baldassarre, Caivano, Dimauro, Gentile, and Visaggio, (2018) as it can provide a new paradigm in its way of delivering education while effectively cutting costs, through scaling back computer resources, while maintaining a reliable and dynamic service. While researchers, and students can access a blend of supportive materials online through built in services like that of Google Apps, this enables the resources to be processed at the infrastructure side not the client side, freeing up processing time of the individual tablet or pc. This according to Alsufyani et al., (2015) will allow for the simplification of students accessing web applications, data centers, and services in real time.

Munawar, Toor, Aslam, and Hamid, (2018) suggests that E-learning can be used to incorporated Virtual Laboratories that will enable the learners to experience latest technologies and techniques to perform tasks for better understanding of concepts and effectively improve performance. Utpal & Majidul (2013) and Burgos, and Corbí (2018). suggests that E-learning in the Cloud, can support the individuals through not being limited to a particular type of software package, while offering the learner their own personal storage space is more secure due to it being located on a variety of different remote servers. Radulescu (2014), Burgos, and Corbí (2018) and Ria, Cox, Quinn, Bakir, and Woolford (2018) has all indicate that they have created a Virtual Laboratory that enables lecturers to design innovate ways to make on-line learning more enjoyable through the use of 'VLCS', E-learning in the Cloud. VLCS uses services to provide features of e-learning to existing Cloud technology to enhance its capabilities while placing the student first 'Personalisation within the Cloud'.

According to Hobbs, et al., (2006) and McLoughlin & Luca (2002) by providing a supporting mechanism through on-line learning, a University can improve Transferable Skills for students to get them ready for industry. These will enable the employer to expect a diverse knowledgebase of skill sets and the capability of individual to be flexible while working in a range of different contexts. Cargill (2004) suggests that with any additional training individuals will be time-pressured, and can be seen as a barrier instead of a skill-development approach.

Methodology

The approach adopted within this research project was one of mixed methods (Creswell and Clark 2010) as it used the combination of quantitative and qualitative data from a number of sources including: an online survey and a focus groups. The main research theme was to identify student's perceptions of Higher Education training; and finally what was their view on the supporting mechanism the university had implemented. The online surveys were distributed through mailing system and 150 students completed the questionnaire. In addition to the online survey, several focus group meetings were held. In total, these involved 20 participants from different disciplines across the university. Three main questions informed the discussions:

- What changes would you like to see to support transferable skills within the Higher Education?
- Are you aware of the importance of transferable skills?
- Carrying out additional Higher Educational Training will help me to stand out within the jobs market?

Using the three questions we will aim to try to find students perceptions on the following hypothesis.

1. Skills Training within Higher Education can have a positive impact on student's perceptions

In total there were 170 students who took part within this research over a 4-month period, which involved 75% (127n) full time student and 25%-part time from cross disciplines. Expanding on the 170 students who took part, a sample demographic table will be used to highlight some of the respondent's categories (Table 1).

FINDINGS AND DISCUSSION

Using the three proposed questions mentioned within the introduction, the first set of analytical data can be divided into two areas: the student's perception of training within Higher Education; and the support they get from their institutions.

Table 1. Demographic table

Measure	Item	No. of Respondents
Gender	Male	106
	Female	64
Type of Study	Full Time	127
	Part Time	43
Length of Study	Year 1	75
	Year 2	47
	Year 3	35
	Year 4	10
	Year 5 +	3

Student's Perception of Higher Education

Using the student's thoughts about Higher Education and the training required for them to complete as an additional learning journey, the researcher explores analytical data gathered that will illustrate current activities and views of the individuals. The analytical data from table 1, shows a 51% (no 87), out of 170 a negative attitude towards training within Higher Education, while 35%, of students asked were favorable with the idea of additional courses. The other 14%, or (24 out of 170) were uncertain within their views towards training within Higher Education.

Table 3, indicated that 63% of participants asked, had agreed that training within Higher Education during their studies has helped them through their studies, while 22% disagree with the whole concept of training.

The focus group was used to explore this theme in more depth and the following quotations provide an illustration of some students' perspectives:

Higher Educational training provides a way of allowing other students to share techniques and also helps with networking.

Provides greater support and helps with issues of isolation of individuals, which has enabled me to share ideas with other students within the research process.

Table 3, indicated that 63% of participants asked, had agreed that training within Higher Education during their studies has helped them through their studies, while 22% disagree with the whole concept of training.

Table 2. 'Attitude towards training'

(Q1) Within my department what is your attitude towards training within Higher Education and Transferable Skills								
Very Unfavorable	Unfavorable	Uncertain	Favorable	Very Favorable	Standard Deviation	Unbiased "n-1"	Standard Error	P-Value
36 (21%)	51 (30%)	24 (14%)	40 (24%)	19 (11%)	12.79	11.44	5.72	0.0005

Table 3. 'Training modules has helped with research approaches'

(Q2) The Training Modules provided by the institution has helped me to do my research?								
Strongly Disagree	Disagree	Neither Agree nor Disagree	Agree	Strongly Agree	Standard Deviation	Unbiased "n-1"	Standard Error	P-Value
30 (18%)	7 (4%)	25 (15%)	62 (36%)	46 (27%)	20.94	18.73	9.36	0.022

Looking at the results from Table 4, 117 (69%) participants out of 170 had indicated that there are well aware of the importance of Higher Educational Training while studying for their PhD. However, looking at the data analysis even though, it is compulsory within 'HE', 20% of students still did not think it was of high importance.

Referring to the student's perspective within Table 4, it is clear that 50% of participants had indicated that additional training within Higher Education would allow them to stand out compared to other candidates. However, 39% (65 out of 170) did disagree with the above statement and looking at the focus group, would indicate some of the individuals thought;

By undergoing additional training within Higher Education, would allow me to become better at a variety of tasks, instead of being specific and focusing on one particular topic.

Support From Institutions

This particular section of analytical data looks at the participant's perception about the support provides for students within Higher Education Training and the different support mechanisms.

The data analysis from table 6 indicates that 66% of postgraduate students asked (111 out of 170) suggested that the range of training modules that supports the diversity of needs within Higher Education can be seen as comprehensive, while 25% of participants highlighted the fact they did not fully agree.

Table 4. 'Aware of transferable skills'

(Q3) I am aware of the importance of transferable skills associated with my studies?								
Strongly Disagree	Disagree	Neither Agree nor Disagree	Agree	Strongly Agree	Standard Deviation	Unbiased "n-1"	Standard Error	P-Value
25 (15%)	8 (5%)	20 (12%)	68 (40%)	49 (29%)	24.16	21.61	10.80	0.04

Table 5. 'Training helps you to stand out in the job market'

(Q4) I think carrying out additional Higher Educational Training will help me to stand out within the jobs market?								
Strongly Disagree	Disagree	Neither Agree nor Disagree	Agree	Strongly Agree	Standard Deviation	Unbiased "n-1"	Standard Error	P-Value
30 (18%)	35 (21%)	20 (12%)	35 (21%)	50 (29%)	21.98	19.66	4.84	0.0149

Table 6. 'Range of Training Modules'

QA) The range of training modules at the University is very Comprehensive?								
Strongly Disagree	**Disagree**	**Neither Agree nor Disagree**	**Agree**	**Strongly Agree**	**Standard Deviation**	**Unbiased "n-1"**	**Standard Error**	**P-Value**
7 (4%)	35 (21%)	17 (10%)	54 (32%)	57 (34%)	22.07	22.07	9.87	0.0279

The next two tables will examine the support from the supervisor through the student's perspective and what other features they would like to see as an aid. Table 6, indicates that that 66% of students thought that their supervisor was very knowledgeable about transferable skills and enable guidance on selecting relevant training modules. However, 17%, neither agreed nor disagreed with their supervisors over this guidance and another 17% had indicated that weren't happy with the support when referred to about transferable skills.

Table 8 builds upon the results from table 7, by indicating that did they find that when a supervisor asks them to do additional training, were they given to much and this is their response; 67% of participants had disagreed, while 27% had suggested they had been given too much to study while carrying out their studies.

Part of the work associated with this research is aimed at providing additional guidance towards the 29% of students who wanted more support on-line, through the use of adaptive pathway or recommender system, which will enable learners to see or select modules based on other pathways from previous years. This research approach of the online recommender system will aid students when discussing possible pathways with the supervisor reducing unnecessary workload; improve

Table 7. 'Supervisor Knowledge'

QB) My Supervisor is very knowledgeable about Transferable Skills?								
Strongly Disagree	**Disagree**	**Neither Agree nor Disagree**	**Agree**	**Strongly Agree**	**Standard Deviation**	**Unbiased "n-1"**	**Standard Error**	**P-Value**
8 (5%)	20 (12%)	29 (17%)	60 (35%)	53 (31%)	21.99	19.673	9.83	0.0275

Table 8. 'Allocation of Training from the supervisor'

QC) The amount of training modules students are asked to do is too much?								
Strongly Disagree	**Disagree**	**Neither Agree nor Disagree**	**Agree**	**Strongly Agree**	**Standard Deviation**	**Unbiased "n-1"**	**Standard Error**	**P-Value**
53 (31%)	61 (36%)	10 (6%)	27 (16%)	19 (11%)	22.02	19.70	9.85	0.004

selection of relevant modules based on knowledge based; and reduced irrelevant distraction from studies.

Data analysis while comparing the P-values to support the following hypothesis' "Do Academic Institutions have the right level of support?"

This particular section presents the data analysis in table 12, P-Values showing the results belonging to the second hypothesis if it is null or not. The values belong to the p-value should be within the fresh hold of or below 0.05 to indicate that the results fall into the 95% of confidence interval.

Referring to the Table 9, the P-Values it is clear that the values are under 0.5 fresh hold and pointing towards a null hypothesis, might have certain areas of supports areas that don't need improving according to trends within the research.

FRAMEWORK DESIGN

Repository

To improve the design of this framework, HEIs should hold a large enough data set from over two years, to enable the repository to allow for multiple options and course pathways. If you are going to tackle the cold start problem, then you could populate the information from degree success stories from previous years to enable the system to learn from or adapt to.

HEI Pathways

The framework design of the 'HEI Pathways', see fig 1 comprises of three main critical components, these are, the Repository, Content-based Filtering and the Contribute-Pathway, which takes into the consideration of the literature found within this research. The HEI Pathway will assist with direct interaction between the supervisors and students through selecting relevant training modules.

Table 9. P-Values

Questions	P-Value
QA	0.0279
QB	0.0275
QC	0.004

Figure 1. 'HEI PATHWAYS'

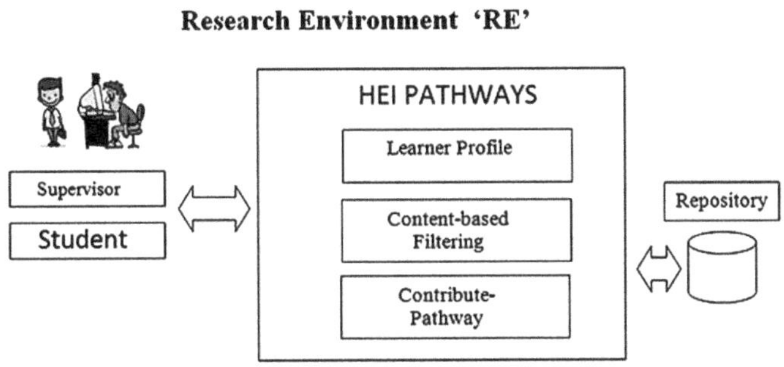

Content-Based

The Content-based Filtering mechanism uses the Learner Profile, to extract attributes of the learner (Stern, Dubeck, and Dick, 2018), which includes disciplines and research topics, before processing and filtering data within the repository. Students can rate the pathways (Chaichumpa, and Temdee, 2018), which has been retrieved with the guidance from the supervisor as this would act as a form of supporting mechanism.

The Filtering Mechanism (FM) extracts and separates two things (A) The Research Topic Area & (B) Previous Students Results belonging to that discipline. To enable FM calculations to work the results are fed into algorithm that stores and keep tracks of the module codes (from each student) as they appear, builds up a record and compares how many times they appear while taking into account the minimum value of credits associated with the Degree Course, for example: See table 10 Number occurrence for Cross Platforms

Once the Pathway has been calculated these are displayed to the individuals with the Supervisor for guidance and approval. For a graphical representation of Table 12, please see Figure 2 for pattern sets of module outcomes.

Table 10. Number occurrence for cross platforms

Module Code	Title of Module	Course Value	No of Occurrence	Code in Venn Diagram
*001	Cross Platforms	20	13	B
*002	Collaborative Development	10	11	F
*003	Mobile Platforms	10	20	S

Figure 2.

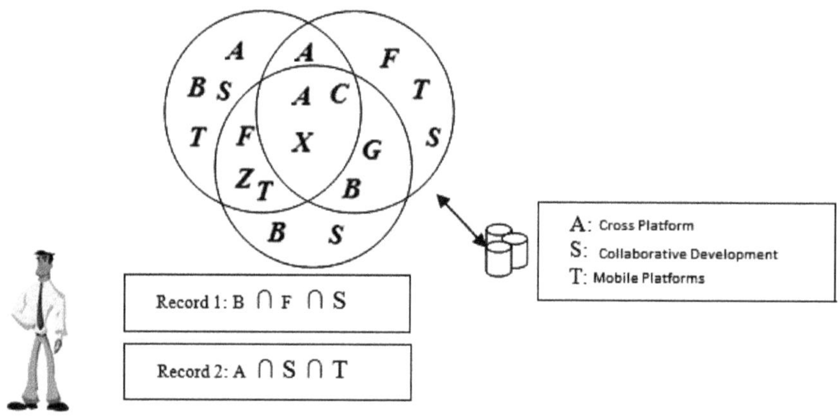

Contribute-Pathway Identified

This particular feature of the HEI Pathway allows individuals to create their own educational pathways building upon the content-based recommendations with the aid of the supervisor for guidance. The Contribute-Pathway, acts similar to the works carried out by Zajaczek et al., (2006) and their research into Schoolbook for Neuroradiology. According to Zajaczek et al., (2006) the idea of Schoolbook is to offer the individual the opportunity to choose a variety of different learning pathways, to decide what learning content to be studied. Once the student has selected a branch of required modules for training, the options are simplified and stored back into the management system.

Using the Contribute-Pathway as a learning aid within e-learning will enable students to structure their time over their journey while gaining the necessary skills required for industry based skills.

Learner Profile

The learner profile is used within this research to hold the details of the student; this contains information about the individual, i.e. learning trait and academic profile. Each element of the learner profile is treated separately.

Limitations

Looking at the statistical analysis, further analysis is needed from a preliminary to a primary investigation with a larger study size, into needs of students and the support for them, from a broader of selection Looking at the challenges this paper presents; 'the supervisor and student's perception thoughts on transferable skills'; these can only be changed from implementing guidelines and additional training from Supervisory Training.

Evaluation

In this paper, we are exploring new ideas and concepts to support HE students through their journey, while offering them a more personalised and tailored educational experience. This approach will enable the students to come together with their supervisors and select suitable educational training needs that will help the individual to benefit from additional transferable skills training. The results do highlight that the students and their supervisors do find that additional training for transferable skills can be overbearing, time-consuming and competing against other priorities (Cargill, 2004). These transferable skills are needed by students within HE as the job market is growing, and individuals are increasingly becoming instrumental consumers. It may be difficult, in light of increasing competitiveness for graduate jobs, but transferable skills offer students a wider opportunity (Costello et al., 2014).

REFERENCES

Albatayneh, N. A., Ghauth, K. I., & Chua, F. F. (2018). Utilizing learners, negative ratings in semantic content-based recommender system for e-learning forum. *Journal of Educational Technology & Society*, *21*(1), 112–125.

Alpay, E., & Walsh, E. (2008). A skills perception inventory for evaluating postgraduate transferable skills development, assessment & *evaluation*. *Higher Education*, *33*(6).

Alsufyani, R., Safdari, F., & Chang, V. (2015). Migration of cloud services and deliveries to higher education. Emerging Software as a Service and Analytics Workshop (ESaaSA 2015), in conjunction with CLOSER 2015.

Alves, P., Amaral, L., & Pires, J. (2008). Case-based reasoning approach to adaptive web-based educaitonal systems. *Eighth IEEE International Conference on Advanced Learning Technologies*, 241-245.

Baldassarre, M. T., Caivano, D., Dimauro, G., Gentile, E., & Visaggio, G. (2018). Cloud computing for education: A systematic mapping study. *IEEE Transactions on Education*, *61*(3), 234–244. doi:10.1109/TE.2018.2796558

Bao, Y., Kehm, B. M., & Ma, Y. (2018). From product to process. the reform of doctoral education in Europe and China. *Studies in Higher Education*, *43*(3), 524–541. doi:10.1080/03075079.2016.1182481

Blaschke, L. M. (2018). Self-determined learning (heutagogy) and digital media creating integrated educational environments for developing lifelong learning skills. In The Digital Turn in Higher Education (pp. 129-140). Springer VS.

Bolton, C., & Rosselli, A. C. (2017). The assessment of transferable skills in a campus recreation program: An exploratory case study on how professionals teach and how student employees learn. *Recreational Sports Journal*, *41*(2), 125–143. doi:10.1123/rsj.2016-0029

Bridge, D., & Dunleavy, K. (2014). If you liked Herlocker et al.'s explanations paper, then you might like this paper too. *Joint Workshop on Interfaces and Human Decision Making in Recommender Systems, in Conjuction with the 8th ACM Conference on Recommender Systems.*

Brodie, P., & Irving, K. (2007). Assessment in work-based learning: Investigating a pedagogical approach to enhance student learning. *Assessment & Evaluation in Higher Education*, *32*(1), 2007. doi:10.1080/02602930600848218

Buchanan, J., Yu, S., Marginson, S. & Wheelahan, L. (2009). *Education, work and economic renewal: an issues paper prepared for the Australian Education Union*. Academic Press.

Burgos, D., & Corbí, A. (2018). Transgenic learning for STEAM subjects and virtual containers for OER. *Distance Education*, 1–16.

Campbell, M., Gibson, W., Hall, A., Richards, D., & Callery, P. (2008). Online vs. face-to-face discussion in a web-based research methods course for postgraduate nursing students: A quasi-experimental study. *International Journal of Nursing Studies*, *45*(5), 750–759. doi:10.1016/j.ijnurstu.2006.12.011 PMID:17306272

Cargill, M. (2004). Transferable skills within research degree: a collaborative genre-based approach to developing publication skills and its implications for research education. *Teaching in Higher Education,* (1).

Carter, M.C. (2018). Tell us what you really think! A new way to measure public opinion. *Australian Defence Force Journal, 203.*

Chadha, D. (2015). A curriculum model for transferable skills development. *Engineering Education: A Journal of the Higher Education Academy*, *1*(1).

Chaichumpa, S., & Temdee, P. (2018). Assessment of student competency for personalised online learning using objective distance. *International Journal of Innovation and Learning*, *23*(1), 19–36. doi:10.1504/IJIL.2018.088789

Chang, V. (2003). The role and effectiveness of e-learning: key issues in an industrial context. *The First International Conference in the United Nations Information Society.*

Chang, V. (2013). Brain segmentation – a case study of biomedical cloud computing for education and research. In Learning Technologies Workshop, Higher Education Academy (HEA). University of Greenwich.

Chang, V. (2015). *The role and effectiveness of e-learning for the industry*. LAP Lambert Academic Publishing.

Chang, V., & Wills, G. (2013). A University of greenwich case study of cloud computing - Education as a Service. In E-Logistics and E Supply Chain Management: Applications for Evolving Business. IGI Global.

Conn, S. S., English, J., Scheffler, F., & Hall, S. (2011). Tag clouds as a pathway to improved pedagogical efficacy in information systems courses: a baseline study involving web 2.0 technologies. *Information Systems Education Journal, 9*(6).

Costello, R. (2015). Supporting the needs of higher educational learners, through the 'Postgraduate Pathways'. *International Journal of Organizational and Collective Intelligence*, *5*(3), 16–31. doi:10.4018/IJOCI.2015070102

Costello, R. (2018). *Gaming Innovations in Higher Education: Emerging Research and Opportunities*. IGI Global. doi:10.4018/978-1-5225-2981-1

Craswell, G. (2007). Deconstructing the skills training debate in doctoral education. *Higher Education Research & Development*, *26*(4), 377–391. doi:10.1080/07294360701658591

Creswell, W. J., & Clark, P. L. V. (2010). *Designing and conducting mixed methods research. Sydney, SAGE Publications*. London: SAGE Publications, Incorporated.

Cryer, P. (1998). Transferable skills, marketability and lifelong learning: The particular case of postgraduate research students. *Studies in Higher Education*, *23*(2), 207–216. doi:10.1080/03075079812331380394

Dennis, C., Smith, S., & Wadsworth, D. (2012). Developing and accessing transferable skills in higher education: A field trial and a way forward. *International Journal of Management and Marketing Academy*, *2*(1), 1–25.

Drachsler, H., Hummel, G. K., & Koper, R. (2008). Personal recommender systems for learners in lifelong learning networks: The requirements, techniques and model. *International Journal of Learning Technology*.

Ellis, M., & Anderson, P. (2018). Teaching and learning through interdisciplinary pedagogies in a second life environment: focus on integration and assessment. In Handbook of Research on Program Development and Assessment Methodologies in K-20 Education (pp. 275-303). IGI Global.

Ghauth, I. K., & Abdullah, A. N. (2010). Learning materials recommendation using good learners' rating and content-based filtering. *Educational Technology Research and Development*.

Gilbert, R., Balatti, J., Turner, P., & Whitehouse, H. (2004). The generic skills debate in research higher degrees. *Higher Education Research & Development, 23*(3), 375–388. doi:10.1080/0729436042000235454

Gokhale, V.A. (2018). Challenges in doctoral research in architecture in India. *International Journal on New Trends in Education & Their Implications, 9*(1).

Goyal, M., & Krishnamurthy, R. (2018). Optimizing student engagement in online learning environments: intuitionistic fuzzy logic in student modeling. In Optimizing Student Engagement in Online Learning Environments (pp. 187-219). IGI Global.

Higher Education Commission. (2013). *Postgraduate education: an independent inquiry by higher education commission.* Available at http://www.policyconnect.org.uk/hec/sites/site_hec/files/report/329/fieldreportdownload/hec-postgraduateeducationreport.pdf

Hinchliffe, W. G., & Jolly, A. (2011). Graduate identity and employability. *British Educational Research Journal, 37*(4), 2011. doi:10.1080/01411926.2010.482200

Hobbs, M., Brown, E., & Gordon, M., (2006, October). Using a virtual world for transferable skills in gaming education. *Virtual World Environment.*

Hryciw, D. H., Tangalakis, K., & Best, G. (2017). Development of transferable skills in a low-SES population through peer assisted study sessions. *Proceedings of The Australian Conference on Science and Mathematics Education,* 69.

Kyewski, E., & Krämer, N. C. (2018). To gamify or not to gamify? an experimental field study of the influence of badges on motivation, activity, and performance in an online learning course. *Computers & Education, 118,* 25–37. doi:10.1016/j.compedu.2017.11.006

Linsay, R., Breen, R., & Jenkins, A. (2002). Academic research and teaching quality: The views of undergraduate and postgraduate students. *Studies in Higher Education, 27*(3), 309–327. doi:10.1080/03075070220000699

Mawson, M., & Haworth, A.C. (2018). Supporting the employability agenda in University Libraries: a case study from the University of Sheffield. *Information and Learning Science.*

McLoughlin, C., & Luca, J. (2002). A Learner-centred approach to developing team skills through web-based learning and assessment. *British Journal of Educational, 33*(5), 571-582.

Munawar, S., Toor, S. K., Aslam, M., & Hamid, M. (2018). Move to smart learning environment: Exploratory research of challenges in computer laboratory and design intelligent virtual laboratory for eLearning Technology. *EURASIA Journal of Mathematics, Science and Technology Education, 14*(5), 1645–1662.

Nägele, C., & Stalder, B. E. (2017). Competence and the need for transferable skills. In Competence-based Vocational and Professional Education (pp. 739-753). Springer.

Radulescu, A. S. (2014). A Perspective on e-learning and cloud computing. *Procedia - Social and Behavioral Sciences,* 141, 1084–1088.

Ria, S., Cox, M. J., Quinn, B. F., Bakir, A., & Woolford, M. J. (2018). A scoring system for assessing learning progression of dental students' clinical skills using haptic virtual workstations. *Journal of Dental Education, 82*(3), 277–285. doi:10.21815/JDE.018.028 PMID:29496806

Royal Society. (2017). *Reforms to the UK's higher education, research and innovation system.* Retrieved from https://royalsociety.org/topics-policy/projects/higher-education-research-innovation-system/

Saiti, A., & Prokopiadou, G. (2008). Post-graduate students and learning environments: Users' perceptions regarding the choice of information sources. *The International Information & Library Review, 40*, 94–103.

Sandars, J., & Schroter, S. (2007). Web 2.0 technologies for undergraduate and postgraduate medical education: An online survey. *Postgraduate Medical Journal, 83*(986), 759–762.

Sherbin, L., & Rashid, R. (2017). Diversity doesn't stick without inclusion. *Harvard Business Review.*

Stern, J. M., Dubeck, M. M., & Dick, A. (2018). Using early grade reading assessment (EGRA) data for targeted instructional support: Learning profiles and instructional needs in Indonesia. *International Journal of Educational Development, 61*, 64–71. doi:10.1016/j.ijedudev.2017.12.003

Veitch, S., Strehlow, K., & Boyd, J. (2018). Supporting university students with socially challenging behaviours through professional development for teaching staff professional development for teaching staff. *Journal of Academic Language and Learning, 12*(1), A156–A167.

Wang, S.-L., & Wu, C.-Y. (2011). Application of context-aware and personalised recommendation to implement an adaptive ubiquitous learning systems. *Expert Systems with Applications*, *38*(9), 831–838. doi:10.1016/j.eswa.2011.02.083

Wu, X. V., Chan, Y. S., Tan, K. H. S., & Wang, W. (2018). A systematic review of online learning programs for nurse preceptors. *Nurse Education Today*, *60*, 11–22. doi:10.1016/j.nedt.2017.09.010 PMID:28987893

Zajaczek, W. E. J., Götz, F., Kupka, T., Behrends, M., Haubitz, B., Donnerstag, F., … Becker, H. (2006). eLearning in education and advanced training in neuroradiology: introduction of a web-based teaching and learning application. *Neuroradiology, 48*(9), 640-646.

Chapter 8
Can Applied On-Job Training Yield Increased Productivity?

Kevin Paul Barrons
Grand Valley State University, USA

ABSTRACT

On-job training (OJT) and the zone of proximal learning (ZPL) remain some of the top innovative approaches to increasing the efficacies required in progressive enterprises. Available data indicate that there is a positive correlation between OJT and cumulated productivity. The ZPL is at the cutting-edge of improving cognitive and affective and sensory practices while OJT upsurge the skillfulness required to boost performance in the value creation system. OJT and ZPL can be juxtaposed to progress explicit knowledge difficult for the competition to mimic. A case study is drawn to illustrate how OJT and the ZPL can be applied in the divided labor to grow specialization and design and implement the technology required to upsurge productivity in a successful organization.

DOI: 10.4018/978-1-5225-7390-6.ch008

INTRODUCTION

Lev Vygotsky did not write his theories with business organizations in mind. He was increasingly influenced by the systemic thinking of the scholars associated with German-American Gestalt psychology movement in which Kurt Lewin and Chris Argyris, among others, were part of. Under the influence of Kurt Lewin's "Topological (and vector) psychology (Lewin, 1936)—Vygotsky introduced the vague notion of the *Zone of proximal development (ZPD)* and identified play of young children as their *leading activity*, that he understood as the main source of the preschoolers' development in terms of emotional, volitional and cognitive development (Wertsch, 1984). Since then, Bandura (2015), Senge (2006) and Barrons (2015) have taken topological studies further to infer that socialization is a part of human development process. Bandura found that learning reproductions are an important source for learning new behaviors and for achieving behavioral change in organizations. For example, in the induction of new employees, the recruit is shown how the job is done and who to consult when in doubt. Senge (2006) propound that only those organizations that can adapt quickly and effectively will be able to excel in their field or market. For example, the organism amoeba which thrives in marshlands replicates itself by breaking into two parts over and over. The numerous organisms adapt to the conditions of the environment and thrive. Within a brief period, the water is chockablock with the organisms. Thus, companies that fail to learn and adapt to the environment in which they do business fail. Barrons (2015) investigated the importance of the ZPD of talent management in the workplace. Barrons advocates to improve cognitive practice an increase in learning in the value creation process in the Zone of Proximal Development (ZPD) environment is essential. Seeing much success is noticed in this newest pedagogy "flipped instruction" design, it has changed various disciplines in business education which can best be applied to the training component of the workforce today. Barrons indicates the key areas of applying the ZPD includes: 1) socialization; 2) anticipation; 3) tacit experience; and, 4) explicit practices. The success of this model continues to create and is leading us towards higher learner motivation, comprehension, and personal achievement.

BACKGROUND INFORMATION

In Yasnitsky and Van der Veer (2015), the Zone of proximal development (ZPD) is Vygotsky's term for the range of tasks that a child is in the process of learning to complete. In the original Vygotsky's writings, this phrase is used in three different meanings. Vygotsky viewed the ZPD to better explain the relationship between

Figure 1. Zone of proximal development
(Barrons, 2015)

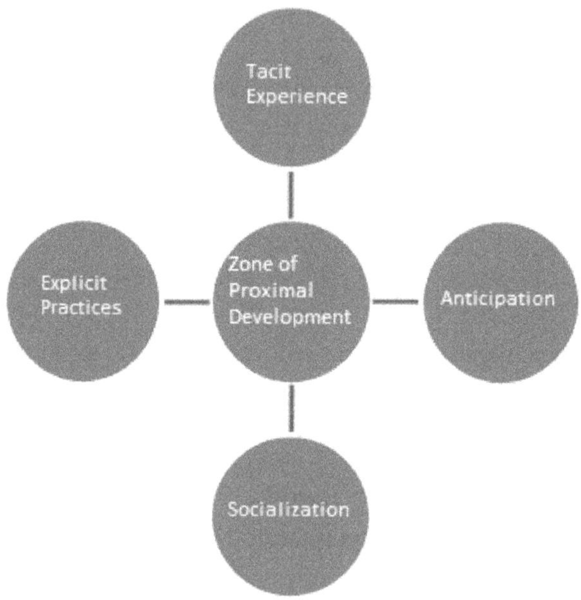

children's learning and cognitive development. Prior to the ZPD, the relation between learning and development could be boiled down to the following three major positions: 1) Development always precedes learning (e.g., constructivism) children first need to meet a particular maturation level before learning can occur 2) Learning and development cannot be separated but instead occur simultaneously (e.g., behaviorism learning is development; and 3) learning and development are separate but interactive processes (e.g., gestaltism) one process always prepares the other process, and vice versa. Vygotsky rejected these three major theories because he believed that learning should always precede development in the ZPD. According to Vygotsky, through the assistance of a more capable person, a child can learn skills or aspects of a skill that goes beyond the child's actual developmental or maturational level. The lower limit of ZPD is the level of skill reached by the child working independently (also referred to as the child's actual developmental level). The upper limit is the level of potential skill that the child can reach with the assistance of a more capable instructor. In this sense, the ZPD provides a perspective view of cognitive development, as opposed to a retrospective view that characterizes development regarding a child's independent capabilities.

Institutional Isomorphism

In DiMaggio and Powel (1983), "The Iron cage" was a term initially employed by Marx Weber to describe bureaucratic control of life in a capitalist society. Weber posited that bureaucratization was caused by competition among those in power such as corporations and individuals in need to control markets. DiMaggio and Powel posited that bureaucratization made organizations more similar but not more efficient. The companies focused on structuration of the organizational field recognized area of institutional life, e.g., supply chain or qualified employees to produce related products and services like those of the competition.

Where Does On-Job Training Learning Fit-In?

DiMaggio and Powel suggested that the structuration process was practice employed by companies to define who they were. The process did not examine the capability required to enhance efficiency and effectiveness. In Senge (2006), the learning organization approach focused on five disciplines needed to structure an efficient and effective organization. The first is Personal mastery a discipline of continually clarifying and deepening our vision, of focusing our energies, of developing patience, and of seeing reality objectively. The second is Mental modeling which are deeply ingrained assumptions, generalizations, or even pictures of images that influence how the stakeholder employees understand the world and how they act. The third involves building a Shared vision - a practice of unearthing shared pictures of the future that foster genuine commitment and enrollment rather than compliance. For example, bureaucratic organizations emphasize paper qualifications as employee entry requirements. They can overlook talent which in most cases is not a fully comprehensive review or certified.

The fourth discipline is about the organization and development of Team learning. It is an opportunity to build effective capacity suspend assumptions and enter genuine thinking together. The last is Systems thinking – the discipline that integrates the other four to chart a high-performance organization. Implementing the five disciplines include many interventions aimed at improving the skills, attitudes, and knowledge needed to produce the goods demanded by customers. On-job training is critical to enable the workforce to continue to learn and improve making effectiveness a reality.

Lack of Continuous Learning

Bolman and Deal (2008) posit that untrained workers harm organizations in many ways: shoddy quality, poor service, higher costs, and costly mistakes. A skilled worker averts unnecessary costs by doing the job right first time correctly and all the time. For example, a high proportion of petrochemical industry accidents involve contract employees. Bolman and Deal argued that in post-invasion Iraq, some of America's more damaging mistakes were the work of private security firms who often employed workers who had less training than their military counterparts. Many organizations are unwilling to invest in human capital development because training costs are immediate and easy to measure; the benefits are long-term and elusive. Pfeffer (1994) suggested that training contractor workers or temporary workers added disincentives. The effects of training programs over long periods of time found consistently positive effects.

Coming Together to Learn

The zone of proximal learning recognizes that learning must occur on the job as well as in the classroom. In Aubrey and Tilliette (1990), a French firm known as Carnaud et Metal Box is the world's third packaging company which puts great emphasis on creating a learning organization. Their mantra is akin to: *He who puts employees first will never come second*, goes a long way to motivate managers to empower the workforce. Aubrey and Tilliette assert that progressive employees give power to employees as well as invest in their development. Empowerment includes keeping employees informed, encouraging autonomy and participation, redesigning work, building effective teams, promoting egalitarianism, and infusing work with meaning.

Providing Information and Support

On-the-job training (OJT) is a type of skill development where a worker learns how to do the work through hands-on experience. It is an opportunity to provide the worker with information and support he or she needs to understand the job at hand. OJT is also an opportunity to flip the classroom for the learner to perfect the dexterity needed to champion performance. By seeing how the job is done, and taking moments to repeat how the specialist does the job, the learner improved the skillfulness required on the job.

Training an employee on the job can be one of the most effective teaching methods because it gives the worker practical experience with the tools and equipment he or she will be working with to get the job done (see Figure 1). By flipping the classroom, the learner builds the confidence to excel performance. In Mupepi (2017), the ZPL enable the workforce to perfect its act. In Figure 1, the middle circle represents the zone of proximal development, students cannot complete tasks unaided but can complete them with guidance. On-the-job training is one of the most common types of training used in the workplace, especially for vocational jobs, such as those in manufacturing (Zereki, 2009). Often, this type of training is unstructured: the new

Figure 2. The ZDL increases as the worker is given more opportunity to learn about his job
(Mupepi, 2014).

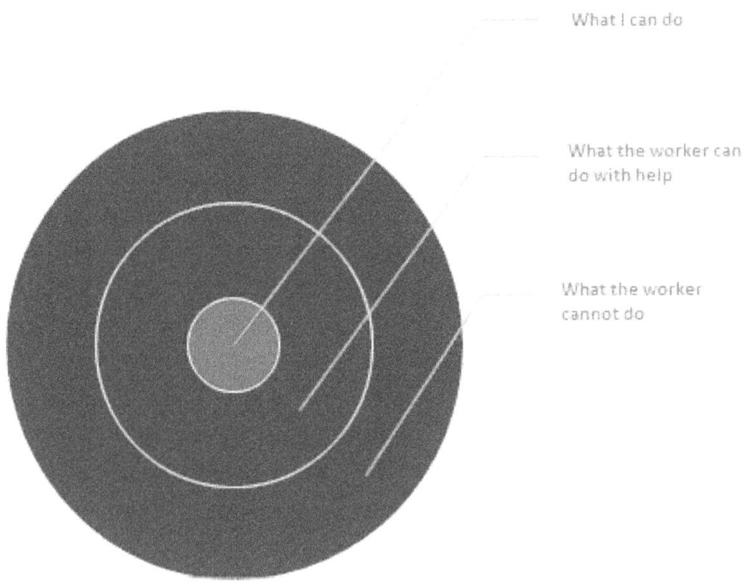

employee is assigned an experienced supervisor, who demonstrates how the job is done. In Mupepi (2014) seating-with-Nelly is a form of skills development in which the novice seat with an experienced seamstress to learn the tricks and ropes of the cutter in a clothing manufacturing industry. The trainee may shadow other workers for several shifts, while learning the steps that make up the job and how to use all the required equipment. Training is usually conducted one-on-one, and the new worker generally can perform the various parts of the job with direct supervision. Vygotsky argues that the novice receives instruction about the job and is shown how to work under the supervision of the expert effectively. The ZPD is the phase where the employee is left to do the job without the expert. It is the difference between what a learner can do without help and what he or she can do with help (see Figure 1).

An Opportunity to Re-Design the Job and Invest in People

Employers often fail to invest the time and resources necessary to develop a cadre of committed and talented employees. Precisely for that reason numerous scholars including Mupepi (2017) and Pfeffer (1994), among many others, have made the case that a skilled and motivated workforce can be designed and implemented to create a powerful source of competitive advantage. Consistent with core on-job training assumptions, high performing companies do a better job of understanding and responding to the needs of both employees and customers. As a result, they redesign the work to constitute the skillsets technology and knowledge the worker needs to master to perform his job effectively.

The Story of the Susman Brothers and Wulfsohn 1901-2005(Macmillan,2017)

This a story of a family business. It has operated in many countries under different names but it is best known as Susman Brothers and Wulfsohn. The focus of its activities has always been in south-central Africa. The story begins in the heyday of imperialism and touches several European empires: the Russian, British, German, and Portuguese and more importantly the African Lozi empire situated on the Zambezi escarpment in Northern Rhodesia in 1899. It started in various places and times: in Russia in 1876, in Cape Town in 1896, in Francis Town in Bechuanaland now Botswana in 1900. Brothers Elie and Harry Susman were pioneer entrepreneurs whose businesses spanned European and African countries during the colonization of Africa.

How Was the Division of Labor Applied?

Adam Smith (1723-1790) wrote a book entitled An Inquiry into the Wealth of Nations which received much acclaim after its first publication in 1776. The book offers the first collected descriptions of what builds a nation's wealth and is today a fundamental work in classical economics. By reflecting upon the division of labor, productivity, and free enterprise, wealth creation can become a reality, all things being equal (Mupepi, 2014).

The Susman Brothers spoke Yiddish and read Max Weber's *Protestant ethic* and Adam Smith's Wealth of Nations and German Economist Werner Sombart *Socialism and the Social Movement in the nineteen centuries.* According to Macmillan (2017), all the readings to which the Susman Brothers were exposed were about socialism except the Bible and Tora. Werner Sombart suggested that Max Weber's *Protestant ethic* was, a Jewish ethic. It could have been combined with the European fifteenth-century Christian monastic practice of working and praying which resulted with the phrase: *to work is to pray.* The Susman Brothers embraced these philosophies to build their African business empire. They laid out plans of their business and decided that they were going to develop and implement the finest meat production company supported with retail outlets of butcheries and groceries to support the growing Copperbelt industries and urban settlements. Thus, the enterprise had a complicated value creation system in which appropriate technology was often applied. Drawing from Adam Smith they defined the labor needed to sustain their vision of the beef industry in Northern Rhodesia (now Zambia). They categorized core business operations to include beef production, meat preparation, meat products transportation and distribution, retail supermarkets and butcheries, and research and development to sustain the enterprise.

Beef Farming and Cold Storage Enterprise

The brothers were pioneers in Northern Rhodesia in 1899. They built the infrastructure for transportation, farming, and much more. The town of Livingstone in Zambia was built by the Susman Brothers, The Livingstone Synagogue, Anglican Church, Livingstone Primary School Civic Center and the roads housing for staff were all built with the proceeds from the brothers' business operations. The pastures and potential farms lay in Southern Angola, Capriv Strip, Namibia, Botswana, and Southern Rhodesia. The company they formed was known as the Susman Brothers and Wulfsohn Group (Private Limited) (Company from now on).

Figure 3. The Core business of the Susman Brothers and Wulfsohn (Macmillan, 2017).

Retail Operations in South Africa

During the twentieth century in southern Africa, diversifying the business was one of the ways entrepreneurs could manage risk. The Company had retail operations in Cape Town, and Johannesburg, South Africa. It was one of the few enterprises encouraged by the British South Africa Company to develop a cash economy in Southern and Northern Rhodesia and Botswana. It had its headquarters situated at Livingstone in Zambia. The Company had to develop the local infrastructure to make many things such as roads and bridges real. The transportation systems at the start were horse and carriage. Later Cecil Rhodes built a railroad that stretched from Cape Town to Cairo to expand the British Empire. In the process, he made a fortune from mining and farming industries. In Livingstone town, the Company built the sewage system and accommodation for its employees. The city was built completely with a Jewish synagogue a school, grocery which doubled up as a post office and butchery stores, among many other structures.

A Political Background and Technology Transfer

The company worked hand in hand with Chief Lewanika of the Lozi who in the scheme of colonization had sought a protectorate of his territory from Queen Victoria in 1880. It can be argued that the Protectorate scheme with many benefits such as technology transfer, education, and building the infrastructure required in an effective economy. Barotseland's status at the onset of the colonial era differed from the other regions which became Zambia. It was the first territory north of the Zambezi to sign a minerals concession and protectorate agreement with the British South Africa Company (BSAC) of Cecil Rhodes. It enabled the BSAC to bring into the country missionaries who built schools and hospitals, engineers and medical professions, among many others, critical in enabling civilization to take place (Gann and Duignan, 1999).

Discovery of Diamonds

By 1880, the kingdom was stabilized, and King Lewanika signed a treaty on 26 June 1889 to provide the kingdom with international recognition as a State. After the discovery of diamonds, King Lewanika began trading with Europe. The first trade concession was signed on 27 June 1889 with Harry Ware, in return, King Lewanika and his kingdom were to be protected. Ware transferred his concession to Cecil Rhodes of the British South Africa Company. Seeking the improvement of the military protection and with the intention to sign a treaty with the British Government, King Lewanika signed on 26 June 1890 the Lochner concession putting

Barotseland under the protection of the British South Africa Company. At that time, there was European administration in Southern Rhodesia, in Nyasaland further East, and the beginnings of European administration in what was then called North-Eastern Rhodesia (centered on Fort Jameson, now Chipata) and North-Western Rhodesia - basically Barotseland. Later, these two were administratively combined as simply "Northern Rhodesia," later divided up in five Provinces and Barotseland, which was treated slightly differently from the rest (Gann and Duignan 1999).

A Trade Agreement With King Lewanika

A large meat abattoir in Livingstone which supplied meat to the Zambians and Copperbelt companies. The Company built at Livingstone attached to the Jewish Synagogue a culture center for local meetings. It also used the facility to introduce Judaism to the Lozi and offered on-job training to employees. As missionaries arrived in Barotseland, they were assisted by the Company to build their accommodation schools and places of worship. Thus, the Company was indirectly involved in the teaching of the English Language and helping missionaries from Europe to get established. They were instrumental in spreading the Judaic ideology among the Tswana and Zambians. The brothers were Jews of Lithuanian provinces of the Russian Empire, Kovno, and Vilna, who were known for their devotion to Orthodox Judaism.

The Barotseland Trading Expedition

The brothers imported consumer goods from Europe through their partners in South Africa and Southern Rhodesia. Technology is transferred by dissemination. Experts from Europe and South Africa came to work with the Company in many projects. For example, cold rooms and refrigeration equipment was installed or built by experts who in turn demonstrated how the technology worked, what to do when it broke down, and how to fix it.

Allan Wack and Shephard a customs clearance agency with offices at Beit Bridge Durban and Salisbury; and Landau Importers with offices in Bulawayo and Salisbury Southern Rhodesia were very important stakeholders in the Susman Brothers and Wulfsohn trading empire. Experts from these companies came to Zambia to show the Susman brothers the paperwork that was required in all import license applications, and the type of technology available from different principals in European cities. For example, the Company was the first to build cold storage facilities in Bulawayo and Livingstone using Germany refrigeration technology. They also commissioned the first refrigeration railroad trucks in 1966 built by a Germany company then known as Capri Limited. In all these enterprises technology transfer and African labor were critical.

Susman Brothers Workforce University

The goal of the Susman Brothers Workforce University was to enable the learners to develop the skillfulness and knowledge they needed to produce the goods and services demanded by the customers. The Barotseland Protectorate Agreement included the provision of an educational system, facilities, and training of teachers and nurses. Vocational education was of paramount importance in the context of economic development. The Company had to build a training center in Livingstone to make on-job training a reality. Workshops to show the employees how equipment and tools could be used were held each time the Company acquired innovative technology. Reading and writing were also treated as a technology that required personal mastery and understanding of the English Language. The workforce as a whole were active learners who tended to retain and understand information best by doing something engaging with it such as discussing or applying it or explaining it to others. "Let's try it and see how it works" or the same active learner's phrase in the local Shona Language "Ngatimboyedza tione Kuti zvirikuyenda nepi" The Susmans were fluent in local languages such as Bemba Lozi or Shona.

Courses such as customer care required the learners to reflect on how the customers could be taken care of by deducing lessons from job specifications.

Reflective Learning

Reflective learners prefer to think about the job at hand first. They tend then to work in groups to share what they know. For example, a farmer and his workers troubled by the leopard breaking into the chicken coup had to reflect about how the leopard was breaking through the security fence to help himself to a chicken dinner each night. Upon reflecting on the behavior of the predator, they learned that the six-foot fence was no deterrent to a leopard that could jump fences and gates up to 10 feet high.

Visual and Verbal Learners

Very few could read and write in the English Language or in their vernacular languages except those who had been privileged to attend missionary schools. Most of the job incumbents were visual and verbal learners. Visual learners remember best when they see pictures, diagrams, flowcharts, demonstrations, and films. The Susman brothers used the workplace as visual aids. For example, in a supermarket customer looking for food could go straight to the food hallways. Those looking for clothing could go either to the menswear or ladies fashion wear. The fixtures and adverts in Mens' and Ladies' departments were designed differently. Somehow ladies are sensitive to fashion while men were penetrating about gender (Frost, 2005).

Building Organizational Strength

The Company moved from strength to strength by building forte through employee engagement. Employee engagement made the difference. In Townsend and Viets (2013), operating income for organizations with high employee engagement improved 19% while it declined 33% over the same period for companies with low employee engagement. Engagement makes a difference in the lives and productivity of employees.

Learning to Increase Productivity

Macmillan (2017) alluded to trial and error as characterizing research and development during the pioneer days. When the railroads reached Livingstone, the Company customized the first refrigerated trucks in the Bulawayo plant of the Zambezi Coachworks. Innovation occurred because of a management team that could work effectively with all employees. They sought to teach the workforce what they needed to know about their jobs. They illustrated that increased output gave life to the business. The courses included the stock control in which the importance of maintaining accurate records was emphasized. The trainee was shown what stock cards looked like and how entries into and out of stock were recorded.

In the handyman repair shop, the trainee was taught how to diagnose and solve problems. For example, electricity blackout in a shop could be caused by many things going wrong: power overload to equipment triggering the fuse box to cut supply or short circuits in equipment. The handyman trainee had to use tools to diagnose circuits and understand the laws of electricity. In Mupepi (2005), learning technical skills among lowly educated implied that each trainee had to be taught the skills he needed to earn a better wage by examining how best the knowledge and skills could be transferred. The handyman training was not all about electrical circuits; it included attending to blocked sewages, broken windowpanes, and fixing all things such as those envisioned in the TV program *Jim'll Fix It* (Gould, 2011).

Courses in Meat Preparation

Meat preparation and packaging skills development were conducted on-site at the abattoirs in Bulawayo Zimbabwe and Livingstone Zambia. The hotel and catering industry at Victoria Falls Chaminuka National and Hwange National Parks were in their infancy but growing very fast. The customers in this industry were the biggest consumers of meat products. They often gave their orders in advance which specified the cuts and type of meat they wanted. Customer specifications became learning aids, how they were written and dates of expected delivery were important in the quality equation. The Company had developed Polish sausages which were intended for export to Europe, but the Company could not meet demand in Southern Rhodesia and South Africa markets alone.

Collaboration With Stakeholders

The Sussman Brothers and Wulfsohn Company could have applied the design of the open system to model a Business useful to mushrooming British colonies in central Africa at that time. The open system approach attracted critical stakeholders such as the BSAC, King Lewanika and others, and emerging state governments. They were critical in the sense that labor was drawn from local authorities, the state administrations provided the rule of law and security in an environment that was shifting from traditional authority to that of colonial rule (Mupepi, 2015). The Company drew its customers, clients or patrons from such an emerging political environment. In Schein (2013), participation in the community is one of these wonderful abstractions that seems to mean something good, yet it is very hard to define in a practical context. For example, in the early day's security of the business depended largely on the local community. In 1900 cattle rustling was rife in Southern Rhodesia, Barotseland, Bechuanaland or Mozambique (Mupepi, 2015). The brothers built amicable relationships with local communities as well as the neighboring states. Their business operations overlapped into neighboring countries as exports. In Northern Rhodesia, they built the bridge at Kazungula to access Angola, Bechuanaland, South Africa, Southern Rhodesia and Southwest Africa. In Livingstone and Lusaka, they supported church-organizations to fund community schools and health centers, churches, synagogues, and many other social amenities. In other words, they were engaged with the community as well as the employees.

Political Engagement

The Sussman brothers articulated diversity and inclusion in the vision of their business. They were very sensitive about who they were and in turn were mindful of the Lozi, Bemba and other ethnic groups that made up their workforce. For example, in each ethnic village where they drew labor, they built a school and a health center which were organized by missionaries. They funded these projects as a way of giving back to the community. In the early 1960s, there were rumors that the Federation of Rhodesia and Nyasaland which had come into existence in September 1953, was going to be disbanded. It was known that the British government wanted to grant independence to Northern Rhodesia and Nyasaland but keep Southern Rhodesia in the fold of the British Empire. African nationalists such as Harry Nkumbulah and Kenneth Kaunda and European politicians such as Roy Welensky were supported by the directors of the Company (Macmillan, 2017).

CONCLUSION

One of the persistent debates surrounding organizational identity is whether it is fixed and immutable. The Sussman Brothers and Wulfsohn Company has recreated itself many times over and operates today using a name associated with an independent state of Zambia.

SUMMARY

Productivity is a social construct among the learners, their instructors, and the learning community. Engaging employees also imply developing and implementing a system-wide performance metrics. The organization should communicate with each other successfully using verbal or written methods. Human beings learn by reading and writing as well by seeing the job being done by the expert.

WAY FORWARD

Creating Engaged Employees

Given the importance of retaining employees for fiscal as well as productivity and humanistic reasons, developing engaged employees is more important than ever. Organization development methods and techniques are the strategies that pull these building blocks together to ignite purpose passion and meaning in the workforce. There is a need to connect purpose and practice ensuring employees understand how they impact the overall goal of the organization. The Sussman Brothers maintained effective communications with all stakeholders...customers, community, employees, suppliers as well as politicians, among others to forge ahead corporate goals. They developed a culture of accountability and professionalism in the organization and discovered that all employees could learn in one way or the other to increase the knowledge useful in doing their work.

CONCLUSION

Constructivism is a learning strategy that contests that learning is an active, contextualized process of constructing knowledge and developing the brashness one needs to perfect performance. Because learners construct knowledge, on-job training becomes interactive engaged and lively. A common misunderstanding regarding constructivism is that instructors or line managers with training responsibilities should never tell the novice anything directly but, instead should always allow them to construct knowledge for themselves.

REFERENCES

Aubrey, B., & Tilliette, B. (1990). *Savoir Faire Savoir*. Paris: Dunoid ISBN.

Bandura, A. (2015). *Moral Disengagement: How People Do Harm and Live with Themselves*. New York, NY: Worth.

Barrons, K. (2015). *Expanding Training Possibilities: Flipping the Zone of Proximal Development For Talent Management*. Academic Press.

Bolman, L. G., & Deal, T. E. (2008). *Reframing Organizations* (4th ed.). San Francisco: Josey Bass.

Gould, L. (2011, October 3). RIP Sir Jimmy: it's all over now. *Mail.*

Lewin, K. (1936). *Principles of topological psychology*. New York: McGraw-Hill. doi:10.1037/10019-000

Macmillan, H. (2017). *An African Trading Empire: The Story of Susman Brothers and Wulfsohn 1901-2005*. New York: Tauris.

Mupepi, M. (2005). *Transforming Village entrepreneurs into sustainable*. Ann Arbor, MI: UMI.

Mupepi, M. (2014, April). Can the division of labor be re-engineered to advance organizational dynamism? *SAGE Open*, 1–6.

Mupepi, M. (2015). *British Imperialism in Zimbabwe: The Organization Development of the First Chimurenga (1883-1904)*. San Diego, CA: Cognella.

Mupepi, M. (2017). *Effective Talent Management Strategies for Organizational Success*. Hershey, PA: IGI Global. doi:10.4018/978-1-5225-1961-4

Pfeffer, J. (1994). *Competitive advantage through people: Unleashing the power of the workforce*. Boston: Harvard Business School Press.

Schein, E. (2013). A Brief and Provocative History of Participation. In J. Vogelsang & M. Townsend (Eds.), *Handbook for Strategic HR*. New York: Amacom.

Senge, P. (2006). *The Fifth Discipline: The Art and Practice of the Learning Organization*. New York: Doubleday.

Townsend, M., & Viets, A. (2013). Introduction. In J. Vogelsang & M. Townsend (Eds.), *Handbook for Strategic HR*. New York: Amacom.

Zaretskii, V. K. (2009). The Zone of Proximal Development What Vygotsky Did Not Have Time to Write. *Journal of Russian & East European Psychology*, *47*(6), 1061–1405. doi:10.2753/RPO1061-0405470604

Compilation of References

Abbariki, M. (2013). Knowledge sharing and work identity. *Knowledge Management: An International Journal*, *12*(2), 45–60.

Abtahi, M. S., Behboudi, L., & Hasanabad, H. M. (2017). Factors Affecting Internet Advertising Adoption in Ad Agencies. *International Journal of Innovation in the Digital Economy*, *8*(4), 18–29. doi:10.4018/IJIDE.2017100102

Age Discrimination in Employment Act of 1967 (ADEA), which protects individuals who are 40 years of age or older. (n.d.). Accessed 04/28/18 https://www.eeoc.gov/laws/statutes/titlevii.cfm

Agrawal, S. (2017). The Impact of Emerging Technologies and Social Media on Different Business(es): Marketing and Management. In O. Rishi & A. Sharma (Eds.), *Maximizing Business Performance and Efficiency Through Intelligent Systems* (pp. 37–49). Hershey, PA: IGI Global. doi:10.4018/978-1-5225-2234-8.ch002

Akhtar, N., & Khan, R. A. (2011). Exploring the paradox of organizational learning and learning organization. *Interdisciplinary Journal of Contemporary Research in Business*, *2*(9), 257–270.

Albatayneh, N. A., Ghauth, K. I., & Chua, F. F. (2018). Utilizing learners, negative ratings in semantic content-based recommender system for e-learning forum. *Journal of Educational Technology & Society*, *21*(1), 112–125.

Alnoukari, M., Razouk, R., & Hanano, A. (2016). BSC-SI, A Framework for Integrating Strategic Intelligence in Corporate Strategic Management. *International Journal of Strategic Information Technology and Applications*, *7*(1), 32–44. doi:10.4018/IJSITA.2016010103

Alnoukari, M., Razouk, R., & Hanano, A. (2016). BSC-SI: A Framework for Integrating Strategic Intelligence in Corporate Strategic Management. *International Journal of Social and Organizational Dynamics in IT*, *5*(2), 1–14. doi:10.4018/IJSODIT.2016070101

Alpay, E., & Walsh, E. (2008). A skills perception inventory for evaluating postgraduate transferable skills development, assessment & *evaluation*. *Higher Education*, *33*(6).

Alsufyani, R., Safdari, F., & Chang, V. (2015). Migration of cloud services and deliveries to higher education. Emerging Software as a Service and Analytics Workshop (ESaaSA 2015), in conjunction with CLOSER 2015.

Altındağ, E. (2016). Current Approaches in Change Management. In A. Goksoy (Ed.), *Organizational Change Management Strategies in Modern Business* (pp. 24–51). Hershey, PA: IGI Global. doi:10.4018/978-1-4666-9533-7.ch002

Alvarez-Dionisi, L. E., Turner, R., & Mittra, M. (2016). Global Project Management Trends. *International Journal of Information Technology Project Management*, *7*(3), 54–73. doi:10.4018/IJITPM.2016070104

Alves, P., Amaral, L., & Pires, J. (2008). Case-based reasoning approach to adaptive web-based educaitonal systems. *Eighth IEEE International Conference on Advanced Learning Technologies*, 241-245.

Anantharaman, R. N., Rajeswari, K. S., Angusamy, A., & Kuppusamy, J. (2017). Role of Self-Efficacy and Collective Efficacy as Moderators of Occupational Stress Among Software Development Professionals. *International Journal of Human Capital and Information Technology Professionals*, *8*(2), 45–58. doi:10.4018/IJHCITP.2017040103

Aninze, F., El-Gohary, H., & Hussain, J. (2018). The Role of Microfinance to Empower Women: The Case of Developing Countries. *International Journal of Customer Relationship Marketing and Management*, *9*(1), 54–78. doi:10.4018/IJCRMM.2018010104

Appolloni, B., Malchiodi, D., & Gaito, S. (2003). *Algorithmic Inference in Machine Learning*. South Australia, Australia: Advanced Knowledge International.

Archer-Brown, C., Marder, B., Calvard, T., & Kowalski, T. (2018). Hybrid social media: Employees' use of a boundary-spanning technology. *New Technology, Work and Employment*, *33*(1), 74–93. doi:10.1111/ntwe.12103

Argyris, C. (1990). *Overcoming Organizational Defenses: Facilitating Organizational Learning*. Boston: Allyn and Bacon.

Argyris, C. (1999). *On Organizational Learning* (2nd ed.). Oxford, UK: Blackwell Publishing.

Argyris, C., & Schön, D. (1978). *Organizational learning: A theory of action perspective*. Reading, MA: Addison Wesley.

Arsenijević, O. M., Orčić, D., & Kastratović, E. (2017). Development of an Optimization Tool for Intangibles in SMEs: A Case Study from Serbia with a Pilot Research in the Prestige by Milka Company. In M. Vemić (Ed.), *Optimal Management Strategies in Small and Medium Enterprises* (pp. 320–347). Hershey, PA: IGI Global. doi:10.4018/978-1-5225-1949-2.ch015

Aryanto, V. D., Wismantoro, Y., & Widyatmoko, K. (2018). Implementing Eco-Innovation by Utilizing the Internet to Enhance Firm's Marketing Performance: Study of Green Batik Small and Medium Enterprises in Indonesia. *International Journal of E-Business Research*, *14*(1), 21–36. doi:10.4018/IJEBR.2018010102

Atiku, S. O., & Fields, Z. (2017). Multicultural Orientations for 21st Century Global Leadership. In N. Baporikar (Ed.), *Management Education for Global Leadership* (pp. 28–51). Hershey, PA: IGI Global. doi:10.4018/978-1-5225-1013-0.ch002

Atiku, S. O., & Fields, Z. (2018). Organisational Learning Dimensions and Talent Retention Strategies for the Service Industries. In N. Baporikar (Ed.), *Global Practices in Knowledge Management for Societal and Organizational Development* (pp. 358–381). Hershey, PA: IGI Global. doi:10.4018/978-1-5225-3009-1.ch017

Aubrey, B., & Tilliette, B. (1990). *Savoir Faire Savoir*. Paris: Dunoid ISBN.

Ávila, L., & Teixeira, L. (2018). The Main Concepts Behind the Dematerialization of Business Processes. In M. Khosrow-Pour, D.B.A. (Ed.), Encyclopedia of Information Science and Technology, Fourth Edition (pp. 888-898). Hershey, PA: IGI Global. doi:10.4018/978-1-5225-2255-3.ch076

Backstrom, L., Huttenlocher, D., Kleinberg, J., & Lan, X. (2006). Group formation in large social networks. *Proceedings of the 12th ACM SIGKDD international conference on Knowledge discovery and data mining - KDD '06*. doi:10.1145/1150402.1150412

Baldassarre, M. T., Caivano, D., Dimauro, G., Gentile, E., & Visaggio, G. (2018). Cloud computing for education: A systematic mapping study. *IEEE Transactions on Education, 61*(3), 234–244. doi:10.1109/TE.2018.2796558

Bandura, A. (2015). *Moral Disengagement: How People Do Harm and Live with Themselves*. New York, NY: Worth.

Bao, Y., Kehm, B. M., & Ma, Y. (2018). From product to process. the reform of doctoral education in Europe and China. *Studies in Higher Education, 43*(3), 524–541. doi:10.1080/03075079.2016.1182481

Barbosa, P., & O'Reilly, A. (2011). *Harvard Trends: Tendências de Gestão*. Porto: Vida Económica.

Barn, B. S., & Barn, R. (2016). An Exploration of Resilience and Values in the Co-Design of Sociotechnical Systems. *International Journal of Systems and Society, 3*(1), 1–17. doi:10.4018/IJSS.2016010101

Barrons, K. (2015). *Expanding Training Possibilities: Flipping the Zone of Proximal Development For Talent Management*. Academic Press.

Bartens, Y., Chunpir, H. I., Schulte, F., & Voß, S. (2017). Business/IT Alignment in Two-Sided Markets: A COBIT 5 Analysis for Media Streaming Business Models. In S. De Haes & W. Van Grembergen (Eds.), *Strategic IT Governance and Alignment in Business Settings* (pp. 82–111). Hershey, PA: IGI Global. doi:10.4018/978-1-5225-0861-8.ch004

Basemsap, K. (2015). Implementing Enterprise Resource Planning. In M. Khosrow-Pour (Ed.), *Encyclopedia of Information Science and Technology* (3rd ed.; pp. 798–807). Hershey, PA: IGI Global. doi:10.4018/978-1-4666-5888-2.ch076

Bashayreh, A. M. (2018). Organizational Culture and Organizational Performance. In W. Lee & F. Sabetzadeh (Eds.), *Contemporary Knowledge and Systems Science* (pp. 50–69). Hershey, PA: IGI Global. doi:10.4018/978-1-5225-5655-8.ch003

Bateson, G. (1972). *Steps to an ecology of mind*. New York, NY: Chandler Publishing Co.

Beal, V. (2016). *ERP - enterprise resource planning*. Accessed 11/14/16 http://www.webopedia.com/term/e/erp.html

Beaulieu, J.-P., Carriere, E. J., & Schoch, C. (2013). The Power of Interactive Collaborative Designs. In J. Vogelsang & M. Townsend (Eds.), Handbook for Strategic HR: Best Practices in Organization Development from OD Network. Academic Press.

Bedell, D. (2011, March). Business Intelligence. *Global Finance,* 46-47.

Bedford, D. A. (2018). Sustainable Knowledge Management Strategies: Aligning Business Capabilities and Knowledge Management Goals. In N. Baporikar (Ed.), *Global Practices in Knowledge Management for Societal and Organizational Development* (pp. 46–73). Hershey, PA: IGI Global. doi:10.4018/978-1-5225-3009-1.ch003

Benmoussa, F., Nakara, W. A., & Jaouen, A. (2016). The Use of Social Media by SMEs in the Tourism Industry. In I. Lee (Ed.), *Encyclopedia of E-Commerce Development, Implementation, and Management* (pp. 2159–2170). Hershey, PA: IGI Global. doi:10.4018/978-1-4666-9787-4.ch155

Berger, P. L., & Luckman, T. (1966). *The social construction of reality*. New York: Anchor Books.

Berger, R. (2016). Indigenous Management and Bottom of Pyramid Countries: The Role of National Institutions. In U. Aung & P. Ordoñez de Pablos (Eds.), *Managerial Strategies and Practice in the Asian Business Sector* (pp. 107–123). Hershey, PA: IGI Global. doi:10.4018/978-1-4666-9758-4.ch007

Bergier, J. (1970). *A Espionagem Industrial*. Porto: Editorial Inova.

Berkman, R. (2008). *The Art of Strategic Listening: Finding Market Intelligence in Blogs and Social Media*. Paramount Market Pub.

Berlin, I. (2004). American Slavery in History and Memory and the Search for Social Justice. *The Journal of American History*, *90*(4), 1251–1268. doi:10.2307/3660347

Bertalanffy, L. v. (1969). *General System Theory*. New York: George Braziller Publishers.

Berthon, P., Pitt, L., Plangger, K., & Shapiro, D. (2012). Marketing meets Web 2.0, social media, and creative consumers: Implications for international marketing strategy. *Business Horizons*, *55*(3), 261–271. doi:10.1016/j.bushor.2012.01.007

Besson, B., & Possin, J. (1996). *Do serviço de informação à inteligência económica: detectar as ameaças e oportunidades da empresa*. Instituto Piaget.

Best, D. (1996a). Business Process and Information Management. In D. Best (Ed.), *The Fourth Resource: Information and its Management*. Hampshire, UK: Aslib/Gower.

Best, D. (1996b). *The Fourth Resource: Information and its Management*. Hampshire, UK: Aslib/Gower.

Beuren, I. M. (1998). *Gerenciamento da informação: um recurso estratégico no processo de gestão empresarial*. São Paulo: Atlas.

Bharwani, S., & Musunuri, D. (2018). Reflection as a Process From Theory to Practice. In M. Khosrow-Pour, D.B.A. (Ed.), Encyclopedia of Information Science and Technology, Fourth Edition (pp. 1529-1539). Hershey, PA: IGI Global. doi:10.4018/978-1-5225-2255-3.ch132

Bhatt, G. D., Wang, Z., & Rodger, J. A. (2017). Information Systems Capabilities and Their Effects on Competitive Advantages: A Study of Chinese Companies. *Information Resources Management Journal*, *30*(3), 41–57. doi:10.4018/IRMJ.2017070103

Bhushan, M., & Yadav, A. (2017). Concept of Cloud Computing in ESB. In R. Bhadoria, N. Chaudhari, G. Tomar, & S. Singh (Eds.), *Exploring Enterprise Service Bus in the Service-Oriented Architecture Paradigm* (pp. 116–127). Hershey, PA: IGI Global. doi:10.4018/978-1-5225-2157-0.ch008

Bhushan, S. (2017). System Dynamics Base-Model of Humanitarian Supply Chain (HSCM) in Disaster Prone Eco-Communities of India: A Discussion on Simulation and Scenario Results. *International Journal of System Dynamics Applications*, *6*(3), 20–37. doi:10.4018/IJSDA.2017070102

Bion, W. R. (1949). Experience in groups, III. *Human Relations*, *2*(1), 13–22. doi:10.1177/001872674900200102

Bion, W. R. (1961). *Experiences in Groups*. London, UK: Tavistock Institute; doi:10.4324/9780203359075

Bion, W. R. (1962). A theory of thinking. *The International Journal of Psycho-Analysis*, 43.

Bion, W. R., & Rickman, J. (1943). Intra-group tensions in therapy. *Lancet*, *2*(6274), 678–781. doi:10.1016/S0140-6736(00)88231-8

Biswas, A., & De, A. K. (2017). On Development of a Fuzzy Stochastic Programming Model with Its Application to Business Management. In S. Trivedi, S. Dey, A. Kumar, & T. Panda (Eds.), *Handbook of Research on Advanced Data Mining Techniques and Applications for Business Intelligence* (pp. 353–378). Hershey, PA: IGI Global. doi:10.4018/978-1-5225-2031-3.ch021

Blaschke, L. M. (2018). Self-determined learning (heutagogy) and digital media creating integrated educational environments for developing lifelong learning skills. In The Digital Turn in Higher Education (pp. 129-140). Springer VS.

Blau, P. M. (1976). *Approaches to the study of social structure*. London, UK: Open Book Publishing.

Blood, R. (2004). *O Livro de Bolso do Weblogue: Conselhos Práticos para Criar e Manter o seu blogue* (1st ed.). Porto: Campo das Letras.

Bohm, D. (2014). *On dialogue*. London: Routledge.

Bolander. (2015). Social networks sales organizations: their development and importance for salesperson performance. *Journal of Marketing: A Quarterly Publication of the American Marketing Association,79*(6), 1-16.

Bolman, L. G., & Deal, T. E. (2008). *Reframing Organizations* (4th ed.). San Francisco: Josey Bass.

Bolton, C., & Rosselli, A. C. (2017). The assessment of transferable skills in a campus recreation program: An exploratory case study on how professionals teach and how student employees learn. *Recreational Sports Journal, 41*(2), 125–143. doi:10.1123/rsj.2016-0029

Boulding, K. E. (1956). General systems theory---the skeleton of science. *Management Science, 2*(3), 197–208. doi:10.1287/mnsc.2.3.197

Bramston, D. (2009). *Basics Product Design: Idea Searching* (1st ed.). Lausanne: Ava Publishing.

Brandi, U., & Elkjaer, B. (2011). Tidsskrift for arbejdsliv. *Organisatorisk læring i organisatorisk forandring, 13*(2), 73- 89.

Bratianu, C. (2015). *Organizational Knowledge Dynamics: Managing Knowledge Creation, Acquisition, Sharing, and Transformation*. Hershey, PA: IGI Global. doi:10.4018/978-1-4666-8318-1

Bridge, D., & Dunleavy, K. (2014). If you liked Herlocker et al.'s explanations paper, then you might like this paper too. *Joint Workshop on Interfaces and Human Decision Making in Recommender Systems, in Conjuction with the 8th ACM Conference on Recommender Systems.*

British Council. (2018). *Equality, diversity and inclusion.* Accessed 04/28?18 https://www.britishcouncil.org/organisation/how-we-work/equality-diversity-inclusion

Brodie, P., & Irving, K. (2007). Assessment in work-based learning: Investigating a pedagogical approach to enhance student learning. *Assessment & Evaluation in Higher Education, 32*(1), 2007. doi:10.1080/02602930600848218

Brophy, P., & Coulling, K. (1996). *Quality Management for Information and Library Managers.* Guildford: Aslib/Gower.

Brown, E. (2012). *Working the Crowd: Social Media Marketing for Business* (2nd ed.). British Informatics Society.

Brown, J. S., & Duguid, P. (1991). Organizational Learning and Communities-of-Practice: Toward a Unified View of Working, Learning, and Innovation. *Organization Science, 2*(1), 40–57. doi:10.1287/orsc.2.1.40

Brown, J., & Duguid, P. (2000). *The Social Life of Information* (1st ed.). Boston: Harvard Business School Press.

Buchanan, J., Yu, S., Marginson, S. & Wheelahan, L. (2009). *Education, work and economic renewal: an issues paper prepared for the Australian Education Union.* Academic Press.

Bücker, J., & Ernste, K. (2018). Use of Brand Heroes in Strategic Reputation Management: The Case of Bacardi, Adidas, and Daimler. In A. Erdemir (Ed.), *Reputation Management Techniques in Public Relations* (pp. 126–150). Hershey, PA: IGI Global. doi:10.4018/978-1-5225-3619-2.ch007

Bureš, V. (2018). Industry 4.0 From the Systems Engineering Perspective: Alternative Holistic Framework Development. In R. Brunet-Thornton & F. Martinez (Eds.), *Analyzing the Impacts of Industry 4.0 in Modern Business Environments* (pp. 199–223). Hershey, PA: IGI Global. doi:10.4018/978-1-5225-3468-6.ch011

Burgelman, R., Christensen, C., & Wheelwright, S. (2009). *Strategic Management of Technology and Innovation* (5th ed.). Singapore: McGraw-Hill.

Burgos, D., & Corbí, A. (2018). Transgenic learning for STEAM subjects and virtual containers for OER. *Distance Education*, 1–16.

Buzady, Z. (2017). Resolving the Magic Cube of Effective Case Teaching: Benchmarking Case Teaching Practices in Emerging Markets – Insights from the Central European University Business School, Hungary. In D. Latusek (Ed.), *Case Studies as a Teaching Tool in Management Education* (pp. 79–103). Hershey, PA: IGI Global. doi:10.4018/978-1-5225-0770-3.ch005

Campatelli, G., Richter, A., & Stocker, A. (2016). Participative Knowledge Management to Empower Manufacturing Workers. *International Journal of Knowledge Management*, *12*(4), 37–50. doi:10.4018/IJKM.2016100103

Campbell, M., Gibson, W., Hall, A., Richards, D., & Callery, P. (2008). Online vs. face-to-face discussion in a web-based research methods course for postgraduate nursing students: A quasi-experimental study. *International Journal of Nursing Studies*, *45*(5), 750–759. doi:10.1016/j.ijnurstu.2006.12.011 PMID:17306272

Canhoto, A. (2013). *Social media as a source of competitive intelligence*. Retrieved 28-02-2013, from http://anacanhoto.com/2013/01/18/social-media-as-a-source-of-competitive-intelligence/

Căpusneanu, S., & Topor, D. I. (2018). Business Ethics and Cost Management in SMEs: Theories of Business Ethics and Cost Management Ethos. In I. Oncioiu (Ed.), *Ethics and Decision-Making for Sustainable Business Practices* (pp. 109–127). Hershey, PA: IGI Global. doi:10.4018/978-1-5225-3773-1.ch007

Cargill, M. (2004). Transferable skills within research degree: a collaborative genre-based approach to developing publication skills and its implications for research education. *Teaching in Higher Education*, (1).

Carlson, N. R., & Heth, C. D. (2010). *Psychology the Science of Behavior*. Ontario, CA: Pearson Education Canada.

Carneiro, A. (2016). Maturity in Health Organization Information Systems: Metrics and Privacy Perspectives. *International Journal of Privacy and Health Information Management*, *4*(2), 1–18. doi:10.4018/IJPHIM.2016070101

Carrera, F. (2009). *Networking: Guia de Sobrevivência Profissional* (1st ed.). Lisboa: Sílabo.

Carrera, F. (2012a). *Comunicar 2.0: a Arte de bem Comunicar no Século XXI* (1st ed.). Lisboa: Sílabo.

Carrera, F. (2012b). *Marketing Digital na Versão 2.0: o que não pode ignorar* (2nd ed.). Lisboa: Sílabo.

Carter, M.C. (2018). Tell us what you really think! A new way to measure public opinion. *Australian Defence Force Journal, 203*.

Castells, M. (2000). *The Information Age: The Rise of the Network Society* (2nd ed.). London: Blackwell.

Castells, M. (2004). *A Galáxia Internet: Reflexões sobre Internet, Negócios e Sociedade*. Lisboa: Fundação Calouste Gulbenkian.

CCE. (2010). *Fair lending: Comptroller's handbook. Consumer Compliance Examination (CCE)*. Retrieved https://www.occ.treas.gov/publications/publications-by-type/comptrollers-handbook/fair-lending/pub-ch-fair-lending.pdf

Central Statistics Office. (2018). *Population Census and Survey United Kingdom*. Cardiff, UK: Central Statistics Office. Accessed 4/17/18 https://www.statisticsauthority.gov.uk/

Chadha, D. (2015). A curriculum model for transferable skills development. *Engineering Education: A Journal of the Higher Education Academy, 1*(1).

Chae, C., Suh, B., Han, S., Han, H., & Lim, D. H. (2018). Enhancing Learner-Driven Informal Learning in a Virtual Practice Community: The Massive Open Online Course (MOOC) as a Learning Solution for Professional Development. In J. Keengwe (Ed.), *Handbook of Research on Digital Content, Mobile Learning, and Technology Integration Models in Teacher Education* (pp. 207–226). Hershey, PA: IGI Global; doi:10.4018/978-1-5225-2953-8.ch011

Chaichumpa, S., & Temdee, P. (2018). Assessment of student competency for personalised online learning using objective distance. *International Journal of Innovation and Learning, 23*(1), 19–36. doi:10.1504/IJIL.2018.088789

Chandan, H. C. (2016). Motivations and Challenges of Female Entrepreneurship in Developed and Developing Economies. In N. Baporikar (Ed.), *Handbook of Research on Entrepreneurship in the Contemporary Knowledge-Based Global Economy* (pp. 260–286). Hershey, PA: IGI Global. doi:10.4018/978-1-4666-8798-1.ch012

Chang, V. (2013). Brain segmentation – a case study of biomedical cloud computing for education and research. In Learning Technologies Workshop, Higher Education Academy (HEA). University of Greenwich.

Chang, V., & Wills, G. (2013). A University of greenwich case study of cloud computing - Education as a Service. In E-Logistics and E Supply Chain Management: Applications for Evolving Business. IGI Global.

Chang, V. (2003). The role and effectiveness of e-learning: key issues in an industrial context. *The First International Conference in the United Nations Information Society*.

Chang, V. (2015). *The role and effectiveness of e-learning for the industry*. LAP Lambert Academic Publishing.

Chang, V. (2016). Review and discussion: E-learning for academia and industry. *International Journal of Information Management*, *36*(3), 476–485. doi:10.1016/j.ijinfomgt.2015.12.007

Chan, R. L., Mo, P. L., & Moon, K. K. (2018). Strategic and Tactical Measures in Managing Enterprise Risks: A Study of the Textile and Apparel Industry. In K. Strang, M. Korstanje, & N. Vajjhala (Eds.), *Research, Practices, and Innovations in Global Risk and Contingency Management* (pp. 1–19). Hershey, PA: IGI Global. doi:10.4018/978-1-5225-4754-9.ch001

Charlier, S. D., Burke-Smalley, L. A., & Fisher, S. L. (2018). Undergraduate Programs in the U.S: A Contextual and Content-Based Analysis. In J. Mendy (Ed.), *Teaching Human Resources and Organizational Behavior at the College Level* (pp. 26–57). Hershey, PA: IGI Global. doi:10.4018/978-1-5225-2820-3.ch002

Chaudhuri, S. (2016). Application of Web-Based Geographical Information System (GIS) in E-Business. In U. Panwar, R. Kumar, & N. Ray (Eds.), *Handbook of Research on Promotional Strategies and Consumer Influence in the Service Sector* (pp. 389–405). Hershey, PA: IGI Global. doi:10.4018/978-1-5225-0143-5.ch023

Chawla, S., & Renesch, J. (1995). *Learning Organizations: Developing Cultures for Tomorrow's Workplace*. Portland, OR: Productivity Press.

Chen, H., Chau, M., & Zeng, D. (2002). CI Spider: A tool for competitive intelligence on the Web. *Decision Support Systems*, *34*(1), 1–17. doi:10.1016/S0167-9236(02)00002-7

Choo, C. W. (2003). *Gestão de informação para a organização inteligente: a arte de explorar o meio ambiente*. Lisboa: Editorial Caminho.

Choudhuri, P. S. (2016). An Empirical Study on the Quality of Services Offered by the Private Life Insurers in Burdwan. In U. Panwar, R. Kumar, & N. Ray (Eds.), *Handbook of Research on Promotional Strategies and Consumer Influence in the Service Sector* (pp. 31–55). Hershey, PA: IGI Global. doi:10.4018/978-1-5225-0143-5.ch002

Christensen, C., Anthony, S., & Roth, E. (2004). *Seeing What's Next: Using the Theories of Innovation to Predict Industry Change*. Harvard Business School Press.

Civil Rights Act of 1964. (n.d.). Retrieved from https://www.eeoc.gov/laws/statutes/titlevii.cfm

Clancy, K. (2018). Rid the sciences of Harassers. *National Geographic*, *233*(5), 15–18.

Clarke, H., & Mezzofiore, G. (2018). *Windrush' scandal forces UK government into U-turn*. Accessed 04/18/2018 https://www.msn.com/en-us/news/us/windrush-scandal-forces-uk-government-into-u-turn/ar-AAvWzLx

Conn, S. S., English, J., Scheffler, F., & Hall, S. (2011). Tag clouds as a pathway to improved pedagogical efficacy in information systems courses: a baseline study involving web 2.0 technologies. *Information Systems Education Journal, 9*(6).

Conway, D. (2005). Transformationalism and return: Home as an enduring fixture and anchor. In *The experience of Return migration: Caribbean Experience*. Aldershort, UK: Ashgate.

Costello, R. (2015). Supporting the needs of higher educational learners, through the 'Postgraduate Pathways'. *International Journal of Organizational and Collective Intelligence*, *5*(3), 16–31. doi:10.4018/IJOCI.2015070102

Costello, R. (2018). *Gaming Innovations in Higher Education: Emerging Research and Opportunities*. IGI Global. doi:10.4018/978-1-5225-2981-1

Craswell, G. (2007). Deconstructing the skills training debate in doctoral education. *Higher Education Research & Development*, *26*(4), 377–391. doi:10.1080/07294360701658591

Creswell, W. J., & Clark, P. L. V. (2010). *Designing and conducting mixed methods research. Sydney, SAGE Publications*. London: SAGE Publications, Incorporated.

Cromwell, J. (2014). More than Slaves and Sugar: Recent Historiography of the Trans-imperial Caribbean and Its Sinew Populations. *History Compass*, *12*(10), 770–783. doi:10.1111/hic3.12192

Cryer, P. (1998). Transferable skills, marketability and lifelong learning: The particular case of postgraduate research students. *Studies in Higher Education*, *23*(2), 207–216. doi:10.1080/03075079812331380394

Cummings, T. G. (1976). Sociotechnical systems: an intervention strategy. In W. W. Burke (Ed.), *Current issues and strategies in organization development* (pp. 187–213). New York: Human Science Press.

Curtis, P. (2006). *Gleaning consumer intelligence from blogs and podcasts*. Retrieved 02-12-2012, from http://www.freepint.com/issues/040506.htm#tips

Daft, R. (2013). *Management*. London, UK: Cengage Learning.

Dahlberg, T., Kivijärvi, H., & Saarinen, T. (2017). IT Investment Consistency and Other Factors Influencing the Success of IT Performance. In S. De Haes & W. Van Grembergen (Eds.), *Strategic IT Governance and Alignment in Business Settings* (pp. 176–208). Hershey, PA: IGI Global. doi:10.4018/978-1-5225-0861-8.ch007

Damnjanović, A. M. (2017). Knowledge Management Optimization through IT and E-Business Utilization: A Qualitative Study on Serbian SMEs. In M. Vemić (Ed.), *Optimal Management Strategies in Small and Medium Enterprises* (pp. 249–267). Hershey, PA: IGI Global. doi:10.4018/978-1-5225-1949-2.ch012

Daneshpour, H. (2017). Integrating Sustainable Development into Project Portfolio Management through Application of Open Innovation. In M. Vemić (Ed.), *Optimal Management Strategies in Small and Medium Enterprises* (pp. 370–387). Hershey, PA: IGI Global. doi:10.4018/978-1-5225-1949-2.ch017

Daniel, A. D., & Reis de Castro, V. (2018). Entrepreneurship Education: How to Measure the Impact on Nascent Entrepreneurs. In A. Carrizo Moreira, J. Guilherme Leitão Dantas, & F. Manuel Valente (Eds.), *Nascent Entrepreneurship and Successful New Venture Creation* (pp. 85–110). Hershey, PA: IGI Global. doi:10.4018/978-1-5225-2936-1.ch004

Davenport, T. (1997). *Information Ecology: Mastering the Information and Knowledge Environment*. New York: Oxford University Press.

Davenport, T., Marchand, D., & Dickson, T. (2004). *Dominando a gestão da informação*. Porto Alegre: Bookmann.

David, F., van der Sijde, P., & van den Besselaar, P. (2016). Enterpreneurial Incentives, Obstacles, and Management in University-Business Co-Operation: The Case of Indonesia. In J. Saiz-Álvarez (Ed.), *Handbook of Research on Social Entrepreneurship and Solidarity Economics* (pp. 499–518). Hershey, PA: IGI Global. doi:10.4018/978-1-5225-0097-1.ch024

David, R., Swami, B. N., & Tangirala, S. (2018). Ethics Impact on Knowledge Management in Organizational Development: A Case Study. In N. Baporikar (Ed.), *Global Practices in Knowledge Management for Societal and Organizational Development* (pp. 19–45). Hershey, PA: IGI Global. doi:10.4018/978-1-5225-3009-1.ch002

Davis, M. C., Challenger, R., Dharshana, N. W. J., & Clegg, C. W. (2014). Advancing socio-technical systems thinking: A call for bravery. Applied Ergonomics, 45(2), 171-180.

Defillippi, R. (2011). *Psychological perspectives in organizational learning a four-quadrant approach* (H. Shipton, Ed.). West Sussex, UK: Wiley.

Delias, P., & Lakiotaki, K. (2018). Discovering Process Horizontal Boundaries to Facilitate Process Comprehension. *International Journal of Operations Research and Information Systems*, *9*(2), 1–31. doi:10.4018/IJORIS.2018040101

Deng, Z., & Luo, L. (2007). An Exploratory Discuss of New Ways for Competitive Intelligence on WEB 2.0. In Integration and Innovation Orient to E-Society (pp. 597-604). Boston: Springer.

Denholm, J., & Lee-Davies, L. (2018). Success Factors for Games in Business and Project Management. In *Enhancing Education and Training Initiatives Through Serious Games* (pp. 34–68). Hershey, PA: IGI Global. doi:10.4018/978-1-5225-3689-5.ch002

Dennis, C., Smith, S., & Wadsworth, D. (2012). Developing and accessing transferable skills in higher education: A field trial and a way forward. *International Journal of Management and Marketing Academy*, *2*(1), 1–25.

Denscombe, M. (2010). *Good Research Guide: For small-scale social research projects* (4th ed.). Berkshire, UK: Open University Press.

Department of Labor Report. (2010). *Employment situation summary*. Accessed 04/29/18 https://www.bls.gov/news.release/empsit.nr0.htm

Deshpande, M. (2017). Best Practices in Management Institutions for Global Leadership: Policy Aspects. In N. Baporikar (Ed.), *Management Education for Global Leadership* (pp. 1–27). Hershey, PA: IGI Global. doi:10.4018/978-1-5225-1013-0.ch001

Deshpande, M. (2018). Policy Perspectives for SMEs Knowledge Management. In N. Baporikar (Ed.), *Knowledge Integration Strategies for Entrepreneurship and Sustainability* (pp. 23–46). Hershey, PA: IGI Global. doi:10.4018/978-1-5225-5115-7.ch002

Dezdar, S. (2017). ERP Implementation Projects in Asian Countries: A Comparative Study on Iran and China. *International Journal of Information Technology Project Management*, *8*(3), 52–68. doi:10.4018/IJITPM.2017070104

Dickins, J. (2013). Social media is an underused opportunity for luxury brands. *Digital Marketing Hub: The Guardian*. Retrieved 14-06-2013, from http://www.guardian.co.uk/media-network/media-network-blog/2013/jun/14/social-media-opportunity-luxury-brands

Dickinson, B. (2015). *Skunkworks Audio Tape*. Amazon Digital Services LLC.

Dimeo, P. (2001). Contemporary developments in Indian football. *Contemporary South Asia*, *10*(2), 251–264. doi:10.1080/09584930120083846

Domingos, D., Martinho, R., & Varajão, J. (2016). Controlled Flexibility in Healthcare Processes: A BPMN-Extension Approach. In M. Cruz-Cunha, I. Miranda, R. Martinho, & R. Rijo (Eds.), *Encyclopedia of E-Health and Telemedicine* (pp. 521–535). Hershey, PA: IGI Global. doi:10.4018/978-1-4666-9978-6.ch040

Domingos, D., Respício, A., & Martinho, R. (2017). Reliability of IoT-Aware BPMN Healthcare Processes. In C. Reis & M. Maximiano (Eds.), *Internet of Things and Advanced Application in Healthcare* (pp. 214–248). Hershey, PA: IGI Global. doi:10.4018/978-1-5225-1820-4.ch008

Dosumu, O., Hussain, J., & El-Gohary, H. (2017). An Exploratory Study of the Impact of Government Policies on the Development of Small and Medium Enterprises in Developing Countries: The Case of Nigeria. *International Journal of Customer Relationship Marketing and Management*, *8*(4), 51–62. doi:10.4018/IJCRMM.2017100104

Drachsler, H., Hummel, G. K., & Koper, R. (2008). Personal recommender systems for learners in lifelong learning networks: The requirements, techniques and model. *International Journal of Learning Technology.*

Drack, M., Apfalter, W., & Pouvreau, D. (2017, March 11). On the Making of a System Theory of Life: Paul A Weiss and Ludwig von Bertalanffy's Conceptual Connection. *The Quarterly Review of Biology*, 349–373. PMID:18217527

Dubé, L., Bourhis, A., & Jacob, R. (2005). The impact of structuring characteristics on the launching of virtual communities of practice. *Journal of Organizational Change Management*, *18*(2), 145–166. doi:10.1108/09534810510589570

Duguid, P. (2005). The Art of Knowing: Social and Tacit Dimensions of Knowledge and the Limits of the Community of Practice. *The Information Society*, *21*(2), 109–118. doi:10.1080/01972240590925311

Durst, S., Bruns, G., & Edvardsson, I. R. (2017). Retaining Knowledge in Smaller Building and Construction Firms. *International Journal of Knowledge and Systems Science*, *8*(3), 1–12. doi:10.4018/IJKSS.2017070101

East, W. E. (1998). *Web-enabled design review and lessons learned.* USACERL Technical Report (ADA344693) CERL-TR-98/31.

Easterby-Smith, M., & Prieto, I. M. (2008). Dynamic capabilities and knowledge management: An integrative role for learning? *British Journal of Management*, *19*(3), 235–249. doi:10.1111/j.1467-8551.2007.00543.x

Economist. (2018). *Diversity and Development.* Accessed 04/28/18 https://www.economist.com/node/2926697

Edvardsson, I. R., & Durst, S. (2017). Outsourcing, Knowledge, and Learning: A Critical Review. *International Journal of Knowledge-Based Organizations*, *7*(2), 13–26. doi:10.4018/IJKBO.2017040102

Edwards, J. S. (2018). Integrating Knowledge Management and Business Processes. In M. Khosrow-Pour, D.B.A. (Ed.), Encyclopedia of Information Science and Technology, Fourth Edition (pp. 5046-5055). Hershey, PA: IGI Global. doi:10.4018/978-1-5225-2255-3.ch437

Eijnatten, F. M. van. (1993). *The Paradigm that Changed the work place.* Stockholm, Sweden: the Swedish Center for Working Life.

Eijnatten, F.M. van & Hoevenaars, A.M. (1989). Modern sociotechnique in the Netherlands. *Gedrag en Organisatie, 2*(4/5), 289-304.

Ejiogu, A. O. (2018). Economics of Farm Management. In *Agricultural Finance and Opportunities for Investment and Expansion* (pp. 56–72). Hershey, PA: IGI Global. doi:10.4018/978-1-5225-3059-6.ch003

Ekanem, I., & Abiade, G. E. (2018). Factors Influencing the Use of E-Commerce by Small Enterprises in Nigeria. *International Journal of ICT Research in Africa and the Middle East*, *7*(1), 37–53. doi:10.4018/IJICTRAME.2018010103

Ekanem, I., & Alrossais, L. A. (2017). Succession Challenges Facing Family Businesses in Saudi Arabia. In P. Zgheib (Ed.), *Entrepreneurship and Business Innovation in the Middle East* (pp. 122–146). Hershey, PA: IGI Global. doi:10.4018/978-1-5225-2066-5.ch007

El Faquih, L., & Fredj, M. (2017). Ontology-Based Framework for Quality in Configurable Process Models. *Journal of Electronic Commerce in Organizations*, *15*(2), 48–60. doi:10.4018/JECO.2017040104

El-Gohary, H., & El-Gohary, Z. (2016). An Attempt to Explore Electronic Marketing Adoption and Implementation Aspects in Developing Countries: The Case of Egypt. *International Journal of Customer Relationship Marketing and Management*, *7*(4), 1 26. doi:10.4018/IJCRMM.2016100101

Elkjaer, B. (2003). Organizational learning with a pragmatic slant. *International Journal of Lifelong Education*, *22*(5), 481–494. doi:10.1080/0260137032000102841

Elkjaer, B. (2013). Organisational Learning as Movements in Practice. *Pedagogy and Teacher Education, Scientific Papers. University of Latvia*, *790*, 22–33.

Ellis, M., & Anderson, P. (2018). Teaching and learning through interdisciplinary pedagogies in a second life environment: focus on integration and assessment. In Handbook of Research on Program Development and Assessment Methodologies in K-20 Education (pp. 275-303). IGI Global.

Emery, F. E., & Trist, E. L. (1981). The causal texture of organizational environments. In F. E. Emery (Ed.), *Systems Thinking* (Vol. 1). London, UK: Penguin Books.

Engel, P. J. H. (2008). Tacit knowledge and Visual Expertise in Medical Diagnostic Reasoning: Implications for medical education. *Medical Teacher*, *30*(7), e184–e188. doi:10.1080/01421590802144260 PMID:18777417

Engeström, Y. (2001). Expansive learning at work: Toward an activity theoretical reconceptualization. *Journal of Education and Work*, *14*(1), 133–156. doi:10.1080/13639080020028747

Engeström, Y., & Kerosuo, H. (2007). From workplace learning to inter-organizational learning and back: The contribution of activity theory. *Journal of Workplace Learning*, *19*(6), 336–342. doi:10.1108/13665620710777084

Engeström, Y., Rantavuori, J., & Kerosuo, H. (2013). Expansive learning in a library: Actions, cycles and deviations from instructional intentions. *Vocations and Learning*, *6*(1), 81–106. doi:10.100712186-012-9089-6

Entico, G. J. (2016). Knowledge Management and the Medical Health Librarians: A Perception Study. In J. Yap, M. Perez, M. Ayson, & G. Entico (Eds.), *Special Library Administration, Standardization and Technological Integration* (pp. 52–77). Hershey, PA: IGI Global. doi:10.4018/978-1-4666-9542-9.ch003

European Union Agency for Fundamental Rights. (2018). *European Convention on Human Rights.* Accessed 04/28/18 http://fra.europa.eu/en/publication/2018/handbook-european-law-non-discrimination

Faisal, M. N., & Talib, F. (2017). Building Ambidextrous Supply Chains in SMEs: How to Tackle the Barriers? *International Journal of Information Systems and Supply Chain Management*, *10*(4), 80–100. doi:10.4018/IJISSCM.2017100105

Falkheimer, J. (2009). On Giddens: Interpreting public relations through Anthony Giddens' structuration and late modernity theory. In O. Ihlen, B. van Ruler, & M. Frederiksson (Eds.), *Public relations and social theory: Key figures and concepts* (pp. 103–119). New York, NY: Routledge.

Fernandes, T. M., Gomes, J., & Romão, M. (2017). Investments in E-Government: A Benefit Management Case Study. *International Journal of Electronic Government Research*, *13*(3), 1–17. doi:10.4018/IJEGR.2017070101

Fernandez, J. P. (1991). *Managing a Diverse Work Force: Regaining the Competitive Edge*. Toronto: Lexington Books.

Fialka, J. (1997). *War by other means: Economic espionage in America* (1st ed.). Norton.

Flamholtz, E., & Randle, Y. (2014). Implications of organizational Life Cycles for Corporate Culture and Climate. In B. Schneider & K. Barbera (Eds.), *The Oxford Handbook of organizational Climate and Culture* (pp. 235–265). OUP.

Flamholtz, E., & Randle, Y. (2014). Implications of organizational Life Cycles for Corporate Culture and Climate. In B. Schneider & K. Barbera (Eds.), *The Oxford Handbook of organizational Climate and Culture, Oxford Library of psychology* (pp. 235–265). OUP.

Focalytic. (2013). Social Media Content Analysis of the 2013 Masters Golf Tournament. *Focal Point*. Retrieved 16-06-2013, from http://www.focalytic.com/Portals/182440/docs/themastersgolfebook.pdf

Fouda, F. A. (2016). A Suggested Curriculum in Career Education to Develop Business Secondary Schools Students' Career Knowledge Management Domains and Professional Thinking. *International Journal of Technology Diffusion*, *7*(2), 42–62. doi:10.4018/IJTD.2016040103

Freeman, Jo. (1991). How 'Sex' Got into Title VII: Persistent Opportunism as a Maker of Public Policy. *Law and Inequality: A Journal of Theory and Practice*, *9*(2), 163–184.

Freiberg, K., & Frieberg, J. (2005). *Guts: Companies that blow the doors off business-as-usual*. New York: Random House.

Gallant, S., & Rios, D. (2014). The organization development consulting process. In B. B. Jones & M. Brazzel (Eds.), *The NTL handbook of organization development and change* (2nd ed.; pp. 153–174). San Francisco, CA: Wiley. doi:10.1002/9781118836170.ch8

Gallardo-Vázquez, D., & Pajuelo-Moreno, M. L. (2016). How Spanish Universities are Promoting Entrepreneurship through Your Own Lines of Teaching and Research? In L. Carvalho (Ed.), *Handbook of Research on Entrepreneurial Success and its Impact on Regional Development* (pp. 431–454). Hershey, PA: IGI Global. doi:10.4018/978-1-4666-9567-2.ch019

Gao, S. S., Oreal, S., & Zhang, J. (2018). Contemporary Financial Risk Management Perceptions and Practices of Small-Sized Chinese Businesses. In I. Management Association (Ed.), Global Business Expansion: Concepts, Methodologies, Tools, and Applications (pp. 917-931). Hershey, PA: IGI Global. doi:10.4018/978-1-5225-5481-3.ch041

Garber, R. (2001). Inteligência competitiva de mercado: como capturar, armazenar, analisar informações de marketing e tomar decisões num mercado competitivo. São Paulo: Madras.

Garet, M. S., Porter, A. C., Desimone, L., Birman, B. F., & Yoon, K. S. (2001, January 1). What Makes Professional Development Effective? Results From a National Sample of Teachers. *American Educational Research Journal, 38*(4), 915–945. doi:10.3102/00028312038004915

Garg, R., & Berning, S. C. (2017). Indigenous Chinese Management Philosophies: Key Concepts and Relevance for Modern Chinese Firms. In B. Christiansen & G. Koc (Eds.), *Transcontinental Strategies for Industrial Development and Economic Growth* (pp. 43–57). Hershey, PA: IGI Global. doi:10.4018/978-1-5225-2160-0.ch003

Gencer, Y. G. (2017). Supply Chain Management in Retailing Business. In U. Akkucuk (Ed.), *Ethics and Sustainability in Global Supply Chain Management* (pp. 197–210). Hershey, PA: IGI Global. doi:10.4018/978-1-5225-2036-8.ch011

Gharajedaghi, J. (2010). *Systems Thinking: Managing Chaos and Complexity a Platform for Designing Business Architecture* (3rd ed.). London, UK: Elsevier.

Ghauth, I. K., & Abdullah, A. N. (2010). Learning materials recommendation using good learners' rating and content-based filtering. *Educational Technology Research and Development.*

Gherardi, S. (2001). From organizational learning to practicebased knowing. *Human Relations, 54*(1), 131–139. doi:10.1177/0018726701541016

Giacosa, E. (2016). Innovation in Luxury Fashion Businesses as a Means for the Regional Development. In L. Carvalho (Ed.), *Handbook of Research on Entrepreneurial Success and its Impact on Regional Development* (pp. 206–222). Hershey, PA: IGI Global. doi:10.4018/978-1-4666-9567-2.ch010

Giacosa, E. (2018). The Increasing of the Regional Development Thanks to the Luxury Business Innovation. In L. Carvalho (Ed.), *Handbook of Research on Entrepreneurial Ecosystems and Social Dynamics in a Globalized World* (pp. 260–273). Hershey, PA: IGI Global. doi:10.4018/978-1-5225-3525-6.ch011

Gianni, M., & Gotzamani, K. (2016). Integrated Management Systems and Information Management Systems: Common Threads. In P. Papajorgji, F. Pinet, A. Guimarães, & J. Papathanasiou (Eds.), *Automated Enterprise Systems for Maximizing Business Performance* (pp. 195–214). Hershey, PA: IGI Global. doi:10.4018/978-1-4666-8841-4.ch011

Gianni, M., Gotzamani, K., & Linden, I. (2016). How a BI-wise Responsible Integrated Management System May Support Food Traceability. *International Journal of Decision Support System Technology, 8*(2), 1–17. doi:10.4018/IJDSST.2016040101

Gibney, P. (2006). The double bind theory: Still crazy-making after all these years. *Psychotherapy in Australia, 12*(3), 48–55.

Giddens, A. (1984). *The constitution of society: Outline of the theory of structuration*. Cambridge, UK: Polity Press.

Gilbert, R., Balatti, J., Turner, P., & Whitehouse, H. (2004). The generic skills debate in research higher degrees. *Higher Education Research & Development, 23*(3), 375–388. doi:10.1080/0729436042000235454

Glykas, M., & George, J. (2017). Quality and Process Management Systems in the UAE Maritime Industry. *International Journal of Productivity Management and Assessment Technologies, 5*(1), 20–39. doi:10.4018/IJPMAT.2017010102

Glykas, M., Valiris, G., Kokkinaki, A., & Koutsoukou, Z. (2018). Banking Business Process Management Implementation. *International Journal of Productivity Management and Assessment Technologies, 6*(1), 50–69. doi:10.4018/IJPMAT.2018010104

Godeluck, S. (2000). *A Explosão da Economia na Internet*. Lisboa: Livros do Brasil.

Gokhale, V.A. (2018). Challenges in doctoral research in architecture in India. *International Journal on New Trends in Education & Their Implications, 9*(1).

Goldman, A. (2011). *Tudo que sei sobre Marketing aprendi com o Google*. S. Paulo: Saraiva.

Gomes, E., & Braga, F. (2001). *Inteligência competitiva: como transformar informação em um negócio lucrativo*. Rio de Janeiro: Campus.

Gomes, J., & Romão, M. (2017). Aligning Information Systems and Technology with Benefit Management and Balanced Scorecard. In S. De Haes & W. Van Grembergen (Eds.), *Strategic IT Governance and Alignment in Business Settings* (pp. 112–131). Hershey, PA: IGI Global. doi:10.4018/978-1-5225-0861-8.ch005

Gomes, J., & Romão, M. (2017). The Balanced Scorecard: Keeping Updated and Aligned with Today's Business Trends. *International Journal of Productivity Management and Assessment Technologies, 5*(2), 1–15. doi:10.4018/IJPMAT.2017070101

Gore, W. J. (1963). Developments in Public Administration. *Public Administration Review*, *23*(1), 51–54. doi:10.2307/973389

Gould, L. (2011, October 3). RIP Sir Jimmy: it's all over now. *Mail.*

Goyal, M., & Krishnamurthy, R. (2018). Optimizing student engagement in online learning environments: intuitionistic fuzzy logic in student modeling. In Optimizing Student Engagement in Online Learning Environments (pp. 187-219). IGI Global.

Grefen, P., & Turetken, O. (2017). Advanced Business Process Management in Networked E-Business Scenarios. *International Journal of E-Business Research*, *13*(4), 70–104. doi:10.4018/IJEBR.2017100105

Guisnel, J. (1997). *Espionagem na Internet: As Guerras no Ciberespaço*. Lisboa: Difusão Cultural.

Guynn, J. (2013). Facebook releases information on NSA requests for user data. *Los Angeles Times*. Retrieved 14-06-2013, from http://www.latimes.com/business/technology/la-fi-tn-facebook-releases-first-information-on-fisa-requests-20130614,0,3315731.story

Haggbloom, S. J., Warnick, J. E., Jones, V. K., Yarbrough, G. L., Russell, T. M., Borecky, C. M., & .... (2002). The 100 most eminent psychologists of the 20th century. *Review of General Psychology*, *6*(2), 139–152. doi:10.1037/1089-2680.6.2.139

Haider, A., & Saetang, S. (2017). Strategic IT Alignment in Service Sector. In S. Rozenes & Y. Cohen (Eds.), *Handbook of Research on Strategic Alliances and Value Co-Creation in the Service Industry* (pp. 231–258). Hershey, PA: IGI Global. doi:10.4018/978-1-5225-2084-9.ch012

Haider, A., & Tang, S. S. (2016). Maximising Value Through IT and Business Alignment: A Case of IT Governance Institutionalisation at a Thai Bank. *International Journal of Technology Diffusion*, *7*(3), 33–58. doi:10.4018/IJTD.2016070104

Hajilari, A. B., Ghadaksaz, M., & Fasghandis, G. S. (2017). Assessing Organizational Readiness for Implementing ERP System Using Fuzzy Expert System Approach. *International Journal of Enterprise Information Systems*, *13*(1), 67–85. doi:10.4018/IJEIS.2017010105

Haldorai, A., Ramu, A., & Murugan, S. (2018). Social Aware Cognitive Radio Networks: Effectiveness of Social Networks as a Strategic Tool for Organizational Business Management. In H. Bansal, G. Shrivastava, G. Nguyen, & L. Stanciu (Eds.), *Social Network Analytics for Contemporary Business Organizations* (pp. 188–202). Hershey, PA: IGI Global. doi:10.4018/978-1-5225-5097-6.ch010

Hall, O. P. Jr. (2017). Social Media Driven Management Education. *International Journal of Knowledge-Based Organizations*, *7*(2), 43–59. doi:10.4018/IJKBO.2017040104

Hanifah, H., Halim, H. A., Ahmad, N. H., & Vafaei-Zadeh, A. (2017). Innovation Culture as a Mediator Between Specific Human Capital and Innovation Performance Among Bumiputera SMEs in Malaysia. In N. Ahmad, T. Ramayah, H. Halim, & S. Rahman (Eds.), *Handbook of Research on Small and Medium Enterprises in Developing Countries* (pp. 261–279). Hershey, PA: IGI Global. doi:10.4018/978-1-5225-2165-5.ch012

Hartlieb, S., & Silvius, G. (2017). Handling Uncertainty in Project Management and Business Development: Similarities and Differences. In Y. Raydugin (Ed.), *Handbook of Research on Leveraging Risk and Uncertainties for Effective Project Management* (pp. 337–362). Hershey, PA: IGI Global. doi:10.4018/978-1-5225-1790-0.ch016

Hassan, A., & Privitera, D. S. (2016). Google AdSense as a Mobile Technology in Education. In J. Holland (Ed.), *Wearable Technology and Mobile Innovations for Next-Generation Education* (pp. 200–223). Hershey, PA: IGI Global. doi:10.4018/978-1-5225-0069-8.ch011

Hassan, A., & Rahimi, R. (2016). Consuming "Innovation" in Tourism: Augmented Reality as an Innovation Tool in Digital Tourism Marketing. In N. Pappas & I. Bregoli (Eds.), *Global Dynamics in Travel, Tourism, and Hospitality* (pp. 130–147). Hershey, PA: IGI Global. doi:10.4018/978-1-5225-0201-2.ch008

Hass, K. B. (2017). Living on the Edge: Managing Project Complexity. In Y. Raydugin (Ed.), *Handbook of Research on Leveraging Risk and Uncertainties for Effective Project Management* (pp. 177–201). Hershey, PA: IGI Global. doi:10.4018/978-1-5225-1790-0.ch009

Hawking, P., & Carmine Sellitto, C. (2017). Developing an Effective Strategy for Organizational Business Intelligence. In M. Tavana (Ed.), *Enterprise Information Systems and the Digitalization of Business Functions* (pp. 222–237). Hershey, PA: IGI Global. doi:10.4018/978-1-5225-2382-6.ch010

Hawking, P., & Sellitto, C. (2017). A Fast-Moving Consumer Goods Company and Business Intelligence Strategy Development. *International Journal of Enterprise Information Systems*, *13*(2), 22–33. doi:10.4018/IJEIS.2017040102

Hawking, P., & Sellitto, C. (2017). Business Intelligence Strategy: Two Case Studies. *International Journal of Business Intelligence Research*, *8*(2), 17–30. doi:10.4018/IJBIR.2017070102

Hawthorne, K., & Cromity, J. (2012, March). Social Search for Market Intelligence. *Online: Exploring Technology & Resources for Information Professionals,* 36-38.

Haynes, J. D., Arockiasamy, S., Al Rashdi, M., & Al Rashdi, S. (2016). Business and E Business Strategies for Coopetition and Thematic Management as a Sustained Basis for Ethics and Social Responsibility in Emerging Markets. In M. Al-Shammari & H. Masri (Eds.), *Ethical and Social Perspectives on Global Business Interaction in Emerging Markets* (pp. 25–39). Hershey, PA: IGI Global. doi:10.4018/978-1-4666-9864-2.ch002

Hee, W. J., Jalleh, G., Lai, H., & Lin, C. (2017). E-Commerce and IT Projects: Evaluation and Management Issues in Australian and Taiwanese Hospitals. *International Journal of Public Health Management and Ethics*, *2*(1), 69–90. doi:10.4018/IJPHME.2017010104

Hernandez, A. A. (2018). Exploring the Factors to Green IT Adoption of SMEs in the Philippines. *Journal of Cases on Information Technology*, *20*(2), 49–66. doi:10.4018/JCIT.2018040104

Hernandez, A. A., & Ona, S. E. (2016). Green IT Adoption: Lessons from the Philippines Business Process Outsourcing Industry. *International Journal of Social Ecology and Sustainable Development*, *7*(1), 1–34. doi:10.4018/IJSESD.2016010101

Herring, J. P. (2002). Tópicos fundamentais de inteligência: processo para identificação e definição de necessidades de inteligência. In Prescott & Miller (Eds.), Inteligência competitiva na prática. Rio de Janeiro: Campus.

Higham, W. (2010). The Next Big Thing: Spotting and Forecasting Consumer Trends for Profit (1ª ed.). Bodmin: Kogan Page.

Higher Education Commission. (2013). *Postgraduate education: an independent inquiry by higher education commission.* Available at http://www.policyconnect.org.uk/hec/sites/site_hec/files/report/329/fieldreportdownload/hec-postgraduateeducationreport.pdf

Hinchliffe, W. G., & Jolly, A. (2011). Graduate identity and employability. *British Educational Research Journal, 37*(4), 2011. doi:10.1080/01411926.2010.482200

Hobbs, M., Brown, E., & Gordon, M., (2006, October). Using a virtual world for transferable skills in gaming education. *Virtual World Environment.*

Hoffman, C. (2013). Change Mastery, Simplified. In J. Vogelsang & M. Townsend (Eds.), *Handbook for Strategic HR*. New York: Amacon.

Hofstede, G. (1993). Cultures and Organizations: Software of the Mind. *Administrative Science Quarterly, 38*(1), 132–134. doi:10.2307/2393257

Hollman, A., Bickford, S., & Hollman, T. (2017). Cyber InSecurity: A Post-Mortem Attempt to Assess Cyber Problems from IT and Business Management Perspectives. *Journal of Cases on Information Technology, 19*(3), 42–70. doi:10.4018/JCIT.2017070104

Holloman, C. (2012). *The Social Media MBA: Your Competitive Edge in Social Media Strategy Development and Delivery* (1st ed.). John Wiley & Sons.

Holsapple, C. W., & Wu, J. (2011). An elusive antecedent of superior firm performance: The knowledge management factor. *Decision Support Systems, 52*(1), 271–283. doi:10.1016/j.dss.2011.08.003

Hortinha, J. (2002). *X-Marketing* (1st ed.). Lisboa: Sílabo.

Howard, J. H. (2004). *Workers at War: Labor in China's Arsenals, 1937–1953.* Stanford, CA: Stanford University Press.

Hryciw, D. H., Tangalakis, K., & Best, G. (2017). Development of transferable skills in a low-SES population through peer assisted study sessions. *Proceedings of The Australian Conference on Science and Mathematics Education,* 69.

Human Rights Act, C. 42. (1998). *An Act to give further effect to rights and freedoms guaranteed under the European Convention on Human Rights.* Westminster: House of Commons.

Igbinakhase, I. (2017). Responsible and Sustainable Management Practices in Developing and Developed Business Environments. In Z. Fields (Ed.), *Collective Creativity for Responsible and Sustainable Business Practice* (pp. 180–207). Hershey, PA: IGI Global. doi:10.4018/978-1-5225-1823-5.ch010

Ilahi, L., Ghannouchi, S. A., & Martinho, R. (2016). A Business Process Management Approach to Home Healthcare Processes: On the Gap between Intention and Reality. In M. Cruz-Cunha, I. Miranda, R. Martinho, & R. Rijo (Eds.), *Encyclopedia of E-Health and Telemedicine* (pp. 439–457). Hershey, PA: IGI Global. doi:10.4018/978-1-4666-9978-6.ch035

Imai, M. (1986). *Kaizen: the key to Japan's competitive success*. New York: McGraw-Hill.

Iwata, J. J., & Hoskins, R. G. (2017). Managing Indigenous Knowledge in Tanzania: A Business Perspective. In P. Jain & N. Mnjama (Eds.), *Managing Knowledge Resources and Records in Modern Organizations* (pp. 198–214). Hershey, PA: IGI Global. doi:10.4018/978-1-5225-1965-2.ch012

Jabeen, F., Ahmad, S. Z., & Alkaabi, S. (2016). The Internationalization Decision-Making of United Arab Emirates Family Businesses. In N. Zakaria, A. Abdul-Talib, & N. Osman (Eds.), *Handbook of Research on Impacts of International Business and Political Affairs on the Global Economy* (pp. 1–22). Hershey, PA: IGI Global. doi:10.4018/978-1-4666-9806-2.ch001

Jain, P. (2017). Ethical and Legal Issues in Knowledge Management Life-Cycle in Business. In P. Jain & N. Mnjama (Eds.), *Managing Knowledge Resources and Records in Modern Organizations* (pp. 82–101). Hershey, PA: IGI Global. doi:10.4018/978-1-5225-1965-2.ch006

Jamali, D., Abdallah, H., & Matar, F. (2016). Opportunities and Challenges for CSR Mainstreaming in Business Schools. *International Journal of Technology and Educational Marketing*, *6*(2), 1–29. doi:10.4018/IJTEM.2016070101

James, S., & Hauli, E. (2017). Holistic Management Education at Tanzanian Rural Development Planning Institute. In N. Baporikar (Ed.), *Management Education for Global Leadership* (pp. 112–136). Hershey, PA: IGI Global. doi:10.4018/978-1-5225-1013-0.ch006

Jamieson, D., & Vogelsang, J. (2013). Changing world of human resources. In J. Vogelsang & M. Townsend (Eds.), *Handbook for Strategic HR*. New York: Amacon.

Janošková, M., Csikósová, A., & Čulková, K. (2018). Measurement of Company Performance as Part of Its Strategic Management. In R. Leon (Ed.), *Managerial Strategies for Business Sustainability During Turbulent Times* (pp. 309–335). Hershey, PA: IGI Global. doi:10.4018/978-1-5225-2716-9.ch017

Jean-Vasile, A., & Alecu, A. (2017). Theoretical and Practical Approaches in Understanding the Influences of Cost-Productivity-Profit Trinomial in Contemporary Enterprises. In A. Jean Vasile & D. Nicolò (Eds.), *Sustainable Entrepreneurship and Investments in the Green Economy* (pp. 28–62). Hershey, PA: IGI Global. doi:10.4018/978-1-5225-2075-7.ch002

Jha, D. G. (2016). Preparing for Information Technology Driven Changes. In S. Tiwari & L. Nafees (Eds.), *Innovative Management Education Pedagogies for Preparing Next-Generation Leaders* (pp. 258–274). Hershey, PA: IGI Global. doi:10.4018/978-1-4666-9691-4.ch015

Johnson, A. (2005). Blogs, Wikis & RSS: Colaborative social communities and the value of distributed CI. *Competitive Intelligence Magazine*. Retrieved 10-02-2013, from http://www.aurorawdc.com/blogswikisrss_scipcimag_20050102.pdf

Joia, L. A., & Correia, J. C. (2018). CIO Competencies From the IT Professional Perspective: Insights From Brazil. *Journal of Global Information Management*, *26*(2), 74–103. doi:10.4018/JGIM.2018040104

Juma, A., & Mzera, N. (2017). Knowledge Management and Records Management and Competitive Advantage in Business. In P. Jain & N. Mnjama (Eds.), *Managing Knowledge Resources and Records in Modern Organizations* (pp. 15–28). Hershey, PA: IGI Global. doi:10.4018/978-1-5225-1965-2.ch002

Juran, J. (1999). *Juran's Quality Handbook* (5th ed.). New York: McGraw-Hill.

K., I., & A, V. (2018). Monitoring and Auditing in the Cloud. In K. Munir (Ed.), *Cloud Computing Technologies for Green Enterprises* (pp. 318-350). Hershey, PA: IGI Global. doi:10.4018/978-1-5225-3038-1.ch013

Kabra, G., Ghosh, V., & Ramesh, A. (2018). Enterprise Integrated Business Process Management and Business Intelligence Framework for Business Process Sustainability. In A. Paul, D. Bhattacharyya, & S. Anand (Eds.), *Green Initiatives for Business Sustainability and Value Creation* (pp. 228–238). Hershey, PA: IGI Global. doi:10.4018/978-1-5225-2662-9.ch010

Kahaner, L. (1997). *Competitive Intelligence: How to gather, analyze, and use information to move your business to the top* (1st ed.). New York: Simon & Schuster.

Kane, G. C. (n.d.). *Why Social Media Will Fundamentally Change Business*. Retrieved from https://sloanreview.mit.edu/article/why-social-media-will-fundamentally-change-business/

Kaoud, M. (2017). Investigation of Customer Knowledge Management: A Case Study Research. *International Journal of Service Science, Management, Engineering, and Technology*, *8*(2), 12–22. doi:10.4018/IJSSMET.2017040102

Kara, M. E., & Fırat, S. Ü. (2016). Sustainability, Risk, and Business Intelligence in Supply Chains. In M. Erdoğdu, T. Arun, & I. Ahmad (Eds.), *Handbook of Research on Green Economic Development Initiatives and Strategies* (pp. 501–538). Hershey, PA: IGI Global. doi:10.4018/978-1-5225-0440-5.ch022

Kassel, A. (2008). *Social Networking: A Research Tool*. Retrieved 15/12/2012, from http://web.fumsi.com/go/article/find/3196

Katuu, S. (2018). A Comparative Assessment of Enterprise Content Management Maturity Models. In N. Gwangwava & M. Mutingi (Eds.), *E-Manufacturing and E-Service Strategies in Contemporary Organizations* (pp. 93–118). Hershey, PA: IGI Global. doi:10.4018/978-1-5225-3628-4.ch005

Kawasaki, G. (2007). *Ten Ways to Use LinkedIn*. Retrieved 05-01-2007, from http://blog.guykawasaki.com

Kaya, Y. (2008). Constructivism: Its Theoretical Underpinnings, Variations, and Implications for Classroom Instruction. *Educational Horizons, 86*(3), 161-172.

Khan, M. A. (2016). MNEs Management Strategies in Developing Countries: Establishing the Context. In M. Khan (Ed.), *Multinational Enterprise Management Strategies in Developing Countries* (pp. 1–33). Hershey, PA: IGI Global. doi:10.4018/978-1-5225-0276-0.ch001

Khan, M. A. (2016). Operational Approaches in Organizational Structure: A Case for MNEs in Developing Countries. In M. Khan (Ed.), *Multinational Enterprise Management Strategies in Developing Countries* (pp. 129–151). Hershey, PA: IGI Global. doi:10.4018/978-1-5225-0276-0.ch007

Kimble, C. (2013). Knowledge management, codification and tacit knowledge. *Information Research, 18*(2).

Kinnunen, S., Ylä-Kujala, A., Marttonen-Arola, S., Kärri, T., & Baglee, D. (2018). Internet of Things in Asset Management: Insights from Industrial Professionals and Academia. *International Journal of Service Science, Management, Engineering, and Technology*, *9*(2), 104–119. doi:10.4018/IJSSMET.2018040105

Kirsch, Brown, & Charley. (2006). Using Patents in Competitive Intelligence. *Competitive Intelligence Magazine*, *9*(1), 17–21.

Klein, A. Z., Sabino de Freitas, A., Machado, L., Freitas, J. C. Jr, Graziola, P. G. Jr, & Schlemmer, E. (2017). Virtual Worlds Applications for Management Education. In L. Tomei (Ed.), *Exploring the New Era of Technology-Infused Education* (pp. 279–299). Hershey, PA: IGI Global. doi:10.4018/978-1-5225-1709-2.ch017

Koeslag, J. H., Saunders, P. T., & Wessels, J. A. (1997). Glucose homeostasis with infinite gain: Further lessons from the Daisyworld parable? *The Journal of Endocrinology*, *134*(2), 187–192. doi:10.1677/joe.0.1540187 PMID:9291828

Koestler, A. (1967). *The Ghost in the machine*. London, UK: Hutchinson.

Kohler, W. (1929). *Gestalt psychology, an introduction to new concepts in modern psychology*. New York: Liveright.

Kolbaek, D. (2012). *Proactive reviews*. Copenhagen: Book on Demand.

Kolbaek, D. (2014). *Learning from experience in the context of work*. Aalborg, Denmark: Aalborg University Press.

Kolbaek, D. (2015). *Proactive Review. In Utilizing Evidence-Based Lessons Learned for Enhanced Organizational Innovation and Change*. Hershey, PA: IGI Global.

Kolb, D. A., & Fry, R. (1975). Toward an applied theory of experiential learning. In C. Cooper (Ed.), *Theories of Group Process*. London, UK: John Wiley.

Kolb, D. A., & Kolb, A. Y. (2011). *The Kolb Learning Style Inventory 4.0*. Prentice-Hall.

Kotler, P., Armstrong, G., Saunders, J., & Wong, V. (1999). *Principles of Marketing* (2nd ed.). Cambridge, UK: Prentice Hall.

Kotze, L. (2013). *Social media increasingly important in competitive intelligence*. Retrieved 08-03-2013, from http://www.ibis.co.za/Competitive-Intelligence-Blog/social-media-increasingly-important-in-competitive-intelligence.html

Kożuch, B., & Jabłoński, A. (2017). Adopting the Concept of Business Models in Public Management. In M. Lewandowski & B. Kożuch (Eds.), *Public Sector Entrepreneurship and the Integration of Innovative Business Models* (pp. 10–46). Hershey, PA: IGI Global. doi:10.4018/978-1-5225-2215-7.ch002

Kumar, J., Adhikary, A., & Jha, A. (2017). Small Active Investors' Perceptions and Preferences Towards Tax Saving Mutual Fund Schemes in Eastern India: An Empirical Note. *International Journal of Asian Business and Information Management, 8*(2), 35–45. doi:10.4018/IJABIM.2017040103

Kyewski, E., & Krämer, N. C. (2018). To gamify or not to gamify? an experimental field study of the influence of badges on motivation, activity, and performance in an online learning course. *Computers & Education, 118*, 25–37. doi:10.1016/j.compedu.2017.11.006

Lanza-Cruz, I., Berlanga, R., & Aramburu, M. (2018). Modeling Analytical Streams for Social Business Intelligence. In Informatics (Vol. 5, No. 3, p. 33). Multidisciplinary Digital Publishing Institute.

Lapowsky, I. (2018). *Are Gay People Better Entrepreneurs?* Accessed 04/28/18 https://www.inc.com/issie-lapowsky/gay-people-make-better-entrepreneurs.html

Lassoued, Y., Bouzguenda, L., & Mahmoud, T. (2016). Context-Aware Business Process Versions Management. *International Journal of e-Collaboration, 12*(3), 7–33. doi:10.4018/IJeC.2016070102

Lavassani, K. M., & Movahedi, B. (2017). Applications Driven Information Systems: Beyond Networks toward Business Ecosystems. *International Journal of Innovation in the Digital Economy, 8*(1), 61–75. doi:10.4018/IJIDE.2017010104

Lave, J., & Wenger, E. (1991). *Situated Learning: Legitimate Peripheral Participation*. Cambridge, UK: Cambridge University Press. doi:10.1017/CBO9780511815355

Lazzareschi, V. H., & Brito, M. S. (2017). Strategic Information Management: Proposal of Business Project Model. In G. Jamil, A. Soares, & C. Pessoa (Eds.), *Handbook of Research on Information Management for Effective Logistics and Supply Chains* (pp. 59–88). Hershey, PA: IGI Global. doi:10.4018/978-1-5225-0973-8.ch004

Lederer, M., Kurz, M., & Lazarov, P. (2017). Usage and Suitability of Methods for Strategic Business Process Initiatives: A Multi Case Study Research. *International Journal of Productivity Management and Assessment Technologies, 5*(1), 40–51. doi:10.4018/IJPMAT.2017010103

Lee, I. (2017). A Social Enterprise Business Model and a Case Study of Pacific Community Ventures (PCV). In V. Potocan, M. Üngan, & Z. Nedelko (Eds.), *Handbook of Research on Managerial Solutions in Non-Profit Organizations* (pp. 182–204). Hershey, PA: IGI Global. doi:10.4018/978-1-5225-0731-4.ch009

Lee, L. J., & Leu, J. (2016). Exploring the Effectiveness of IT Application and Value Method in the Innovation Performance of Enterprise. *International Journal of Enterprise Information Systems, 12*(2), 47–65. doi:10.4018/IJEIS.2016040104

Lee, Y. (2016). Alignment Effect of Entrepreneurial Orientation and Marketing Orientation on Firm Performance. *International Journal of Customer Relationship Marketing and Management, 7*(4), 58–69. doi:10.4018/IJCRMM.2016100104

Leonard, H. (2013). *Blogs Outrank Social Networks In Influence*. Retrieved 09-03-2013, from http://www.businessinsider.com/blog-influence-outranks-social-networks-2013-3

Leon, L. A., Seal, K. C., Przasnyski, Z. H., & Wiedenman, I. (2017). Skills and Competencies Required for Jobs in Business Analytics: A Content Analysis of Job Advertisements Using Text Mining. *International Journal of Business Intelligence Research, 8*(1), 1–25. doi:10.4018/IJBIR.2017010101

Leu, J., Lee, L. J., & Krischke, A. (2016). Value Engineering-Based Method for Implementing the ISO14001 System in the Green Supply Chains. *International Journal of Strategic Decision Sciences, 7*(4), 1–20. doi:10.4018/IJSDS.2016100101

Leven, P., Holmstrom, J., & Mathiassen, L. (2014). Managing research and innovation networks: Evidence from a government sponsored cross-industry program. *Research Policy, 43*(1), 156–168. doi:10.1016/j.respol.2013.08.004

Levy, C. L., & Elias, N. I. (2017). SOHO Users' Perceptions of Reliability and Continuity of Cloud-Based Services. In M. Moore (Ed.), *Cybersecurity Breaches and Issues Surrounding Online Threat Protection* (pp. 248–287). Hershey, PA: IGI Global. doi:10.4018/978-1-5225-1941-6.ch011

Levy, M. (2018). Change Management Serving Knowledge Management and Organizational Development: Reflections and Review. In N. Baporikar (Ed.), *Global Practices in Knowledge Management for Societal and Organizational Development* (pp. 256–270). Hershey, PA: IGI Global. doi:10.4018/978-1-5225-3009-1.ch012

Lewandowski, M. (2017). Public Organizations and Business Model Innovation: The Role of Public Service Design. In M. Lewandowski & B. Kożuch (Eds.), *Public Sector Entrepreneurship and the Integration of Innovative Business Models* (pp. 47–72). Hershey, PA: IGI Global. doi:10.4018/978-1-5225-2215-7.ch003

Lewin, K. (1943). Defining the "Field at a Given Time." Psychological Review, 50, 292-310.

Lewin, K. (1946). Action research and minority problems. *The Journal of Social Issues, 2*(4), 34–46. doi:.1946.tb02295.x doi:10.1111/j.1540-4560

Lewin, K. (1936). *Principles of topological psychology*. New York: McGraw-Hill. doi:10.1037/10019-000

Lewin, K. (1943). Defining the Field at a Given Time. *Psychological Review*, *50*(3), 292–310. doi:10.1037/h0062738

Lewin, K. (1946). Action research and minority problems. *The Journal of Social Issues*, *2*(4), 34–46. doi:10.1111/j.1540-4560.1946.tb02295.x

Lewin, K. (1946). Research on minority problems. *Technology Review*, *48*(3).

Lewin, K. (1951). *Field theory in social science*. New York: Harper.

Lewin, K., Lippitt, R., & White, R. K. (1939). Patterns of aggressive behavior in experimentally created 'social climates'. *The Journal of Social Psychology*, *10*(2), 271–299. doi:10.1080/00224545.1939.9713366

Lhannaoui, H., Kabbaj, M. I., & Bakkoury, Z. (2017). A Survey of Risk-Aware Business Process Modelling. *International Journal of Risk and Contingency Management*, *6*(3), 14–26. doi:10.4018/IJRCM.2017070102

Liaropoulos, A. (2006). Revolutions in warfare: Paradigms and Historical evidence: the Napoleonic and First World War Revolutions in Military Affairs. *The Journal of Military History*, *70*(2), 363–384. doi:10.1353/jmh.2006.0106

Libert, B., & Spector, J. (2009). *Muitas Cabeças Pensam Melhor: Como mobilizar o poder das multidões para o seu negócio* (1st ed.). Porto: Lua de Papel.

Li, J., Sun, W., Jiang, W., Yang, H., & Zhang, L. (2017). How the Nature of Exogenous Shocks and Crises Impact Company Performance?: The Effects of Industry Characteristics. *International Journal of Risk and Contingency Management*, *6*(4), 40–55. doi:10.4018/IJRCM.2017100103

Linsay, R., Breen, R., & Jenkins, A. (2002). Academic research and teaching quality: The views of undergraduate and postgraduate students. *Studies in Higher Education*, *27*(3), 309–327. doi:10.1080/03075070220000699

Long, S. (2016). *Transforming experience in organization: A framework for organizational research and consultancy*. Melbourne, Australia: Karnac Books.

Lu, C., & Liu, S. (2016). Cultural Tourism O2O Business Model Innovation-A Case Study of CTrip. *Journal of Electronic Commerce in Organizations*, *14*(2), 16–31. doi:10.4018/JECO.2016040102

Machen, B., Hosseini, M. R., Wood, A., & Bakhshi, J. (2016). An Investigation into using SAP-PS as a Multidimensional Project Control System (MPCS). *International Journal of Enterprise Information Systems*, *12*(2), 66–81. doi:10.4018/IJEIS.2016040105

Macmillan, H. (2017). *An African Trading Empire: The Story of Susman Brothers and Wulfsohn 1901-2005*. New York: Tauris.

Malega, P. (2017). Small and Medium Enterprises in the Slovak Republic: Status and Competitiveness of SMEs in the Global Markets and Possibilities of Optimization. In M. Vemić (Ed.), *Optimal Management Strategies in Small and Medium Enterprises* (pp. 102–124). Hershey, PA: IGI Global. doi:10.4018/978-1-5225-1949-2.ch006

Malewska, K. M. (2017). Intuition in Decision-Making on the Example of a Non-Profit Organization. In V. Potocan, M. Üngan, & Z. Nedelko (Eds.), *Handbook of Research on Managerial Solutions in Non-Profit Organizations* (pp. 378–399). Hershey, PA: IGI Global. doi:10.4018/978-1-5225-0731-4.ch018

Marchand, D., & Horton, F. Jr. (1986). *Infotrends: Profiting from your Information Resources*. John Wiley & Sons.

Maroofi, F. (2017). Entrepreneurial Orientation and Organizational Learning Ability Analysis for Innovation and Firm Performance. In N. Baporikar (Ed.), *Innovation and Shifting Perspectives in Management Education* (pp. 144–165). Hershey, PA: IGI Global. doi:10.4018/978-1-5225-1019-2.ch007

Marrow, A. J. (1977). *The practical theorist; the life and work of Kurt Lewin*. New York: Teacher's College.

Martinet, B., & Marti, Y. (1995). *A Inteligência Económica: os olhos e os ouvidos da empresa*. Instituto Piaget.

Martins, P. V., & Zacarias, M. (2017). A Web-based Tool for Business Process Improvement. *International Journal of Web Portals*, *9*(2), 68–84. doi:10.4018/IJWP.2017070104

Matthies, B., & Coners, A. (2017). Exploring the Conceptual Nature of e-Business Projects. *Journal of Electronic Commerce in Organizations*, *15*(3), 33–63. doi:10.4018/JECO.2017070103

Mawson, M., & Haworth, A.C. (2018). Supporting the employability agenda in University Libraries: a case study from the University of Sheffield. *Information and Learning Science*.

Mayeh, M. (2012, December). *Understanding the Role of Social Media Monitoring in Generating External Intelligence*. Retrieved from https://dro.deakin.edu.au/eserv/DU:30049105/scheepers-understandingtherole-2012.pdf

McDermott, R., & Archibald, D. (2010). Harnessing Your Staff's Informal Networks. *Harvard Business Review*, *88*(3). PMID:20402051

McGee, J. V., & Prusak, L. (1995). *Gerenciamento estratégico da informação: aumente a competitividade e a eficiência de sua empresa utilizando a informação como uma ferramenta estratégica*. Rio de Janeiro: Campus.

McHugh, D., Groves, D., & Alker, A. (1998). Managing learning: What do we learn from a learning organization? *The Learning Organization*, *5*(5), 209–220. doi:10.1108/09696479810238215

McInerney, C. (2002). Knowledge Management and the Dynamic Nature of Knowledge. *Journal of the American Society for Information Science and Technology*, *53*(12), 1009–1018. doi:10.1002/asi.10109

McKee, J. (2018). Architecture as a Tool to Solve Business Planning Problems. In M. Khosrow-Pour, D.B.A. (Ed.), Encyclopedia of Information Science and Technology, Fourth Edition (pp. 573-586). Hershey, PA: IGI Global. doi:10.4018/978-1-5225-2255-3.ch050

McLoughlin, C., & Luca, J. (2002). A Learner-centred approach to developing team skills through web-based learning and assessment. *British Journal of Educational*, *33*(5), 571-582.

McMurray, A. J., Cross, J., & Caponecchia, C. (2018). The Risk Management Profession in Australia: Business Continuity Plan Practices. In N. Bajgoric (Ed.), *Always-On Enterprise Information Systems for Modern Organizations* (pp. 112–129). Hershey, PA: IGI Global. doi:10.4018/978-1-5225-3704-5.ch006

Meddah, I. H., & Belkadi, K. (2018). Mining Patterns Using Business Process Management. In R. Hamou (Ed.), *Handbook of Research on Biomimicry in Information Retrieval and Knowledge Management* (pp. 78–89). Hershey, PA: IGI Global. doi:10.4018/978-1-5225-3004-6.ch005

Mendes, L. (2017). TQM and Knowledge Management: An Integrated Approach Towards Tacit Knowledge Management. In D. Jaziri-Bouagina & G. Jamil (Eds.), *Handbook of Research on Tacit Knowledge Management for Organizational Success* (pp. 236–263). Hershey, PA: IGI Global. doi:10.4018/978-1-5225-2394-9.ch009

Miller, A. (2007). *Social Tools for Business Use: Messages from a Web 2.0 Conference*. Retrieved from http://web.fumsi.com/go/article/find/3916

Miller, E. C., & Rice, A. K. (1967). *Systems of organization: the control of task and sentient boundaries*. London, UK: Tavistock Publications.

Miller, J. (2002). *O milênio da inteligência competitiva*. Porto Alegre. *The Bookman*.

Milliken, F. J. (1989). Three types of perceived uncertainty about the environment: State, effect and response uncertainty. *Academy of Management Review*, *12*(1), 133–143. doi:10.5465/amr.1987.4306502

Mingers, J., & White, L. (2010). A review of the recent contribution of systems thinking to operational research and management science. *European Journal of Operational Research*, *207*(3), 1147–1161. doi:10.1016/j.ejor.2009.12.019

Mnjama, N. M. (2017). Preservation of Recorded Information in Public and Private Sector Organizations. In P. Jain & N. Mnjama (Eds.), *Managing Knowledge Resources and Records in Modern Organizations* (pp. 149–167). Hershey, PA: IGI Global. doi:10.4018/978-1-5225-1965-2.ch009

Mohr, J., Sengupta, S., & Slater, S. (2010). *Marketing of High-Technology Products and Innovations* (3rd ed.). Pearson.

Mokoqama, M., & Fields, Z. (2017). Principles of Responsible Management Education (PRME): Call for Responsible Management Education. In Z. Fields (Ed.), *Collective Creativity for Responsible and Sustainable Business Practice* (pp. 229–241). Hershey, PA: IGI Global. doi:10.4018/978-1-5225-1823-5.ch012

Mordecai, V. (2013a). 4 Things Social Media Analysis Can Tell You About Your Business. *Focal Point: Focalytic*. Retrieved 23-05-2013, from http://www.focalytic.com/focal-point/bid/291330/4-Things-Social-Media-Analysis-Can-Tell-You-About-Your-Business

Mordecai, V. (2013b). What Businesses Can Gain from a Custom Social Media Listening Tool. *Focal Point: Focalytic*. Retrieved 20-05-2013, from http://www.focalytic.com/focal-point/bid/291331/What-Businesses-Can-Gain-from-a-Custom-Social-Media-Listening-Tool

Mordecai, V. (2013c). What Is Competitive Intelligence? *Focal Point: Focalytic*. Retrieved 14-06-2013, from http://www.focalytic.com/focal-point/bid/297577/What-Is-Competitive-Intelligence

Munawar, S., Toor, S. K., Aslam, M., & Hamid, M. (2018). Move to smart learning environment: Exploratory research of challenges in computer laboratory and design intelligent virtual laboratory for eLearning Technology. *EURASIA Journal of Mathematics, Science and Technology Education*, *14*(5), 1645–1662.

Muniapan, B. (2017). Philosophy and Management: The Relevance of Vedanta in Management. In P. Ordóñez de Pablos (Ed.), *Managerial Strategies and Solutions for Business Success in Asia* (pp. 124–139). Hershey, PA: IGI Global. doi:10.4018/978-1-5225-1886-0.ch007

Muniapan, B., Gregory, M. L., & Ling, L. A. (2016). Marketing Education in Sarawak: Looking at It from the Employers' Viewpoint. In B. Smith & A. Porath (Eds.), *Global Perspectives on Contemporary Marketing Education* (pp. 112–130). Hershey, PA: IGI Global. doi:10.4018/978-1-4666-9784-3.ch008

Mupepi, M. G., & Mupepi, S. C. (2018). Amplifying the Significance of Systems Thinking in Organization. In M. Khosrow-Pour, D.B.A. (Ed.), Encyclopedia of Information Science and Technology, Fourth Edition (pp. 551-562). Hershey, PA: IGI Global. doi:10.4018/978-1-5225-2255-3.ch048

Mupepi, M., & Mupepi, S. (2015b). *Inside social constructs: MBAA International Conference March 25-27*. Chicago: Palmer House Hilton.

Mupepi, Tenkasi, & Sorensen. (2013). Creating High Impact Organizations in the SADC: Adapting OD Methods and Practices. In *Handbook for Strategic HR: Best Practices in Organization Development.* New York: Amacon.

Mupepi, G. M., Ram, V. T., Sorensen, P. F., & Mupepi, S. C. (2013). Creating high impact organization in the SADC: Adapting OD Methods and Practices. In J. Vogelsang, M. Townsend, & ... (Eds.), *Handbook for Strategic HR: Best Practices in Organization Development from OD Network.* New York: AMACOM.

Mupepi, M. (2005). *Transforming Village entrepreneurs into sustainable.* Ann Arbor, MI: UMI.

Mupepi, M. (2014). Can the Division of Labor Be Re-Engineered to Advance Organizational Dynamism? *SAGE Open*, *4*(2). doi:10.1177/2158244014536404

Mupepi, M. (2014, April). Can the division of labor be re-engineered to advance organizational dynamism? *SAGE Open*, 1–6.

Mupepi, M. (2015). *British Imperialism in Zimbabwe: The Organization Development of the First Chimurenga (1883-1904).* San Diego, CA: Cognella.

Mupepi, M. (2017b). Deconstructing Talent: Understanding know-how in organization. In M. Mupepi (Ed.), *Effective Talent Management Strategies for Organizational Success* (pp. 83–100). Hershey, PA: IGI Global; doi:10.4018/978-1-5225-1961-4.ch007

Mupepi, M. (2017b). *Effective Talent Management Strategies for Organizational Success.* Hershey, PA: IGI Global; doi:10.4018/978-1-5225-1961-4

Mupepi, M. G. (2017a). Using Communities of Practice to Identify Competencies. In K. Rasmussen, P. Northrup, & R. Colson (Eds.), *Handbook of Research on Competency-Based Education in University Settings* (pp. 157–167). Hershey, PA: IGI Global; doi:10.4018/978-1-5225-0932-5.ch008

Mupepi, M. G., Essila, J. C., Mensah, A. O., & Mupepi, S. C. (2018). Alternate Techniques to Chart Practicality in Organizations. In N. Baporikar (Ed.), *Knowledge Integration Strategies for Entrepreneurship and Sustainability* (pp. 334–352). Hershey, PA: IGI Global. doi:10.4018/978-1-5225-5115-7.ch016

Mupepi, M. G., & Mupepi, S. C. (2017). The Structure of Talent: A Co-Constructed Competency Perspective. In M. Mupepi (Ed.), *Effective Talent Management Strategies for Organizational Success* (pp. 57–73). Hershey, PA: IGI Global. doi:10.4018/978-1-5225-1961-4.ch005

Mupepi, M. G., Tenkasi, R. V., Sorensen, P. F., & Mupepi, S. C. (2013). Creating High Impact Organization in the SADC: Adapting OD Methods and Practices. In J. Vogelsang & M. Townsend (Eds.), *Handbook for Strategic HR*. New York: Amacon.

Mupepi, M., & Mupepi, S. (2015a). Charting Highly Productive Organization: Wrapping it all in Social Constructs. *International Journal of Productivity Management and Assessment Technologies*, *3*(1), 13–30. doi:10.4018/IJPMAT.2015010102

Murad, S. E., & Dowaji, S. (2017). Using Value-Based Approach for Managing Cloud-Based Services. In A. Turuk, B. Sahoo, & S. Addya (Eds.), *Resource Management and Efficiency in Cloud Computing Environments* (pp. 33–60). Hershey, PA: IGI Global. doi:10.4018/978-1-5225-1721-4.ch002

Mutahar, A. M., Daud, N. M., Thurasamy, R., Isaac, O., & Abdulsalam, R. (2018). The Mediating of Perceived Usefulness and Perceived Ease of Use: The Case of Mobile Banking in Yemen. *International Journal of Technology Diffusion*, *9*(2), 21–40. doi:10.4018/IJTD.2018040102

Myrtle, P. (2017). *Diversity in Organization*. London, UK: Cengage.

Nägele, C., & Stalder, B. E. (2017). Competence and the need for transferable skills. In Competence-based Vocational and Professional Education (pp. 739-753). Springer.

Naidoo, V. (2017). E-Learning and Management Education at African Universities. In N. Baporikar (Ed.), *Management Education for Global Leadership* (pp. 181–201). Hershey, PA: IGI Global. doi:10.4018/978-1-5225-1013-0.ch009

Naidoo, V., & Igbinakhase, I. (2018). Opportunities and Challenges of Knowledge Retention in SMEs. In N. Baporikar (Ed.), *Knowledge Integration Strategies for Entrepreneurship and Sustainability* (pp. 70–94). Hershey, PA: IGI Global. doi:10.4018/978-1-5225-5115-7.ch004

National Statistics Office. (2018). *Population of the United Kingdom*. Accessed 04/29/18 https://www.bing.com/search?q=population+of+the+uk&form=EDGEAR&qs=AS&cvid=3d330c3445684ce08cb35d6070a58aea&cc=US&setlang=en-US&PC=HCTS

Nayak, S., & Prabhu, N. (2017). Paradigm Shift in Management Education: Need for a Cross Functional Perspective. In N. Baporikar (Ed.), *Management Education for Global Leadership* (pp. 241–255). Hershey, PA: IGI Global. doi:10.4018/978-1-5225-1013-0.ch012

Ndede-Amadi, A. A. (2016). Student Interest in the IS Specialization as Predictor of the Success Potential of New Information Systems Programmes within the Schools of Business in Kenyan Public Universities. *International Journal of Information Systems and Social Change*, *7*(2), 63–79. doi:10.4018/IJISSC.2016040104

Nedelko, Z., & Potocan, V. (2016). Management Practices for Processes Optimization: Case of Slovenia. In G. Alor-Hernández, C. Sánchez-Ramírez, & J. García-Alcaraz (Eds.), *Handbook of Research on Managerial Strategies for Achieving Optimal Performance in Industrial Processes* (pp. 545–561). Hershey, PA: IGI Global. doi:10.4018/978-1-5225-0130-5.ch025

Nedelko, Z., & Potocan, V. (2017). Management Solutions in Non-Profit Organizations: Case of Slovenia. In V. Potocan, M. Üngan, & Z. Nedelko (Eds.), *Handbook of Research on Managerial Solutions in Non-Profit Organizations* (pp. 1–22). Hershey, PA: IGI Global. doi:10.4018/978-1-5225-0731-4.ch001

Nedelko, Z., & Potocan, V. (2017). Priority of Management Tools Utilization among Managers: International Comparison. In V. Wang (Ed.), *Encyclopedia of Strategic Leadership and Management* (pp. 1083–1094). Hershey, PA: IGI Global. doi:10.4018/978-1-5225-1049-9.ch075

Nedelko, Z., Raudeliūnienė, J., & Črešnar, R. (2018). Knowledge Dynamics in Supply Chain Management. In N. Baporikar (Ed.), *Knowledge Integration Strategies for Entrepreneurship and Sustainability* (pp. 150–166). Hershey, PA: IGI Global. doi:10.4018/978-1-5225-5115-7.ch008

Negroponte, N. (1995). *Being Digital*. New York: Knopf.

Ng, A. Y. (2012). *Deep Learning of Invariant Features via Simulated Fixations in Video*. Accessed 05/10/18 http://papers.nips.cc/author/andrew-y-ng-1853

Nguyen, H. T., & Hipsher, S. A. (2018). Innovation and Creativity Used by Private Sector Firms in a Resources-Constrained Environment. In S. Hipsher (Ed.), *Examining the Private Sector's Role in Wealth Creation and Poverty Reduction* (pp. 219–238). Hershey, PA: IGI Global. doi:10.4018/978-1-5225-3117-3.ch010

Nickelsen, N. C. M., & Elkjaer, B. (2014, April). *Performing task integration – the dilemmas of relational coordination and knowledge sharing*. Paper presented at the Organizational Learning and Knowledge Capabilities Conference, Oslo, Norway.

Nonaka, I. (1991, November-December). The knowledge creating company. *Harvard Business Review*, *69*, 96–104.

Nonaka, I., & Takeuchi, H. (1995). *The knowledge creating company: how Japanese companies create the dynamics of innovation*. New York: Oxford University Press.

Nonaka, I., & Takeuchi, H. (1995). *The knowledge-creating company*. New York, NY: Oxford University Press.

Nonaka, I., Toyama, R., & Konno, N. (2000). SECI, *Ba* and leadership: A unified model of dynamic knowledge creation. *Long Range Planning*, *33*(1), 5–34. doi:10.1016/S0024-6301(99)00115-6

Norris & Laub. (2018). *As America Changes, Some Anxious Whites Feel Left Behind Demographic shifts rippling across the nation are fueling fears that their culture and standing are under threat*. Academic Press.

Norris, M., & Laub, G. (2018, April). As America changes, some anxious whites feel left behind. *National Geographic*. Retrieved from https://www.nationalgeographic.com/magazine/2018/04/race-rising-anxiety-white-america/

Nycz, M., & Pólkowski, Z. (2016). Business Intelligence as a Modern IT Supporting Management of Local Government Units in Poland. *International Journal of Knowledge and Systems Science*, *7*(4), 1–18. doi:10.4018/IJKSS.2016100101

O'Keeffe, T. (2002). Organizational Learning: A new perspective. *Journal of European Industrial Training*, *26*(2), 130–141. doi:10.1108/03090590210422012

Obaji, N. O., Senin, A. A., & Olugu, M. U. (2016). Supportive Government Policy as a Mechanism for Business Incubation Performance in Nigeria. *International Journal of Information Systems and Social Change*, *7*(4), 52–66. doi:10.4018/IJISSC.2016100103

Obicci, P. A. (2017). Risk Sharing in a Partnership. In *Risk Management Strategies in Public-Private Partnerships* (pp. 115–152). Hershey, PA: IGI Global. doi:10.4018/978-1-5225-2503-5.ch004

Obidallah, W. J., & Raahemi, B. (2017). Managing Changes in Service Oriented Virtual Organizations: A Structural and Procedural Framework to Facilitate the Process of Change. *Journal of Electronic Commerce in Organizations*, *15*(1), 59–83. doi:10.4018/JECO.2017010104

Ojala, M. (2012, July). Minding Your Own Business: Social Media Invades Business Research. *Online: Exploring Technology & Resources for Information Professionals,* 51-53.

Ojasalo, J., & Ojasalo, K. (2016). Service Logic Business Model Canvas for Lean Development of SMEs and Start-Ups. In N. Baporikar (Ed.), *Handbook of Research on Entrepreneurship in the Contemporary Knowledge-Based Global Economy* (pp. 217–243). Hershey, PA: IGI Global. doi:10.4018/978-1-4666-8798-1.ch010

Ojo, O. (2017). Impact of Innovation on the Entrepreneurial Success in Selected Business Enterprises in South-West Nigeria. *International Journal of Innovation in the Digital Economy, 8*(2), 29–38. doi:10.4018/IJIDE.2017040103

Okdinawati, L., Simatupang, T. M., & Sunitiyoso, Y. (2017). Multi-Agent Reinforcement Learning for Value Co-Creation of Collaborative Transportation Management (CTM). *International Journal of Information Systems and Supply Chain Management, 10*(3), 84–95. doi:10.4018/IJISSCM.2017070105

Orna, E. (1999). *Practical Information Policies* (2nd ed.). Cambridge, UK: Gower.

Ortner, E., Mevius, M., Wiedmann, P., & Kurz, F. (2016). Design of Interactional Decision Support Applications for E-Participation in Smart Cities. *International Journal of Electronic Government Research, 12*(2), 18–38. doi:10.4018/IJEGR.2016040102

Pal, K. (2018). Building High Quality Big Data-Based Applications in Supply Chains. In A. Kumar & S. Saurav (Eds.), *Supply Chain Management Strategies and Risk Assessment in Retail Environments* (pp. 1–24). Hershey, PA: IGI Global. doi:10.4018/978-1-5225-3056-5.ch001

Palos-Sanchez, P. R., & Correia, M. B. (2018). Perspectives of the Adoption of Cloud Computing in the Tourism Sector. In J. Rodrigues, C. Ramos, P. Cardoso, & C. Henriques (Eds.), *Handbook of Research on Technological Developments for Cultural Heritage and eTourism Applications* (pp. 377–400). Hershey, PA: IGI Global. doi:10.4018/978-1-5225-2927-9.ch018

Parry, V. K., & Lind, M. L. (2016). Alignment of Business Strategy and Information Technology Considering Information Technology Governance, Project Portfolio Control, and Risk Management. *International Journal of Information Technology Project Management, 7*(4), 21–37. doi:10.4018/IJITPM.2016100102

Pashkova, N., Trujillo-Barrera, A., Apostolakis, G., Van Dijk, G., Drakos, P. D., & Baourakis, G. (2016). Business Management Models of Microfinance Institutions (MFIs) in Africa: A Study into Their Enabling Environments. *International Journal of Food and Beverage Manufacturing and Business Models*, *1*(2), 63–82. doi:10.4018/IJFBMBM.2016070105

Patiño, B. E. (2017). New Generation Management by Convergence and Individual Identity: A Systemic and Human-Oriented Approach. In N. Baporikar (Ed.), *Innovation and Shifting Perspectives in Management Education* (pp. 119–143). Hershey, PA: IGI Global. doi:10.4018/978-1-5225-1019-2.ch006

Pawliczek, A., & Rössler, M. (2017). Knowledge of Management Tools and Systems in SMEs: Knowledge Transfer in Management. In A. Bencsik (Ed.), *Knowledge Management Initiatives and Strategies in Small and Medium Enterprises* (pp. 180–203). Hershey, PA: IGI Global. doi:10.4018/978-1-5225-1642-2.ch009

Pejic-Bach, M., Omazic, M. A., Aleksic, A., & Zoroja, J. (2018). Knowledge-Based Decision Making: A Multi-Case Analysis. In R. Leon (Ed.), *Managerial Strategies for Business Sustainability During Turbulent Times* (pp. 160–184). Hershey, PA: IGI Global. doi:10.4018/978-1-5225-2716-9.ch009

Penzias, A. (1989). *Ideas and Information: Managing in a High-Tech World*. New York: W. W. Norton.

Penzias, A. (1995). *Harmony: Business, Technology & Life After Paperwork*. Harper Collins.

Perano, M., Hysa, X., & Calabrese, M. (2018). Strategic Planning, Cultural Context, and Business Continuity Management: Business Cases in the City of Shkoder. In A. Presenza & L. Sheehan (Eds.), *Geopolitics and Strategic Management in the Global Economy* (pp. 57–77). Hershey, PA: IGI Global. doi:10.4018/978-1-5225-2673-5.ch004

Pereira, R., Mira da Silva, M., & Lapão, L. V. (2017). IT Governance Maturity Patterns in Portuguese Healthcare. In S. De Haes & W. Van Grembergen (Eds.), *Strategic IT Governance and Alignment in Business Settings* (pp. 24–52). Hershey, PA: IGI Global. doi:10.4018/978-1-5225-0861-8.ch002

Pérez-Uribe, R. I., Torres, D. A., Jurado, S. P., & Prada, D. M. (2018). Cloud Tools for the Development of Project Management in SMEs. In R. Perez-Uribe, C. Salcedo-Perez, & D. Ocampo-Guzman (Eds.), *Handbook of Research on Intrapreneurship and Organizational Sustainability in SMEs* (pp. 95–120). Hershey, PA: IGI Global. doi:10.4018/978-1-5225-3543-0.ch005

Perez-Uribe, R., & Ocampo-Guzman, D. (2016). Conflict within Colombian Family Owned SMEs: An Explosive Blend between Feelings and Business. In J. Saiz-Álvarez (Ed.), *Handbook of Research on Social Entrepreneurship and Solidarity Economics* (pp. 329–354). Hershey, PA: IGI Global. doi:10.4018/978-1-5225-0097-1.ch017

Petrisor, I., & Cozmiuc, D. (2017). Global Supply Chain Management Organization at Siemens in the Advent of Industry 4.0. In L. Saglietto & C. Cezanne (Eds.), *Global Intermediation and Logistics Service Providers* (pp. 123–142). Hershey, PA: IGI Global. doi:10.4018/978-1-5225-2133-4.ch007

Pfeffer, J. (1994). *Competitive advantage through people: Unleashing the power of the workforce*. Boston: Harvard Business School Press.

Phillips, L. (2011). *The promise of dialogue: The dialogic turn in the production and communication of knowledge*. Amsterdam: John Benjamins Pub. Co. doi:10.1075/ds.12

Pierce, J. M., Velliaris, D. M., & Edwards, J. (2017). A Living Case Study: A Journey Not a Destination. In N. Silton (Ed.), *Exploring the Benefits of Creativity in Education, Media, and the Arts* (pp. 158–178). Hershey, PA: IGI Global. doi:10.4018/978-1-5225-0504-4.ch008

Platsis, G. (2018). The Human Factor: Cyber Security's Greatest Challenge. *International Journal of Public Administration in the Digital Age*, *5*(2), 23–39. doi:10.4018/IJPADA.2018040103

Polanyi, M. (1966). *The Tacit Dimension*. Chicago: University of Chicago Press.

Porter, M. E., & Millar, V. E. (1985). How information gives you competitive advantage. *Harvard Business Review*, *63*(4), 149–160.

Prahalad, C., & Hamel, G. (1990). The core competence of the corporation. *Harvard Business Review*, *68*, 79–91.

Prescott, J. E., & Miller, S. H. (2002). *Inteligência competitiva na prática: técnicas e práticas bem sucedidas para conquistar mercados*. Rio de Janeiro: Campus.

Prior, V. (2006). *Competitive Intelligence: An Introduction*. Retrieved 06-10-2008 from http://www.freepint.com/issues/050106.htm#feature

Prior, V. (2007). *DIY Detection: Competitive Intelligence for SMEs*. Retrieved from http://web.freepint.com/go/features/2483

Qualman, E. (2010). *Socialnomics: Como os media sociais estão a transformar o modo como vivemos e como fazemos negócios* (1st ed.). Lisboa: Presença.

Qvortrup, L. (2000). *Det hyperkomplekse samfund: 14 fortællinger om informationssamfundet* (2nd ed.). København: Gyldendal.

Radosavljevic, M., & Andjelkovic, A. (2017). Multi-Criteria Decision Making Approach for Choosing Business Process for the Improvement: Upgrading of the Six Sigma Methodology. In J. Stanković, P. Delias, S. Marinković, & S. Rochhia (Eds.), *Tools and Techniques for Economic Decision Analysis* (pp. 225–247). Hershey, PA: IGI Global. doi:10.4018/978-1-5225-0959-2.ch011

Radovic, V. M. (2017). Corporate Sustainability and Responsibility and Disaster Risk Reduction: A Serbian Overview. In M. Camilleri (Ed.), *CSR 2.0 and the New Era of Corporate Citizenship* (pp. 147–164). Hershey, PA: IGI Global. doi:10.4018/978-1-5225-1842-6.ch008

Radulescu, A. S. (2014). A Perspective on e-learning and cloud computing. *Procedia - Social and Behavioral Sciences,* 141, 1084–1088.

Raghunath, K. M., Devi, S. L., & Patro, C. S. (2018). Impact of Risk Assessment Models on Risk Factors: A Holistic Outlook. In K. Strang, M. Korstanje, & N. Vajjhala (Eds.), *Research, Practices, and Innovations in Global Risk and Contingency Management* (pp. 134–153). Hershey, PA: IGI Global. doi:10.4018/978-1-5225-4754-9.ch008

Raley & Lucas. (2006). Stereotype or Success? *Journal of Homosexuality, 51*(2), 19-38.

Raman, A., & Goyal, D. P. (2017). Extending IMPLEMENT Framework for Enterprise Information Systems Implementation to Information System Innovation. In M. Tavana (Ed.), *Enterprise Information Systems and the Digitalization of Business Functions* (pp. 137–177). Hershey, PA: IGI Global. doi:10.4018/978-1-5225-2382-6.ch007

Rao, M. (2003). *Leading with knowledge*. New Delhi: TATA McGraw-Hill.

Rao, Y., & Zhang, Y. (2017). The Construction and Development of Academic Library Digital Special Subject Databases. In L. Ruan, Q. Zhu, & Y. Ye (Eds.), *Academic Library Development and Administration in China* (pp. 163–183). Hershey, PA: IGI Global. doi:10.4018/978-1-5225-0550-1.ch010

Rasquilha, L. (2010). *Tendências e Gestão da Inovação: como aplicar as tendências na estratégia de inovação empresarial*. Lousã: Verlag Dashöfer.

Ravasan, A. Z., Mohammadi, M. M., & Hamidi, H. (2018). An Investigation Into the Critical Success Factors of Implementing Information Technology Service Management Frameworks. In K. Jakobs (Ed.), *Corporate and Global Standardization Initiatives in Contemporary Society* (pp. 200–218). Hershey, PA: IGI Global. doi:10.4018/978-1-5225-5320-5.ch009

Redman, T. (1996). *Data Quality for the Information Age*. Norwood: Artech House.

Renna, P., Izzo, C., & Romaniello, T. (2016). The Business Process Management Systems to Support Continuous Improvements. In W. Nuninger & J. Châtelet (Eds.), *Handbook of Research on Quality Assurance and Value Management in Higher Education* (pp. 237–256). Hershey, PA: IGI Global. doi:10.4018/978-1-5225-0024-7.ch009

Revelli, C. (2000). *Inteligência estratégica na Internet: como desenvolver eficazmente actividades de monitorização e de pesquisa nas redes*. Instituto Piaget.

Rezaie, S., Mirabedini, S. J., & Abtahi, A. (2018). Designing a Model for Implementation of Business Intelligence in the Banking Industry. *International Journal of Enterprise Information Systems*, *14*(1), 77–103. doi:10.4018/IJEIS.2018010105

Rho, S., & Vasilakos, A. V. (2018). *Intelligent collaborative system and service in value network for enterprise computing*. Academic Press.

Ria, S., Cox, M. J., Quinn, B. F., Bakir, A., & Woolford, M. J. (2018). A scoring system for assessing learning progression of dental students' clinical skills using haptic virtual workstations. *Journal of Dental Education*, *82*(3), 277–285. doi:10.21815/JDE.018.028 PMID:29496806

Ribault, J.-M., Martinet, B., & Lebidois, D. (1995). *A Gestão das Tecnologias* (1st ed.). Lisboa: D. Quixote.

Riccò, R. (2016). Diversity Management: Bringing Equality, Equity, and Inclusion in the Workplace. In J. Prescott (Ed.), *Handbook of Research on Race, Gender, and the Fight for Equality* (pp. 335–359). Hershey, PA: IGI Global. doi:10.4018/978-1-5225-0047-6.ch015

Rich, B. R., & Janos, L. (2015). *A personal memoir of my years of Lockheed.* New York: Simon and Schuster Audio Books.

Rioch, M. J. (1970). The work of Wilfred Bion. Psychiatry, 33, 56–66. Smith, E. A. (2001). The role of tacit and explicit knowledge in the workplace. *Journal of Knowledge Management*, *5*(4), 311–321.

Robles, F. (2012). *A look at what happened the night Trayvon Martin died.* Accessed 04/29/18 http://www.tampabay.com/news/publicsafety/crime/a-look-at-what-happened-the-night-trayvon-martin-died/1223083

Rogers, E. M. (1983). *Diffusion of innovations.* New York: Free Press.

Romano, L., Grimaldi, R., & Colasuonno, F. S. (2017). Demand Management as a Success Factor in Project Portfolio Management. In L. Romano (Ed.), *Project Portfolio Management Strategies for Effective Organizational Operations* (pp. 202–219). Hershey, PA: IGI Global. doi:10.4018/978-1-5225-2151-8.ch008

Rostek, K. B. (2016). Risk Management: Role and Importance in Business Organization. In D. Jakóbczak (Ed.), *Analyzing Risk through Probabilistic Modeling in Operations Research* (pp. 149–178). Hershey, PA: IGI Global. doi:10.4018/978-1-4666-9458-3.ch007

Rouhani, S., & Savoji, S. R. (2016). A Success Assessment Model for BI Tools Implementation: An Empirical Study of Banking Industry. *International Journal of Business Intelligence Research*, *7*(1), 25–44. doi:10.4018/IJBIR.2016010103

Royal Society. (2017). *Reforms to the UK's higher education, research and innovation system.* Retrieved from https://royalsociety.org/topics-policy/projects/higher-education-research-innovation-system/

Ruan, Z. (2016). A Corpus-Based Functional Analysis of Complex Nominal Groups in Written Business Discourse: The Case of "Business". *International Journal of Computer-Assisted Language Learning and Teaching*, *6*(2), 74–90. doi:10.4018/IJCALLT.2016040105

Ruhi, U. (2018). Towards an Interdisciplinary Socio-Technical Definition of Virtual Communities. In M. Khosrow-Pour, D.B.A. (Ed.), Encyclopedia of Information Science and Technology, Fourth Edition (pp. 4278-4295). Hershey, PA: IGI Global. doi:10.4018/978-1-5225-2255-3.ch371

Russell, M. (2011). *Mining the Social Web: Analyzing Data from Facebook, Twitter, LinkedIn, and Other Social Media Sites* (1st ed.). O'Reilly Media.

Rustmann, F., Jr. (2002). CIA, Inc.: Espionage and the Craft of Business Intelligence (1ª ed.). Dulles: Brassey's.

Ryan, J., Doster, B., Daily, S., & Lewis, C. (2016). A Case Study Perspective for Balanced Perioperative Workflow Achievement through Data-Driven Process Improvement. *International Journal of Healthcare Information Systems and Informatics*, *11*(3), 19–41. doi:10.4018/IJHISI.2016070102

Safari, M. R., & Jiang, Q. (2018). The Theory and Practice of IT Governance Maturity and Strategies Alignment: Evidence From Banking Industry. *Journal of Global Information Management*, *26*(2), 127–146. doi:10.4018/JGIM.2018040106

Safko, L. (2010). *The Social Media Bible: Tactics, Tools & Strategies for Business Success* (2nd ed.). Hoboken, NJ: John Wiley & Sons.

Sage, N. (2013). *How to create business value from social intelligence*. Retrieved 30-05-2013, from http://www.computerweekly.com/opinion/How-to-create-business-value-from-social-intelligence

Saha, D. (2018). *Advances in Data Communications and Networking for Digital Business Transformation*. Hershey, PA: IGI Global; doi:10.4018/978-1-5225-5323-6

Sahoo, J., Pati, B., & Mohanty, B. (2017). Knowledge Management as an Academic Discipline: An Assessment. In B. Gunjal (Ed.), *Managing Knowledge and Scholarly Assets in Academic Libraries* (pp. 99–126). Hershey, PA: IGI Global. doi:10.4018/978-1-5225-1741-2.ch005

Saini, D. (2017). Relevance of Teaching Values and Ethics in Management Education. In N. Baporikar (Ed.), *Management Education for Global Leadership* (pp. 90–111). Hershey, PA: IGI Global. doi:10.4018/978-1-5225-1013-0.ch005

Saiti, A., & Prokopiadou, G. (2008). Post-graduate students and learning environments: Users' perceptions regarding the choice of information sources. *The International Information & Library Review*, *40*, 94–103.

Salas, E., Diazgranandos, D., Klein, C., Burke, C. S., Stagl, K. C., Goodwin, G. F., & Halpin, S. M. (2008). Does Team Training Improve Team Performance? A Meta-Analysis. *Human Factors: the Journal of the Human Factors and Ergonomics Society.*, *50*(6), 903–933. doi:10.1518/001872008X375009 PMID:19292013

Sambhanthan, A. (2017). Assessing and Benchmarking Sustainability in Organisations: An Integrated Conceptual Model. *International Journal of Systems and Service-Oriented Engineering*, *7*(4), 22–43. doi:10.4018/IJSSOE.2017100102

Sambhanthan, A., & Potdar, V. (2017). A Study of the Parameters Impacting Sustainability in Information Technology Organizations. *International Journal of Knowledge-Based Organizations*, *7*(3), 27–39. doi:10.4018/IJKBO.2017070103

Sánchez-Fernández, M. D., & Manríquez, M. R. (2018). The Entrepreneurial Spirit Based on Social Values: The Digital Generation. In P. Isaias & L. Carvalho (Eds.), *User Innovation and the Entrepreneurship Phenomenon in the Digital Economy* (pp. 173–193). Hershey, PA: IGI Global. doi:10.4018/978-1-5225-2826-5.ch009

Sanchez-Ruiz, L., & Blanco, B. (2017). Process Management for SMEs: Barriers, Enablers, and Benefits. In M. Vemić (Ed.), *Optimal Management Strategies in Small and Medium Enterprises* (pp. 293–319). Hershey, PA: IGI Global. doi:10.4018/978-1-5225-1949-2.ch014

Sandars, J., & Schroter, S. (2007). Web 2.0 technologies for undergraduate and postgraduate medical education: An online survey. *Postgraduate Medical Journal*, *83*(986), 759–762.

Sanz, L. F., Gómez-Pérez, J., & Castillo-Martinez, A. (2018). Analysis of the European ICT Competence Frameworks. In V. Ahuja & S. Rathore (Eds.), *Multidisciplinary Perspectives on Human Capital and Information Technology Professionals* (pp. 225–245). Hershey, PA: IGI Global. doi:10.4018/978-1-5225-5297-0.ch012

Sarvepalli, A., & Godin, J. (2017). Business Process Management in the Classroom. *Journal of Cases on Information Technology*, *19*(2), 17–28. doi:10.4018/JCIT.2017040102

Satpathy, B., & Muniapan, B. (2016). Ancient Wisdom for Transformational Leadership and Its Insights from the Bhagavad-Gita. In U. Aung & P. Ordoñez de Pablos (Eds.), *Managerial Strategies and Practice in the Asian Business Sector* (pp. 1–10). Hershey, PA: IGI Global. doi:10.4018/978-1-4666-9758-4.ch001

Saygili, E. E., Ozturkoglu, Y., & Kocakulah, M. C. (2017). End Users' Perceptions of Critical Success Factors in ERP Applications. *International Journal of Enterprise Information Systems, 13*(4), 58–75. doi:10.4018/IJEIS.2017100104

Saygili, E. E., & Saygili, A. T. (2017). Contemporary Issues in Enterprise Information Systems: A Critical Review of CSFs in ERP Implementations. In M. Tavana (Ed.), *Enterprise Information Systems and the Digitalization of Business Functions* (pp. 120–136). Hershey, PA: IGI Global. doi:10.4018/978-1-5225-2382-6.ch006

Schaffer, N. (2011). *Maximizing LinkedIn for Sales and Social Media Marketing: An Unofficial, Practical Guide to Selling & Developing B2B Business on LinkedIn.* CreateSpace Independent Publishing Platform.

Schein, E. (2013). *Corporate culture: How to think ab out and define culture.* In *Handbook for Strategic HR: Best practices in Organization Development.* New York: Amacon.

Schein, E. (2013). A Brief and Provocative History of Participation. In J. Vogelsang & M. Townsend (Eds.), *Handbook for Strategic HR*. New York: Amacom.

Schein, E. (2013). Corporate culture: How to think ab out and define culture. In E. Vogelsang & M. Townsend (Eds.), *Handbook for Strategic HR: Best practices in Organization Development*. New York: Amacon.

Scott, D. (2008). *As Novas Regras de Marketing e Relações Públicas: Como usar os blogues, o podcasting, os media online e as notas informativas para chegar directamente aos consumidores*. Porto: Ideias de Ler.

Seidenstricker, S., & Antonino, A. (2018). Business Model Innovation-Oriented Technology Management for Emergent Technologies. In M. Khosrow-Pour, D.B.A. (Ed.), Encyclopedia of Information Science and Technology, Fourth Edition (pp. 4560-4569). Hershey, PA: IGI Global. doi:10.4018/978-1-5225-2255-3.ch396

Senaratne, S., & Gunarathne, A. D. (2017). Excellence Perspective for Management Education from a Global Accountants' Hub in Asia. In N. Baporikar (Ed.), *Management Education for Global Leadership* (pp. 158–180). Hershey, PA: IGI Global. doi:10.4018/978-1-5225-1013-0.ch008

Senge, P. M. (1990). The art and practice of the learning organization. *The new paradigm in business: Emerging strategies for leadership and organizational change*, 126-138. Retrieved from http://www.giee.ntnu.edu.tw/files/archive/380_9e53918d

Senge, P., & Kleiner, A. (1999). The Dance of Change. New York: Currency Doubleday.

Senge, P. (1990). *The Fifth Discipline: The art and practice of the learning organization*. New York: Doubleday.

Senge, P. (2006). *The Fifth Discipline: The Art and Practice of the Learning Organization*. New York: Doubleday.

Sensuse, D. I., & Cahyaningsih, E. (2018). Knowledge Management Models: A Summative Review. *International Journal of Information Systems in the Service Sector*, *10*(1), 71–100. doi:10.4018/IJISSS.2018010105

Sensuse, D. I., Wibowo, W. C., & Cahyaningsih, E. (2016). Indonesian Government Knowledge Management Model: A Theoretical Model. *Information Resources Management Journal*, *29*(1), 91–108. doi:10.4018/irmj.2016010106

Seth, M., Goyal, D., & Kiran, R. (2017). Diminution of Impediments in Implementation of Supply Chain Management Information System for Enhancing its Effectiveness in Indian Automobile Industry. *Journal of Global Information Management*, *25*(3), 1–20. doi:10.4018/JGIM.2017070101

Seyal, A. H., & Rahman, M. N. (2017). Investigating Impact of Inter-Organizational Factors in Measuring ERP Systems Success: Bruneian Perspectives. In M. Tavana (Ed.), *Enterprise Information Systems and the Digitalization of Business Functions* (pp. 178–204). Hershey, PA: IGI Global. doi:10.4018/978-1-5225-2382-6.ch008

Shaikh, A. A., & Karjaluoto, H. (2016). On Some Misconceptions Concerning Digital Banking and Alternative Delivery Channels. *International Journal of E-Business Research*, *12*(3), 1–16. doi:10.4018/IJEBR.2016070101

Shams, S. M. (2016). Stakeholder Relationship Management in Online Business and Competitive Value Propositions: Evidence from the Sports Industry. *International Journal of Online Marketing*, *6*(2), 1–17. doi:10.4018/IJOM.2016040101

Shamsuzzoha, A. (2016). Management of Risk and Resilience within Collaborative Business Network. In R. Addo-Tenkorang, J. Kantola, P. Helo, & A. Shamsuzzoha (Eds.), *Supply Chain Strategies and the Engineer-to-Order Approach* (pp. 143–159). Hershey, PA: IGI Global. doi:10.4018/978-1-5225-0021-6.ch008

Shapiro, C., & Varian, H. (1999). *Information Rules: A Strategic Guide to the Network Economy* (1st ed.). Boston: Harvard Business School Press.

Shaqrah, A. A. (2018). Analyzing Business Intelligence Systems Based on 7s Model of McKinsey. *International Journal of Business Intelligence Research*, *9*(1), 53–63. doi:10.4018/IJBIR.2018010104

Sharma, A. J. (2017). Enhancing Sustainability through Experiential Learning in Management Education. In N. Baporikar (Ed.), *Management Education for Global Leadership* (pp. 256–274). Hershey, PA: IGI Global. doi:10.4018/978-1-5225-1013-0.ch013

Sherbin, L., & Rashid, R. (2017). Diversity doesn't stick without inclusion. *Harvard Business Review*.

Shetty, K. P. (2017). Responsible Global Leadership: Ethical Challenges in Management Education. In N. Baporikar (Ed.), *Innovation and Shifting Perspectives in Management Education* (pp. 194–223). Hershey, PA: IGI Global. doi:10.4018/978-1-5225-1019-2.ch009

Sinthupundaja, J., & Kohda, Y. (2017). Effects of Corporate Social Responsibility and Creating Shared Value on Sustainability. *International Journal of Sustainable Entrepreneurship and Corporate Social Responsibility*, *2*(1), 27–38. doi:10.4018/IJSECSR.2017010103

Škarica, I., & Hrgović, A. V. (2018). Implementation of Total Quality Management Principles in Public Health Institutes in the Republic of Croatia. *International Journal of Productivity Management and Assessment Technologies*, *6*(1), 1–16. doi:10.4018/IJPMAT.2018010101

Skunkworks, L. (2016). *Lockheed SR-71 Blackbird*. Accessed 11/14/16 http://www.bing.com/images/search?q=skunk+works&view=

Smuts, H., Kotzé, P., Van der Merwe, A., & Loock, M. (2017). Framework for Managing Shared Knowledge in an Information Systems Outsourcing Context. *International Journal of Knowledge Management*, *13*(4), 1–30. doi:10.4018/IJKM.2017100101

Soares, E. R., & Zaidan, F. H. (2016). Information Architecture and Business Modeling in Modern Organizations of Information Technology: Professional Career Plan in Organizations IT. In G. Jamil, J. Poças Rascão, F. Ribeiro, & A. Malheiro da Silva (Eds.), *Handbook of Research on Information Architecture and Management in Modern Organizations* (pp. 439–457). Hershey, PA: IGI Global. doi:10.4018/978-1-4666-8637-3.ch020

Sousa, M. J., Cruz, R., Dias, I., & Caracol, C. (2017). Information Management Systems in the Supply Chain. In G. Jamil, A. Soares, & C. Pessoa (Eds.), *Handbook of Research on Information Management for Effective Logistics and Supply Chains* (pp. 469–485). Hershey, PA: IGI Global. doi:10.4018/978-1-5225-0973-8.ch025

Spears, R., Ellemers, N., & Doosje, B. (2005). Let me count the ways in which I respect thee: Does competence compensate or compromise lack of liking from the group? *European Journal of Social Psychology*, *35*(2), 263–279. doi:10.1002/ejsp.248

Spencer, J. (2012). Ways of being. *Philosophy Compass*, *7*(12), 910–918. doi:10.1111/j.1747-9991.2012.00527.x

Spremic, M., Turulja, L., & Bajgoric, N. (2018). Two Approaches in Assessing Business Continuity Management Attitudes in the Organizational Context. In N. Bajgoric (Ed.), *Always-On Enterprise Information Systems for Modern Organizations* (pp. 159–183). Hershey, PA: IGI Global. doi:10.4018/978-1-5225-3704-5.ch008

Steckerl, S. (2007). *Survival Guide: Online Social Networking*. Retrieved 12/12/2012, from http://web.fumsi.com/go/article/use/2346

Steenkamp, A. L. (2018). Some Insights in Computer Science and Information Technology. In *Examining the Changing Role of Supervision in Doctoral Research Projects: Emerging Research and Opportunities* (pp. 113–133). Hershey, PA: IGI Global. doi:10.4018/978-1-5225-2610-0.ch005

Stern, J. M., Dubeck, M. M., & Dick, A. (2018). Using early grade reading assessment (EGRA) data for targeted instructional support: Learning profiles and instructional needs in Indonesia. *International Journal of Educational Development*, *61*, 64–71. doi:10.1016/j.ijedudev.2017.12.003

Stichweh, R. (2011). Systems Theory. In B. Badie & ... (Eds.), *International Encyclopedia of Political Science* (Vol. 8, pp. 2579–2582). New York: Sage. doi:10.4135/9781412959636.n597

Stoner, J. A. F., Wankel, C. B., & Werner, F. M. (1999). The Need for continuous improvement. In Juran's Quality Handbook (5th ed.). New York: McGraw-Hill.

Studdard, N., Dawson, M., Burton, S. L., Jackson, N., Leonard, B., Quisenberry, W., & Rahim, E. (2016). Nurturing Social Entrepreneurship and Building Social Entrepreneurial Self-Efficacy: Focusing on Primary and Secondary Schooling to Develop Future Social Entrepreneurs. In Z. Fields (Ed.), *Incorporating Business Models and Strategies into Social Entrepreneurship* (pp. 154–175). Hershey, PA: IGI Global. doi:10.4018/978-1-4666-8748-6.ch010

Sun, Z. (2016). A Framework for Developing Management Intelligent Systems. *International Journal of Systems and Service-Oriented Engineering*, *6*(1), 37–53. doi:10.4018/IJSSOE.2016010103

Surowiecki, J. (2007). *A Sabedoria das Multidões: Como a inteligência colectiva transforma a economia e a sociedade* (1st ed.). Porto: Lua de Papel.

Swami, B., & Mphele, G. T. (2016). Problems Preventing Growth of Small Entrepreneurs: A Case Study of a Few Small Entrepreneurs in Botswana Sub-Urban Areas. In N. Baporikar (Ed.), *Handbook of Research on Entrepreneurship in the Contemporary Knowledge-Based Global Economy* (pp. 479–508). Hershey, PA: IGI Global. doi:10.4018/978-1-4666-8798-1.ch020

Syahirah, S. S. S., Bibi, H. F., & Bazli, H. M. (2018). Leadership, Policy and Governance in Malaysia: A Study on Gen Y Perception and Expectation. In *International Conference on Kansei Engineering & Emotion Research* (pp. 683-691). Springer.

Tabach, A., & Croteau, A. (2017). Configurations of Information Technology Governance Practices and Business Unit Performance. *International Journal of IT/Business Alignment and Governance*, *8*(2), 1–27. doi:10.4018/IJITBAG.2017070101

Taborda, J. P., & Ferreira, M. D. (2002). *Competitive intelligence: conceitos, práticas e benefícios*. Pergaminho.

Talaue, G. M., & Iqbal, T. (2017). Assessment of e-Business Mode of Selected Private Universities in the Philippines and Pakistan. *International Journal of Online Marketing*, *7*(4), 63–77. doi:10.4018/IJOM.2017100105

Tambo, T. (2018). Fashion Retail Innovation: About Context, Antecedents, and Outcome in Technological Change Projects. In I. Management Association (Ed.), Fashion and Textiles: Breakthroughs in Research and Practice (pp. 233-260). Hershey, PA: IGI Global. doi:10.4018/978-1-5225-3432-7.ch010

Tambo, T., & Mikkelsen, O. E. (2016). Fashion Supply Chain Optimization: Linking Make-to-Order Purchasing and B2B E-Commerce. In S. Joshi & R. Joshi (Eds.), *Designing and Implementing Global Supply Chain Management* (pp. 1–21). Hershey, PA: IGI Global. doi:10.4018/978-1-4666-9720-1.ch001

Tam, G. C. (2017). Project Manager Sustainability Competence. In *Managerial Strategies and Green Solutions for Project Sustainability* (pp. 178–207). Hershey, PA: IGI Global. doi:10.4018/978-1-5225-2371-0.ch008

Tandon, K. (2016). Innovative Andragogy: The Paradigm Shift to Heutagogy. In S. Tiwari & L. Nafees (Eds.), *Innovative Management Education Pedagogies for Preparing Next-Generation Leaders* (pp. 238–257). Hershey, PA: IGI Global. doi:10.4018/978-1-4666-9691-4.ch014

Tantau, A. D., & Frăţilă, L. C. (2018). Information and Management System for Renewable Energy Business. In *Entrepreneurship and Business Development in the Renewable Energy Sector* (pp. 200–244). Hershey, PA: IGI Global. doi:10.4018/978-1-5225-3625-3.ch006

Tapscott, D., & Williams, A. (2008). Wikinomics: A Nova Economia das Multidões Inteligentes (1ª ed.). Matosinhos: Quidnovi.

Tapscott, D. (1995). *The Digital Economy: Promise and Peril in the Age of Networked Intelligence*. New York: McGraw-Hill.

Tapscott, D. (1999). *Creating Value in the Network Economy*. Boston: Harvard Business School Press.

Tapscott, D., Ticoll, D., & Lowy, A. (2000). *Digital Capital: Harnessing the Power of Business Webs*. Boston: Harvard Business School Press.

Teixeira, N., Pardal, P. N., & Rafael, B. G. (2018). Internationalization, Financial Performance, and Organizational Challenges: A Success Case in Portugal. In L. Carvalho (Ed.), *Handbook of Research on Entrepreneurial Ecosystems and Social Dynamics in a Globalized World* (pp. 379–423). Hershey, PA: IGI Global. doi:10.4018/978-1-5225-3525-6.ch017

Tenkasi, R. V., & Mohrman, S. (1999). Global change as contextual collaborative knowledge creation. In D. L. Cooperrider & J. E. Dutton (Eds.), *Organizational Dimensions of Global Change: No limits to cooperation*. Thousand Oaks, CA: Sage. doi:10.4135/9781452231419.n5

The Entrepreneur. (2015). *Bootstrapping your start-up*. Retrieved from http://www.entrepreneur.com/article/55776

Thiel, K. (2012). *Creating Usable Customer Intelligence from Social Media Data: Network Analytics meets Text Mining*. Retrieved from http://www.knime.org/files/knime_social_media_white_paper.pdf

Townsend, M., & Viets, A. (2013). Introduction. In J. Vogelsang & M. Townsend (Eds.), *Handbook for Strategic HR*. New York: Amacom.

Trad, A., & Kalpić, D. (2018). The Business Transformation Framework, Agile Project and Change Management. In M. Khosrow-Pour, D.B.A. (Ed.), Encyclopedia of Information Science and Technology, Fourth Edition (pp. 620-635). Hershey, PA: IGI Global. doi:10.4018/978-1-5225-2255-3.ch054

Trad, A., & Kalpić, D. (2016). The E-Business Transformation Framework for E-Commerce Architecture-Modeling Projects. In I. Lee (Ed.), *Encyclopedia of E-Commerce Development, Implementation, and Management* (pp. 733–753). Hershey, PA: IGI Global. doi:10.4018/978-1-4666-9787-4.ch052

Trad, A., & Kalpić, D. (2016). The E-Business Transformation Framework for E-Commerce Control and Monitoring Pattern. In I. Lee (Ed.), *Encyclopedia of E-Commerce Development, Implementation, and Management* (pp. 754–777). Hershey, PA: IGI Global. doi:10.4018/978-1-4666-9787-4.ch053

Trad, A., & Kalpić, D. (2018). The Business Transformation and Enterprise Architecture Framework: The Financial Engineering E-Risk Management and E-Law Integration. In B. Sergi, F. Fidanoski, M. Ziolo, & V. Naumovski (Eds.), *Regaining Global Stability After the Financial Crisis* (pp. 46–65). Hershey, PA: IGI Global. doi:10.4018/978-1-5225-4026-7.ch003

Trist, E., & Bamforth, K. (1951). Some Social and Psychological Consequences of the Longwall Method of Coal-Getting. *Human Relations*, *4*(1), 1–38. doi:10.1177/001872675100400101

Trott, P. (2008). *Innovation Management and New Product Development* (4th ed.). Essex, UK: Prentice Hall | Financial Times.

Tsvetovat, M., & Kouznetsov, A. (2011). *Social Network Analysis for Startups: Finding connections on the social web* (1st ed.). O'Reilly Media.

Turchi, S. (2012). Estratégias de Marketing Digital e E-Commerce. S. Paulo: Atlas.

Turulja, L., & Bajgoric, N. (2018). Business Continuity and Information Systems: A Systematic Literature Review. In N. Bajgoric (Ed.), *Always-On Enterprise Information Systems for Modern Organizations* (pp. 60–87). Hershey, PA: IGI Global. doi:10.4018/978-1-5225-3704-5.ch004

Umberto, E. (1992). *Interpretation and Overinterpretation.* Cambridge, UK: Cambridge University Press.

van Wessel, R. M., de Vries, H. J., & Ribbers, P. M. (2016). Business Benefits through Company IT Standardization. In K. Jakobs (Ed.), *Effective Standardization Management in Corporate Settings* (pp. 34–53). Hershey, PA: IGI Global. doi:10.4018/978-1-4666-9737-9.ch003

van Winkelen, C., & McKenzie, J. (2011). *Knowledge works*. Chichester, UK: Wiley.

Vancouver, J. B. (1996). Living systems theory as a paradigm for organizational behavior: Understanding humans, organizations, and social processes. *Behavioral Science, 41*(3), 165–204. doi:10.1002/bs.3830410301 PMID:8856949

Vargas-Hernández, J. G. (2017). Professional Integrity in Business Management Education. In N. Baporikar (Ed.), *Management Education for Global Leadership* (pp. 70–89). Hershey, PA: IGI Global. doi:10.4018/978-1-5225-1013-0.ch004

Vasista, T. G., & AlAbdullatif, A. M. (2017). Role of Electronic Customer Relationship Management in Demand Chain Management: A Predictive Analytic Approach. *International Journal of Information Systems and Supply Chain Management, 10*(1), 53–67. doi:10.4018/IJISSCM.2017010104

Veitch, S., Strehlow, K., & Boyd, J. (2018). Supporting university students with socially challenging behaviours through professional development for teaching staff professional development for teaching staff. *Journal of Academic Language and Learning, 12*(1), A156–A167.

Vergidis, K. (2016). Rediscovering Business Processes: Definitions, Patterns, and Modelling Approaches. In P. Papajorgji, F. Pinet, A. Guimarães, & J. Papathanasiou (Eds.), *Automated Enterprise Systems for Maximizing Business Performance* (pp. 97–122). Hershey, PA: IGI Global. doi:10.4018/978-1-4666-8841-4.ch007

Vieru, D., & Bourdeau, S. (2017). Survival in the Digital Era: A Digital Competence-Based Multi-Case Study in the Canadian SME Clothing Industry. *International Journal of Social and Organizational Dynamics in IT, 6*(1), 17–34. doi:10.4018/IJSODIT.2017010102

Vijayan, G., & Kamarulzaman, N. H. (2017). An Introduction to Sustainable Supply Chain Management and Business Implications. In M. Khan, M. Hussain, & M. Ajmal (Eds.), *Green Supply Chain Management for Sustainable Business Practice* (pp. 27–50). Hershey, PA: IGI Global. doi:10.4018/978-1-5225-0635-5.ch002

Vince, R. (2012). The Contradictions of Impact: Action Learning and Power in Organizations. *Action Learning Research and Practice*, *9*(3), 209–218. doi:10.1080/14767333.2012.722356

Vince, R., & Gabriel, Y. (2011). *Organizations, Learning and Emotion* (H. Shipton, Ed.). West Sussex, UK: Wiley.

Vlachvei, A., & Notta, O. (2017). Firm Competitiveness: Theories, Evidence, and Measurement. In A. Vlachvei, O. Notta, K. Karantininis, & N. Tsounis (Eds.), *Factors Affecting Firm Competitiveness and Performance in the Modern Business World* (pp. 1–42). Hershey, PA: IGI Global. doi:10.4018/978-1-5225-0843-4.ch001

Vliet, V. (2010). *Single and Double Loop learning model.* Retrieved 3/27/18 http://www.toolshero.com

von Bertalanffy, L. (1934). Untersuchungen über die Gesetzlichkeit des Wachstums. I. Allgemeine Grundlagen der Theorie; mathematische und physiologische Gesetzlichkeiten des Wachstums bei Wassertieren. *Arch. Entwicklungsmech.*, *131*, 613–652. PMID:28353935

Von Bertalanffy, L. (1950). An Outline of General System Theory. *The British Journal for the Philosophy of Science*, *1*, 114–129.

von Krogh, G. (2012). How Does Social Software Change Kopwledge Management Toward a Strategic Research Agenda? *The Journal of Strategic Information Systems*, *21*(2), 154–164. doi:10.1016/j.jsis.2012.04.003

von Krogh, G., Ichijo, K., & Nonaka, I. (2000). *Enabling knowledge creation.* New York, NY: Oxford University Press. doi:10.1007/978-1-349-62753-0

von Rosing, M., Fullington, N., & Walker, J. (2016). Using the Business Ontology and Enterprise Standards to Transform Three Leading Organizations. *International Journal of Conceptual Structures and Smart Applications*, *4*(1), 71–99. doi:10.4018/IJCSSA.2016010104

von Rosing, M., & von Scheel, H. (2016). Using the Business Ontology to Develop Enterprise Standards. *International Journal of Conceptual Structures and Smart Applications*, *4*(1), 48–70. doi:10.4018/IJCSSA.2016010103

Vygotsky, L. S. (1978). *Mind and society: The development of higher psychological processes.* Cambridge, MA: Harvard University Press.

Walczak, S. (2016). Artificial Neural Networks and other AI Applications for Business Management Decision Support. *International Journal of Sociotechnology and Knowledge Development*, *8*(4), 1–20. doi:10.4018/IJSKD.2016100101

Wamba, S. F., Akter, S., Kang, H., Bhattacharya, M., & Upal, M. (2016). The Primer of Social Media Analytics. *Journal of Organizational and End User Computing*, *28*(2), 1–12. doi:10.4018/JOEUC.2016040101

Wang, C. L., & Ahmed, P. K. (2003). Organizational learning: A critical review. *The Learning Organization*, *10*(1), 8–17. doi:10.1108/09696470310457469

Wang, C., Schofield, M., Li, X., & Ou, X. (2017). Do Chinese Students in Public and Private Higher Education Institutes Perform at Different Level in One of the Leadership Skills: Critical Thinking?: An Exploratory Comparison. In V. Wang (Ed.), *Encyclopedia of Strategic Leadership and Management* (pp. 160–181). Hershey, PA: IGI Global. doi:10.4018/978-1-5225-1049-9.ch013

Wang, F., Raisinghani, M. S., Mora, M., & Wang, X. (2016). Strategic E-Business Management through a Balanced Scored Card Approach. In I. Lee (Ed.), *Encyclopedia of E-Commerce Development, Implementation, and Management* (pp. 361–386). Hershey, PA: IGI Global. doi:10.4018/978-1-4666-9787-4.ch027

Wang, J. (2017). Multi-Agent based Production Management Decision System Modelling for the Textile Enterprise. *Journal of Global Information Management*, *25*(4), 1–15. doi:10.4018/JGIM.2017100101

Wang, S.-L., & Wu, C.-Y. (2011). Application of context-aware and personalised recommendation to implement an adaptive ubiquitous learning systems. *Expert Systems with Applications*, *38*(9), 831–838. doi:10.1016/j.eswa.2011.02.083

Ward, J., & Peppard, J. (2002). *Strategic Planning for Information Systems* (3rd ed.). Chichester, UK: John Wiley & Sons.

Webster, F. (2000). *Theories of the Information Society*. Cornwall, UK: Routledge.

Wegerif, R. (2007). *Dialogic education and technology. Expanding the space of learning*. New York, NY: Springer. doi:10.1007/978-0-387-71142-3

Weiss, A. (2008). *If They Only Knew: Finding Competitive Intelligence from the Web Sites of Your Competitors*. Retrieved 21/01/2013, from http://web.fumsi.com/go/article/find/3355

Wertsch, J. (1984). *Vygotsky the social formation of Mind*. London, UK: Wiley Ltd.

Whyte, F. W. (1943). *[1991]. Street Corner Society* (4th ed.). Chicago: University of Chicago Press.

Wiedemann, A., & Gewald, H. (2017). Examining Cross-Domain Alignment: The Correlation of Business Strategy, IT Management, and IT Business Value. *International Journal of IT/Business Alignment and Governance*, *8*(1), 17–31. doi:10.4018/IJITBAG.2017010102

Wilkinson, D. M. (2006). *Fundamental Processes in Ecology: An Earth Systems Approach*. Oxford University Press. doi:10.1093/acprof:oso/9780198568469.001.0001

Williams, B., & Hummelbrunner, R. (2010). *Systems concepts in action: A practitioner's toolkit*. New York: Stanford University Press.

Wilson, T. (1985). Information Management. *The Electronic Library*, *3*(1), 62–66. doi:10.1108/eb044644 PMID:2498741

Wilson, T. (1987). Information for business. The business of information. *Aslib Proceedings*, *39*(10), 275–279. doi:10.1108/eb051066

Winkler, I. (1997). *Corporate Espionage: What it is, why it's happening in your company, what you must do about it*. Prima Publishing.

Wolf, R., & Thiel, M. (2018). Advancing Global Business Ethics in China: Reducing Poverty Through Human and Social Welfare. In S. Hipsher (Ed.), *Examining the Private Sector's Role in Wealth Creation and Poverty Reduction* (pp. 67–84). Hershey, PA: IGI Global. doi:10.4018/978-1-5225-3117-3.ch004

Wormell, I. (1990). *Information Quality: Definitions and Dimensions*. London: Taylor Graham.

Wright, S. (2005). *The Civil Rights Act of 1964: Landmark Antidiscrimination Legislation*. The Rosen Publishing Group.

Wu, J., Ding, F., Xu, M., Mo, Z., & Jin, A. (2016). Investigating the Determinants of Decision-Making on Adoption of Public Cloud Computing in E-government. *Journal of Global Information Management*, *24*(3), 71–89. doi:10.4018/JGIM.2016070104

Wu, X. V., Chan, Y. S., Tan, K. H. S., & Wang, W. (2018). A systematic review of online learning programs for nurse preceptors. *Nurse Education Today*, *60*, 11–22. doi:10.1016/j.nedt.2017.09.010 PMID:28987893

Xu, L., & de Vrieze, P. (2016). Building Situational Applications for Virtual Enterprises. In I. Lee (Ed.), *Encyclopedia of E-Commerce Development, Implementation, and Management* (pp. 715–724). Hershey, PA: IGI Global. doi:10.4018/978-1-4666-9787-4.ch050

Yablonsky, S. (2018). Innovation Platforms: Data and Analytics Platforms. In *Multi-Sided Platforms (MSPs) and Sharing Strategies in the Digital Economy: Emerging Research and Opportunities* (pp. 72–95). Hershey, PA: IGI Global. doi:10.4018/978-1-5225-5457-8.ch003

Yap, C. S., Cheng, B. L., Mohamad Hussain, N., & Ahmad, R. (2018). Innovativeness, market intelligence practices, and firm performance of small-and medium-sized tour operators. *Tourism and Hospitality Research, 18*(2), 143–151. doi:10.1177/1467358416636931

Yin, C. Y. (2018). Measuring organizational impacts by integrating competitive intelligence into executive information system. *Journal of Intelligent Manufacturing, 29*(3), 533–547. doi:10.100710845-015-1135-4

Yusoff, A., Ahmad, N. H., & Halim, H. A. (2017). Agropreneurship among Gen Y in Malaysia: The Role of Academic Institutions. In N. Ahmad, T. Ramayah, H. Halim, & S. Rahman (Eds.), *Handbook of Research on Small and Medium Enterprises in Developing Countries* (pp. 23–47). Hershey, PA: IGI Global. doi:10.4018/978-1-5225-2165-5.ch002

Zajaczek, W. E. J., Götz, F., Kupka, T., Behrends, M., Haubitz, B., Donnerstag, F., … Becker, H. (2006). eLearning in education and advanced training in neuroradiology: introduction of a web-based teaching and learning application. *Neuroradiology, 48*(9), 640-646.

Zanin, F., Comuzzi, E., & Costantini, A. (2018). The Effect of Business Strategy and Stock Market Listing on the Use of Risk Assessment Tools. In *Management Control Systems in Complex Settings: Emerging Research and Opportunities* (pp. 145–168). Hershey, PA: IGI Global. doi:10.4018/978-1-5225-3987-2.ch007

Zaretskii, V. K. (2009). The Zone of Proximal Development What Vygotsky Did Not Have Time to Write. *Journal of Russian & East European Psychology, 47*(6), 1061–1405. doi:10.2753/RPO1061-0405470604

Zarrella, D. (2009). *The Social Media Marketing Book* (1st ed.). O'Reilly Media.

Zarrella, D. (2013). *The Science of Marketing: When to Tweet, What to Post, How to Blog, and Other Proven Strategies*. John Wiley & Sons.

Zgheib, P. W. (2017). Corporate Innovation and Intrapreneurship in the Middle East. In P. Zgheib (Ed.), *Entrepreneurship and Business Innovation in the Middle East* (pp. 37–56). Hershey, PA: IGI Global. doi:10.4018/978-1-5225-2066-5.ch003

Related References

To continue our tradition of advancing information science and technology research, we have compiled a list of recommended IGI Global readings. These references will provide additional information and guidance to further enrich your knowledge and assist you with your own research and future publications.

Abtahi, M. S., Behboudi, L., & Hasanabad, H. M. (2017). Factors Affecting Internet Advertising Adoption in Ad Agencies. *International Journal of Innovation in the Digital Economy*, *8*(4), 18–29. doi:10.4018/IJIDE.2017100102

Agrawal, S. (2017). The Impact of Emerging Technologies and Social Media on Different Business(es): Marketing and Management. In O. Rishi & A. Sharma (Eds.), *Maximizing Business Performance and Efficiency Through Intelligent Systems* (pp. 37–49). Hershey, PA: IGI Global. doi:10.4018/978-1-5225-2234-8.ch002

Alnoukari, M., Razouk, R., & Hanano, A. (2016). BSC-SI: A Framework for Integrating Strategic Intelligence in Corporate Strategic Management. *International Journal of Social and Organizational Dynamics in IT*, *5*(2), 1–14. doi:10.4018/IJSODIT.2016070101

Alnoukari, M., Razouk, R., & Hanano, A. (2016). BSC-SI, A Framework for Integrating Strategic Intelligence in Corporate Strategic Management. *International Journal of Strategic Information Technology and Applications*, *7*(1), 32–44. doi:10.4018/IJSITA.2016010103

Altındağ, E. (2016). Current Approaches in Change Management. In A. Goksoy (Ed.), *Organizational Change Management Strategies in Modern Business* (pp. 24–51). Hershey, PA: IGI Global. doi:10.4018/978-1-4666-9533-7.ch002

Alvarez-Dionisi, L. E., Turner, R., & Mittra, M. (2016). Global Project Management Trends. *International Journal of Information Technology Project Management, 7*(3), 54–73. doi:10.4018/IJITPM.2016070104

Anantharaman, R. N., Rajeswari, K. S., Angusamy, A., & Kuppusamy, J. (2017). Role of Self-Efficacy and Collective Efficacy as Moderators of Occupational Stress Among Software Development Professionals. *International Journal of Human Capital and Information Technology Professionals, 8*(2), 45–58. doi:10.4018/IJHCITP.2017040103

Aninze, F., El-Gohary, H., & Hussain, J. (2018). The Role of Microfinance to Empower Women: The Case of Developing Countries. *International Journal of Customer Relationship Marketing and Management, 9*(1), 54–78. doi:10.4018/IJCRMM.2018010104

Arsenijević, O. M., Orčić, D., & Kastratović, E. (2017). Development of an Optimization Tool for Intangibles in SMEs: A Case Study from Serbia with a Pilot Research in the Prestige by Milka Company. In M. Vemić (Ed.), *Optimal Management Strategies in Small and Medium Enterprises* (pp. 320–347). Hershey, PA: IGI Global. doi:10.4018/978-1-5225-1949-2.ch015

Aryanto, V. D., Wismantoro, Y., & Widyatmoko, K. (2018). Implementing Eco-Innovation by Utilizing the Internet to Enhance Firm's Marketing Performance: Study of Green Batik Small and Medium Enterprises in Indonesia. *International Journal of E-Business Research, 14*(1), 21–36. doi:10.4018/IJEBR.2018010102

Atiku, S. O., & Fields, Z. (2017). Multicultural Orientations for 21st Century Global Leadership. In N. Baporikar (Ed.), *Management Education for Global Leadership* (pp. 28–51). Hershey, PA: IGI Global. doi:10.4018/978-1-5225-1013-0.ch002

Atiku, S. O., & Fields, Z. (2018). Organisational Learning Dimensions and Talent Retention Strategies for the Service Industries. In N. Baporikar (Ed.), *Global Practices in Knowledge Management for Societal and Organizational Development* (pp. 358–381). Hershey, PA: IGI Global. doi:10.4018/978-1-5225-3009-1.ch017

Ávila, L., & Teixeira, L. (2018). The Main Concepts Behind the Dematerialization of Business Processes. In M. Khosrow-Pour, D.B.A. (Ed.), Encyclopedia of Information Science and Technology, Fourth Edition (pp. 888-898). Hershey, PA: IGI Global. doi:10.4018/978-1-5225-2255-3.ch076

Bartens, Y., Chunpir, H. I., Schulte, F., & Voß, S. (2017). Business/IT Alignment in Two-Sided Markets: A COBIT 5 Analysis for Media Streaming Business Models. In S. De Haes & W. Van Grembergen (Eds.), *Strategic IT Governance and Alignment in Business Settings* (pp. 82–111). Hershey, PA: IGI Global. doi:10.4018/978-1-5225-0861-8.ch004

Bashayreh, A. M. (2018). Organizational Culture and Organizational Performance. In W. Lee & F. Sabetzadeh (Eds.), *Contemporary Knowledge and Systems Science* (pp. 50–69). Hershey, PA: IGI Global. doi:10.4018/978-1-5225-5655-8.ch003

Bedford, D. A. (2018). Sustainable Knowledge Management Strategies: Aligning Business Capabilities and Knowledge Management Goals. In N. Baporikar (Ed.), *Global Practices in Knowledge Management for Societal and Organizational Development* (pp. 46–73). Hershey, PA: IGI Global. doi:10.4018/978-1-5225-3009-1.ch003

Benmoussa, F., Nakara, W. A., & Jaouen, A. (2016). The Use of Social Media by SMEs in the Tourism Industry. In I. Lee (Ed.), *Encyclopedia of E-Commerce Development, Implementation, and Management* (pp. 2159–2170). Hershey, PA: IGI Global. doi:10.4018/978-1-4666-9787-4.ch155

Berger, R. (2016). Indigenous Management and Bottom of Pyramid Countries: The Role of National Institutions. In U. Aung & P. Ordoñez de Pablos (Eds.), *Managerial Strategies and Practice in the Asian Business Sector* (pp. 107–123). Hershey, PA: IGI Global. doi:10.4018/978-1-4666-9758-4.ch007

Bharwani, S., & Musunuri, D. (2018). Reflection as a Process From Theory to Practice. In M. Khosrow-Pour, D.B.A. (Ed.), Encyclopedia of Information Science and Technology, Fourth Edition (pp. 1529-1539). Hershey, PA: IGI Global. doi:10.4018/978-1-5225-2255-3.ch132

Bhatt, G. D., Wang, Z., & Rodger, J. A. (2017). Information Systems Capabilities and Their Effects on Competitive Advantages: A Study of Chinese Companies. *Information Resources Management Journal, 30*(3), 41–57. doi:10.4018/IRMJ.2017070103

Bhushan, M., & Yadav, A. (2017). Concept of Cloud Computing in ESB. In R. Bhadoria, N. Chaudhari, G. Tomar, & S. Singh (Eds.), *Exploring Enterprise Service Bus in the Service-Oriented Architecture Paradigm* (pp. 116–127). Hershey, PA: IGI Global. doi:10.4018/978-1-5225-2157-0.ch008

Bhushan, S. (2017). System Dynamics Base-Model of Humanitarian Supply Chain (HSCM) in Disaster Prone Eco-Communities of India: A Discussion on Simulation and Scenario Results. *International Journal of System Dynamics Applications, 6*(3), 20–37. doi:10.4018/IJSDA.2017070102

Biswas, A., & De, A. K. (2017). On Development of a Fuzzy Stochastic Programming Model with Its Application to Business Management. In S. Trivedi, S. Dey, A. Kumar, & T. Panda (Eds.), *Handbook of Research on Advanced Data Mining Techniques and Applications for Business Intelligence* (pp. 353–378). Hershey, PA: IGI Global. doi:10.4018/978-1-5225-2031-3.ch021

Bücker, J., & Ernste, K. (2018). Use of Brand Heroes in Strategic Reputation Management: The Case of Bacardi, Adidas, and Daimler. In A. Erdemir (Ed.), *Reputation Management Techniques in Public Relations* (pp. 126–150). Hershey, PA: IGI Global. doi:10.4018/978-1-5225-3619-2.ch007

Bureš, V. (2018). Industry 4.0 From the Systems Engineering Perspective: Alternative Holistic Framework Development. In R. Brunet-Thornton & F. Martinez (Eds.), *Analyzing the Impacts of Industry 4.0 in Modern Business Environments* (pp. 199–223). Hershey, PA: IGI Global. doi:10.4018/978-1-5225-3468-6.ch011

Buzady, Z. (2017). Resolving the Magic Cube of Effective Case Teaching: Benchmarking Case Teaching Practices in Emerging Markets – Insights from the Central European University Business School, Hungary. In D. Latusek (Ed.), *Case Studies as a Teaching Tool in Management Education* (pp. 79–103). Hershey, PA: IGI Global. doi:10.4018/978-1-5225-0770-3.ch005

Campatelli, G., Richter, A., & Stocker, A. (2016). Participative Knowledge Management to Empower Manufacturing Workers. *International Journal of Knowledge Management, 12*(4), 37–50. doi:10.4018/IJKM.2016100103

Căpusneanu, S., & Topor, D. I. (2018). Business Ethics and Cost Management in SMEs: Theories of Business Ethics and Cost Management Ethos. In I. Oncioiu (Ed.), *Ethics and Decision-Making for Sustainable Business Practices* (pp. 109–127). Hershey, PA: IGI Global. doi:10.4018/978-1-5225-3773-1.ch007

Carneiro, A. (2016). Maturity in Health Organization Information Systems: Metrics and Privacy Perspectives. *International Journal of Privacy and Health Information Management, 4*(2), 1–18. doi:10.4018/IJPHIM.2016070101

Chan, R. L., Mo, P. L., & Moon, K. K. (2018). Strategic and Tactical Measures in Managing Enterprise Risks: A Study of the Textile and Apparel Industry. In K. Strang, M. Korstanje, & N. Vajjhala (Eds.), *Research, Practices, and Innovations in Global Risk and Contingency Management* (pp. 1–19). Hershey, PA: IGI Global. doi:10.4018/978-1-5225-4754-9.ch001

Chandan, H. C. (2016). Motivations and Challenges of Female Entrepreneurship in Developed and Developing Economies. In N. Baporikar (Ed.), *Handbook of Research on Entrepreneurship in the Contemporary Knowledge-Based Global Economy* (pp. 260–286). Hershey, PA: IGI Global. doi:10.4018/978-1-4666-8798-1.ch012

Charlier, S. D., Burke-Smalley, L. A., & Fisher, S. L. (2018). Undergraduate Programs in the U.S: A Contextual and Content-Based Analysis. In J. Mendy (Ed.), *Teaching Human Resources and Organizational Behavior at the College Level* (pp. 26–57). Hershey, PA: IGI Global. doi:10.4018/978-1-5225-2820-3.ch002

Chaudhuri, S. (2016). Application of Web-Based Geographical Information System (GIS) in E-Business. In U. Panwar, R. Kumar, & N. Ray (Eds.), *Handbook of Research on Promotional Strategies and Consumer Influence in the Service Sector* (pp. 389–405). Hershey, PA: IGI Global. doi:10.4018/978-1-5225-0143-5.ch023

Choudhuri, P. S. (2016). An Empirical Study on the Quality of Services Offered by the Private Life Insurers in Burdwan. In U. Panwar, R. Kumar, & N. Ray (Eds.), *Handbook of Research on Promotional Strategies and Consumer Influence in the Service Sector* (pp. 31–55). Hershey, PA: IGI Global. doi:10.4018/978-1-5225-0143-5.ch002

Dahlberg, T., Kivijärvi, H., & Saarinen, T. (2017). IT Investment Consistency and Other Factors Influencing the Success of IT Performance. In S. De Haes & W. Van Grembergen (Eds.), *Strategic IT Governance and Alignment in Business Settings* (pp. 176–208). Hershey, PA: IGI Global. doi:10.4018/978-1-5225-0861-8.ch007

Damnjanović, A. M. (2017). Knowledge Management Optimization through IT and E-Business Utilization: A Qualitative Study on Serbian SMEs. In M. Vemić (Ed.), *Optimal Management Strategies in Small and Medium Enterprises* (pp. 249–267). Hershey, PA: IGI Global. doi:10.4018/978-1-5225-1949-2.ch012

Daneshpour, H. (2017). Integrating Sustainable Development into Project Portfolio Management through Application of Open Innovation. In M. Vemić (Ed.), *Optimal Management Strategies in Small and Medium Enterprises* (pp. 370–387). Hershey, PA: IGI Global. doi:10.4018/978-1-5225-1949-2.ch017

Daniel, A. D., & Reis de Castro, V. (2018). Entrepreneurship Education: How to Measure the Impact on Nascent Entrepreneurs. In A. Carrizo Moreira, J. Guilherme Leitão Dantas, & F. Manuel Valente (Eds.), *Nascent Entrepreneurship and Successful New Venture Creation* (pp. 85–110). Hershey, PA: IGI Global. doi:10.4018/978-1-5225-2936-1.ch004

David, F., van der Sijde, P., & van den Besselaar, P. (2016). Enterpreneurial Incentives, Obstacles, and Management in University-Business Co-Operation: The Case of Indonesia. In J. Saiz-Álvarez (Ed.), *Handbook of Research on Social Entrepreneurship and Solidarity Economics* (pp. 499–518). Hershey, PA: IGI Global. doi:10.4018/978-1-5225-0097-1.ch024

David, R., Swami, B. N., & Tangirala, S. (2018). Ethics Impact on Knowledge Management in Organizational Development: A Case Study. In N. Baporikar (Ed.), *Global Practices in Knowledge Management for Societal and Organizational Development* (pp. 19–45). Hershey, PA: IGI Global. doi:10.4018/978-1-5225-3009-1.ch002

Delias, P., & Lakiotaki, K. (2018). Discovering Process Horizontal Boundaries to Facilitate Process Comprehension. *International Journal of Operations Research and Information Systems*, *9*(2), 1–31. doi:10.4018/IJORIS.2018040101

Denholm, J., & Lee-Davies, L. (2018). Success Factors for Games in Business and Project Management. In *Enhancing Education and Training Initiatives Through Serious Games* (pp. 34–68). Hershey, PA: IGI Global. doi:10.4018/978-1-5225-3689-5.ch002

Deshpande, M. (2017). Best Practices in Management Institutions for Global Leadership: Policy Aspects. In N. Baporikar (Ed.), *Management Education for Global Leadership* (pp. 1–27). Hershey, PA: IGI Global. doi:10.4018/978-1-5225-1013-0.ch001

Deshpande, M. (2018). Policy Perspectives for SMEs Knowledge Management. In N. Baporikar (Ed.), *Knowledge Integration Strategies for Entrepreneurship and Sustainability* (pp. 23–46). Hershey, PA: IGI Global. doi:10.4018/978-1-5225-5115-7.ch002

Dezdar, S. (2017). ERP Implementation Projects in Asian Countries: A Comparative Study on Iran and China. *International Journal of Information Technology Project Management*, *8*(3), 52–68. doi:10.4018/IJITPM.2017070104

Domingos, D., Martinho, R., & Varajão, J. (2016). Controlled Flexibility in Healthcare Processes: A BPMN-Extension Approach. In M. Cruz-Cunha, I. Miranda, R. Martinho, & R. Rijo (Eds.), *Encyclopedia of E-Health and Telemedicine* (pp. 521–535). Hershey, PA: IGI Global. doi:10.4018/978-1-4666-9978-6.ch040

Domingos, D., Respício, A., & Martinho, R. (2017). Reliability of IoT-Aware BPMN Healthcare Processes. In C. Reis & M. Maximiano (Eds.), *Internet of Things and Advanced Application in Healthcare* (pp. 214–248). Hershey, PA: IGI Global. doi:10.4018/978-1-5225-1820-4.ch008

Dosumu, O., Hussain, J., & El-Gohary, H. (2017). An Exploratory Study of the Impact of Government Policies on the Development of Small and Medium Enterprises in Developing Countries: The Case of Nigeria. *International Journal of Customer Relationship Marketing and Management*, *8*(4), 51–62. doi:10.4018/IJCRMM.2017100104

Durst, S., Bruns, G., & Edvardsson, I. R. (2017). Retaining Knowledge in Smaller Building and Construction Firms. *International Journal of Knowledge and Systems Science*, *8*(3), 1–12. doi:10.4018/IJKSS.2017070101

Edvardsson, I. R., & Durst, S. (2017). Outsourcing, Knowledge, and Learning: A Critical Review. *International Journal of Knowledge-Based Organizations*, *7*(2), 13–26. doi:10.4018/IJKBO.2017040102

Edwards, J. S. (2018). Integrating Knowledge Management and Business Processes. In M. Khosrow-Pour, D.B.A. (Ed.), Encyclopedia of Information Science and Technology, Fourth Edition (pp. 5046-5055). Hershey, PA: IGI Global. doi:10.4018/978-1-5225-2255-3.ch437

Ejiogu, A. O. (2018). Economics of Farm Management. In *Agricultural Finance and Opportunities for Investment and Expansion* (pp. 56–72). Hershey, PA: IGI Global. doi:10.4018/978-1-5225-3059-6.ch003

Ekanem, I., & Abiade, G. E. (2018). Factors Influencing the Use of E-Commerce by Small Enterprises in Nigeria. *International Journal of ICT Research in Africa and the Middle East*, *7*(1), 37–53. doi:10.4018/IJICTRAME.2018010103

Ekanem, I., & Alrossais, L. A. (2017). Succession Challenges Facing Family Businesses in Saudi Arabia. In P. Zgheib (Ed.), *Entrepreneurship and Business Innovation in the Middle East* (pp. 122–146). Hershey, PA: IGI Global. doi:10.4018/978-1-5225-2066-5.ch007

El Faquih, L., & Fredj, M. (2017). Ontology-Based Framework for Quality in Configurable Process Models. *Journal of Electronic Commerce in Organizations*, *15*(2), 48–60. doi:10.4018/JECO.2017040104

El-Gohary, H., & El-Gohary, Z. (2016). An Attempt to Explore Electronic Marketing Adoption and Implementation Aspects in Developing Countries: The Case of Egypt. *International Journal of Customer Relationship Marketing and Management*, *7*(4), 1–26. doi:10.4018/IJCRMM.2016100101

Entico, G. J. (2016). Knowledge Management and the Medical Health Librarians: A Perception Study. In J. Yap, M. Perez, M. Ayson, & G. Entico (Eds.), *Special Library Administration, Standardization and Technological Integration* (pp. 52–77). Hershey, PA: IGI Global. doi:10.4018/978-1-4666-9542-9.ch003

Faisal, M. N., & Talib, F. (2017). Building Ambidextrous Supply Chains in SMEs: How to Tackle the Barriers? *International Journal of Information Systems and Supply Chain Management, 10*(4), 80–100. doi:10.4018/IJISSCM.2017100105

Fernandes, T. M., Gomes, J., & Romão, M. (2017). Investments in E-Government: A Benefit Management Case Study. *International Journal of Electronic Government Research, 13*(3), 1–17. doi:10.4018/IJEGR.2017070101

Fouda, F. A. (2016). A Suggested Curriculum in Career Education to Develop Business Secondary Schools Students' Career Knowledge Management Domains and Professional Thinking. *International Journal of Technology Diffusion, 7*(2), 42–62. doi:10.4018/IJTD.2016040103

Gallardo-Vázquez, D., & Pajuelo-Moreno, M. L. (2016). How Spanish Universities are Promoting Entrepreneurship through Your Own Lines of Teaching and Research? In L. Carvalho (Ed.), *Handbook of Research on Entrepreneurial Success and its Impact on Regional Development* (pp. 431–454). Hershey, PA: IGI Global. doi:10.4018/978-1-4666-9567-2.ch019

Gao, S. S., Oreal, S., & Zhang, J. (2018). Contemporary Financial Risk Management Perceptions and Practices of Small-Sized Chinese Businesses. In I. Management Association (Ed.), Global Business Expansion: Concepts, Methodologies, Tools, and Applications (pp. 917-931). Hershey, PA: IGI Global. doi:10.4018/978-1-5225-5481-3.ch041

Garg, R., & Berning, S. C. (2017). Indigenous Chinese Management Philosophies: Key Concepts and Relevance for Modern Chinese Firms. In B. Christiansen & G. Koc (Eds.), *Transcontinental Strategies for Industrial Development and Economic Growth* (pp. 43–57). Hershey, PA: IGI Global. doi:10.4018/978-1-5225-2160-0.ch003

Gencer, Y. G. (2017). Supply Chain Management in Retailing Business. In U. Akkucuk (Ed.), *Ethics and Sustainability in Global Supply Chain Management* (pp. 197–210). Hershey, PA: IGI Global. doi:10.4018/978-1-5225-2036-8.ch011

Giacosa, E. (2016). Innovation in Luxury Fashion Businesses as a Means for the Regional Development. In L. Carvalho (Ed.), *Handbook of Research on Entrepreneurial Success and its Impact on Regional Development* (pp. 206–222). Hershey, PA: IGI Global. doi:10.4018/978-1-4666-9567-2.ch010

Giacosa, E. (2018). The Increasing of the Regional Development Thanks to the Luxury Business Innovation. In L. Carvalho (Ed.), *Handbook of Research on Entrepreneurial Ecosystems and Social Dynamics in a Globalized World* (pp. 260–273). Hershey, PA: IGI Global. doi:10.4018/978-1-5225-3525-6.ch011

Gianni, M., & Gotzamani, K. (2016). Integrated Management Systems and Information Management Systems: Common Threads. In P. Papajorgji, F. Pinet, A. Guimarães, & J. Papathanasiou (Eds.), *Automated Enterprise Systems for Maximizing Business Performance* (pp. 195–214). Hershey, PA: IGI Global. doi:10.4018/978-1-4666-8841-4.ch011

Gianni, M., Gotzamani, K., & Linden, I. (2016). How a BI-wise Responsible Integrated Management System May Support Food Traceability. *International Journal of Decision Support System Technology*, *8*(2), 1–17. doi:10.4018/IJDSST.2016040101

Glykas, M., & George, J. (2017). Quality and Process Management Systems in the UAE Maritime Industry. *International Journal of Productivity Management and Assessment Technologies*, *5*(1), 20–39. doi:10.4018/IJPMAT.2017010102

Glykas, M., Valiris, G., Kokkinaki, A., & Koutsoukou, Z. (2018). Banking Business Process Management Implementation. *International Journal of Productivity Management and Assessment Technologies*, *6*(1), 50–69. doi:10.4018/IJPMAT.2018010104

Gomes, J., & Romão, M. (2017). The Balanced Scorecard: Keeping Updated and Aligned with Today's Business Trends. *International Journal of Productivity Management and Assessment Technologies*, *5*(2), 1–15. doi:10.4018/IJPMAT.2017070101

Gomes, J., & Romão, M. (2017). Aligning Information Systems and Technology with Benefit Management and Balanced Scorecard. In S. De Haes & W. Van Grembergen (Eds.), *Strategic IT Governance and Alignment in Business Settings* (pp. 112–131). Hershey, PA: IGI Global. doi:10.4018/978-1-5225-0861-8.ch005

Grefen, P., & Turetken, O. (2017). Advanced Business Process Management in Networked E-Business Scenarios. *International Journal of E-Business Research*, *13*(4), 70–104. doi:10.4018/IJEBR.2017100105

Haider, A., & Saetang, S. (2017). Strategic IT Alignment in Service Sector. In S. Rozenes & Y. Cohen (Eds.), *Handbook of Research on Strategic Alliances and Value Co-Creation in the Service Industry* (pp. 231–258). Hershey, PA: IGI Global. doi:10.4018/978-1-5225-2084-9.ch012

Haider, A., & Tang, S. S. (2016). Maximising Value Through IT and Business Alignment: A Case of IT Governance Institutionalisation at a Thai Bank. *International Journal of Technology Diffusion*, *7*(3), 33–58. doi:10.4018/IJTD.2016070104

Hajilari, A. B., Ghadaksaz, M., & Fasghandis, G. S. (2017). Assessing Organizational Readiness for Implementing ERP System Using Fuzzy Expert System Approach. *International Journal of Enterprise Information Systems*, *13*(1), 67–85. doi:10.4018/IJEIS.2017010105

Haldorai, A., Ramu, A., & Murugan, S. (2018). Social Aware Cognitive Radio Networks: Effectiveness of Social Networks as a Strategic Tool for Organizational Business Management. In H. Bansal, G. Shrivastava, G. Nguyen, & L. Stanciu (Eds.), *Social Network Analytics for Contemporary Business Organizations* (pp. 188–202). Hershey, PA: IGI Global. doi:10.4018/978-1-5225-5097-6.ch010

Hall, O. P. Jr. (2017). Social Media Driven Management Education. *International Journal of Knowledge-Based Organizations*, *7*(2), 43–59. doi:10.4018/IJKBO.2017040104

Hanifah, H., Halim, H. A., Ahmad, N. H., & Vafaei-Zadeh, A. (2017). Innovation Culture as a Mediator Between Specific Human Capital and Innovation Performance Among Bumiputera SMEs in Malaysia. In N. Ahmad, T. Ramayah, H. Halim, & S. Rahman (Eds.), *Handbook of Research on Small and Medium Enterprises in Developing Countries* (pp. 261–279). Hershey, PA: IGI Global. doi:10.4018/978-1-5225-2165-5.ch012

Hartlieb, S., & Silvius, G. (2017). Handling Uncertainty in Project Management and Business Development: Similarities and Differences. In Y. Raydugin (Ed.), *Handbook of Research on Leveraging Risk and Uncertainties for Effective Project Management* (pp. 337–362). Hershey, PA: IGI Global. doi:10.4018/978-1-5225-1790-0.ch016

Hass, K. B. (2017). Living on the Edge: Managing Project Complexity. In Y. Raydugin (Ed.), *Handbook of Research on Leveraging Risk and Uncertainties for Effective Project Management* (pp. 177–201). Hershey, PA: IGI Global. doi:10.4018/978-1-5225-1790-0.ch009

Hassan, A., & Privitera, D. S. (2016). Google AdSense as a Mobile Technology in Education. In J. Holland (Ed.), *Wearable Technology and Mobile Innovations for Next-Generation Education* (pp. 200–223). Hershey, PA: IGI Global. doi:10.4018/978-1-5225-0069-8.ch011

Hassan, A., & Rahimi, R. (2016). Consuming “Innovation” in Tourism: Augmented Reality as an Innovation Tool in Digital Tourism Marketing. In N. Pappas & I. Bregoli (Eds.), *Global Dynamics in Travel, Tourism, and Hospitality* (pp. 130–147). Hershey, PA: IGI Global. doi:10.4018/978-1-5225-0201-2.ch008

Hawking, P., & Carmine Sellitto, C. (2017). Developing an Effective Strategy for Organizational Business Intelligence. In M. Tavana (Ed.), *Enterprise Information Systems and the Digitalization of Business Functions* (pp. 222–237). Hershey, PA: IGI Global. doi:10.4018/978-1-5225-2382-6.ch010

Hawking, P., & Sellitto, C. (2017). A Fast-Moving Consumer Goods Company and Business Intelligence Strategy Development. *International Journal of Enterprise Information Systems*, *13*(2), 22–33. doi:10.4018/IJEIS.2017040102

Hawking, P., & Sellitto, C. (2017). Business Intelligence Strategy: Two Case Studies. *International Journal of Business Intelligence Research*, *8*(2), 17–30. doi:10.4018/IJBIR.2017070102

Haynes, J. D., Arockiasamy, S., Al Rashdi, M., & Al Rashdi, S. (2016). Business and E Business Strategies for Coopetition and Thematic Management as a Sustained Basis for Ethics and Social Responsibility in Emerging Markets. In M. Al-Shammari & H. Masri (Eds.), *Ethical and Social Perspectives on Global Business Interaction in Emerging Markets* (pp. 25–39). Hershey, PA: IGI Global. doi:10.4018/978-1-4666-9864-2.ch002

Hee, W. J., Jalleh, G., Lai, H., & Lin, C. (2017). E-Commerce and IT Projects: Evaluation and Management Issues in Australian and Taiwanese Hospitals. *International Journal of Public Health Management and Ethics*, *2*(1), 69–90. doi:10.4018/IJPHME.2017010104

Hernandez, A. A. (2018). Exploring the Factors to Green IT Adoption of SMEs in the Philippines. *Journal of Cases on Information Technology*, *20*(2), 49–66. doi:10.4018/JCIT.2018040104

Hernandez, A. A., & Ona, S. E. (2016). Green IT Adoption: Lessons from the Philippines Business Process Outsourcing Industry. *International Journal of Social Ecology and Sustainable Development*, *7*(1), 1–34. doi:10.4018/IJSESD.2016010101

Hollman, A., Bickford, S., & Hollman, T. (2017). Cyber InSecurity: A Post-Mortem Attempt to Assess Cyber Problems from IT and Business Management Perspectives. *Journal of Cases on Information Technology*, *19*(3), 42–70. doi:10.4018/JCIT.2017070104

Igbinakhase, I. (2017). Responsible and Sustainable Management Practices in Developing and Developed Business Environments. In Z. Fields (Ed.), *Collective Creativity for Responsible and Sustainable Business Practice* (pp. 180–207). Hershey, PA: IGI Global. doi:10.4018/978-1-5225-1823-5.ch010

Ilahi, L., Ghannouchi, S. A., & Martinho, R. (2016). A Business Process Management Approach to Home Healthcare Processes: On the Gap between Intention and Reality. In M. Cruz-Cunha, I. Miranda, R. Martinho, & R. Rijo (Eds.), *Encyclopedia of E-Health and Telemedicine* (pp. 439–457). Hershey, PA: IGI Global. doi:10.4018/978-1-4666-9978-6.ch035

Iwata, J. J., & Hoskins, R. G. (2017). Managing Indigenous Knowledge in Tanzania: A Business Perspective. In P. Jain & N. Mnjama (Eds.), *Managing Knowledge Resources and Records in Modern Organizations* (pp. 198–214). Hershey, PA: IGI Global. doi:10.4018/978-1-5225-1965-2.ch012

Jabeen, F., Ahmad, S. Z., & Alkaabi, S. (2016). The Internationalization Decision-Making of United Arab Emirates Family Businesses. In N. Zakaria, A. Abdul-Talib, & N. Osman (Eds.), *Handbook of Research on Impacts of International Business and Political Affairs on the Global Economy* (pp. 1–22). Hershey, PA: IGI Global. doi:10.4018/978-1-4666-9806-2.ch001

Jain, P. (2017). Ethical and Legal Issues in Knowledge Management Life-Cycle in Business. In P. Jain & N. Mnjama (Eds.), *Managing Knowledge Resources and Records in Modern Organizations* (pp. 82–101). Hershey, PA: IGI Global. doi:10.4018/978-1-5225-1965-2.ch006

Jamali, D., Abdallah, H., & Matar, F. (2016). Opportunities and Challenges for CSR Mainstreaming in Business Schools. *International Journal of Technology and Educational Marketing*, *6*(2), 1–29. doi:10.4018/IJTEM.2016070101

James, S., & Hauli, E. (2017). Holistic Management Education at Tanzanian Rural Development Planning Institute. In N. Baporikar (Ed.), *Management Education for Global Leadership* (pp. 112–136). Hershey, PA: IGI Global. doi:10.4018/978-1-5225-1013-0.ch006

Janošková, M., Csikósová, A., & Čulková, K. (2018). Measurement of Company Performance as Part of Its Strategic Management. In R. Leon (Ed.), *Managerial Strategies for Business Sustainability During Turbulent Times* (pp. 309–335). Hershey, PA: IGI Global. doi:10.4018/978-1-5225-2716-9.ch017

Jean-Vasile, A., & Alecu, A. (2017). Theoretical and Practical Approaches in Understanding the Influences of Cost-Productivity-Profit Trinomial in Contemporary Enterprises. In A. Jean Vasile & D. Nicolò (Eds.), *Sustainable Entrepreneurship and Investments in the Green Economy* (pp. 28–62). Hershey, PA: IGI Global. doi:10.4018/978-1-5225-2075-7.ch002

Jha, D. G. (2016). Preparing for Information Technology Driven Changes. In S. Tiwari & L. Nafees (Eds.), *Innovative Management Education Pedagogies for Preparing Next-Generation Leaders* (pp. 258–274). Hershey, PA: IGI Global. doi:10.4018/978-1-4666-9691-4.ch015

Joia, L. A., & Correia, J. C. (2018). CIO Competencies From the IT Professional Perspective: Insights From Brazil. *Journal of Global Information Management, 26*(2), 74–103. doi:10.4018/JGIM.2018040104

Juma, A., & Mzera, N. (2017). Knowledge Management and Records Management and Competitive Advantage in Business. In P. Jain & N. Mnjama (Eds.), *Managing Knowledge Resources and Records in Modern Organizations* (pp. 15–28). Hershey, PA: IGI Global. doi:10.4018/978-1-5225-1965-2.ch002

K., I., & A, V. (2018). Monitoring and Auditing in the Cloud. In K. Munir (Ed.), *Cloud Computing Technologies for Green Enterprises* (pp. 318-350). Hershey, PA: IGI Global. doi:10.4018/978-1-5225-3038-1.ch013

Kabra, G., Ghosh, V., & Ramesh, A. (2018). Enterprise Integrated Business Process Management and Business Intelligence Framework for Business Process Sustainability. In A. Paul, D. Bhattacharyya, & S. Anand (Eds.), *Green Initiatives for Business Sustainability and Value Creation* (pp. 228–238). Hershey, PA: IGI Global. doi:10.4018/978-1-5225-2662-9.ch010

Kaoud, M. (2017). Investigation of Customer Knowledge Management: A Case Study Research. *International Journal of Service Science, Management, Engineering, and Technology, 8*(2), 12–22. doi:10.4018/IJSSMET.2017040102

Kara, M. E., & Fırat, S. Ü. (2016). Sustainability, Risk, and Business Intelligence in Supply Chains. In M. Erdoğdu, T. Arun, & I. Ahmad (Eds.), *Handbook of Research on Green Economic Development Initiatives and Strategies* (pp. 501–538). Hershey, PA: IGI Global. doi:10.4018/978-1-5225-0440-5.ch022

Katuu, S. (2018). A Comparative Assessment of Enterprise Content Management Maturity Models. In N. Gwangwava & M. Mutingi (Eds.), *E-Manufacturing and E-Service Strategies in Contemporary Organizations* (pp. 93–118). Hershey, PA: IGI Global. doi:10.4018/978-1-5225-3628-4.ch005

Khan, M. A. (2016). MNEs Management Strategies in Developing Countries: Establishing the Context. In M. Khan (Ed.), *Multinational Enterprise Management Strategies in Developing Countries* (pp. 1–33). Hershey, PA: IGI Global. doi:10.4018/978-1-5225-0276-0.ch001

Khan, M. A. (2016). Operational Approaches in Organizational Structure: A Case for MNEs in Developing Countries. In M. Khan (Ed.), *Multinational Enterprise Management Strategies in Developing Countries* (pp. 129–151). Hershey, PA: IGI Global. doi:10.4018/978-1-5225-0276-0.ch007

Kinnunen, S., Ylä-Kujala, A., Marttonen-Arola, S., Kärri, T., & Baglee, D. (2018). Internet of Things in Asset Management: Insights from Industrial Professionals and Academia. *International Journal of Service Science, Management, Engineering, and Technology*, *9*(2), 104–119. doi:10.4018/IJSSMET.2018040105

Klein, A. Z., Sabino de Freitas, A., Machado, L., Freitas, J. C. Jr, Graziola, P. G. Jr, & Schlemmer, E. (2017). Virtual Worlds Applications for Management Education. In L. Tomei (Ed.), *Exploring the New Era of Technology-Infused Education* (pp. 279–299). Hershey, PA: IGI Global. doi:10.4018/978-1-5225-1709-2.ch017

Kożuch, B., & Jabłoński, A. (2017). Adopting the Concept of Business Models in Public Management. In M. Lewandowski & B. Kożuch (Eds.), *Public Sector Entrepreneurship and the Integration of Innovative Business Models* (pp. 10–46). Hershey, PA: IGI Global. doi:10.4018/978-1-5225-2215-7.ch002

Kumar, J., Adhikary, A., & Jha, A. (2017). Small Active Investors' Perceptions and Preferences Towards Tax Saving Mutual Fund Schemes in Eastern India: An Empirical Note. *International Journal of Asian Business and Information Management*, *8*(2), 35–45. doi:10.4018/IJABIM.2017040103

Lassoued, Y., Bouzguenda, L., & Mahmoud, T. (2016). Context-Aware Business Process Versions Management. *International Journal of e-Collaboration*, *12*(3), 7–33. doi:10.4018/IJeC.2016070102

Lavassani, K. M., & Movahedi, B. (2017). Applications Driven Information Systems: Beyond Networks toward Business Ecosystems. *International Journal of Innovation in the Digital Economy*, *8*(1), 61–75. doi:10.4018/IJIDE.2017010104

Lazzareschi, V. H., & Brito, M. S. (2017). Strategic Information Management: Proposal of Business Project Model. In G. Jamil, A. Soares, & C. Pessoa (Eds.), *Handbook of Research on Information Management for Effective Logistics and Supply Chains* (pp. 59–88). Hershey, PA: IGI Global. doi:10.4018/978-1-5225-0973-8.ch004

Lederer, M., Kurz, M., & Lazarov, P. (2017). Usage and Suitability of Methods for Strategic Business Process Initiatives: A Multi Case Study Research. *International Journal of Productivity Management and Assessment Technologies*, *5*(1), 40–51. doi:10.4018/IJPMAT.2017010103

Lee, I. (2017). A Social Enterprise Business Model and a Case Study of Pacific Community Ventures (PCV). In V. Potocan, M. Ünğan, & Z. Nedelko (Eds.), *Handbook of Research on Managerial Solutions in Non-Profit Organizations* (pp. 182–204). Hershey, PA: IGI Global. doi:10.4018/978-1-5225-0731-4.ch009

Lee, L. J., & Leu, J. (2016). Exploring the Effectiveness of IT Application and Value Method in the Innovation Performance of Enterprise. *International Journal of Enterprise Information Systems*, *12*(2), 47–65. doi:10.4018/IJEIS.2016040104

Lee, Y. (2016). Alignment Effect of Entrepreneurial Orientation and Marketing Orientation on Firm Performance. *International Journal of Customer Relationship Marketing and Management*, *7*(4), 58–69. doi:10.4018/IJCRMM.2016100104

Leon, L. A., Seal, K. C., Przasnyski, Z. H., & Wiedenman, I. (2017). Skills and Competencies Required for Jobs in Business Analytics: A Content Analysis of Job Advertisements Using Text Mining. *International Journal of Business Intelligence Research*, *8*(1), 1–25. doi:10.4018/IJBIR.2017010101

Leu, J., Lee, L. J., & Krischke, A. (2016). Value Engineering-Based Method for Implementing the ISO14001 System in the Green Supply Chains. *International Journal of Strategic Decision Sciences*, *7*(4), 1–20. doi:10.4018/IJSDS.2016100101

Levy, C. L., & Elias, N. I. (2017). SOHO Users' Perceptions of Reliability and Continuity of Cloud-Based Services. In M. Moore (Ed.), *Cybersecurity Breaches and Issues Surrounding Online Threat Protection* (pp. 248–287). Hershey, PA: IGI Global. doi:10.4018/978-1-5225-1941-6.ch011

Levy, M. (2018). Change Management Serving Knowledge Management and Organizational Development: Reflections and Review. In N. Baporikar (Ed.), *Global Practices in Knowledge Management for Societal and Organizational Development* (pp. 256–270). Hershey, PA: IGI Global. doi:10.4018/978-1-5225-3009-1.ch012

Lewandowski, M. (2017). Public Organizations and Business Model Innovation: The Role of Public Service Design. In M. Lewandowski & B. Kożuch (Eds.), *Public Sector Entrepreneurship and the Integration of Innovative Business Models* (pp. 47–72). Hershey, PA: IGI Global. doi:10.4018/978-1-5225-2215-7.ch003

Lhannaoui, H., Kabbaj, M. I., & Bakkoury, Z. (2017). A Survey of Risk-Aware Business Process Modelling. *International Journal of Risk and Contingency Management*, *6*(3), 14–26. doi:10.4018/IJRCM.2017070102

Li, J., Sun, W., Jiang, W., Yang, H., & Zhang, L. (2017). How the Nature of Exogenous Shocks and Crises Impact Company Performance?: The Effects of Industry Characteristics. *International Journal of Risk and Contingency Management*, *6*(4), 40–55. doi:10.4018/IJRCM.2017100103

Lu, C., & Liu, S. (2016). Cultural Tourism O2O Business Model Innovation-A Case Study of CTrip. *Journal of Electronic Commerce in Organizations*, *14*(2), 16–31. doi:10.4018/JECO.2016040102

Machen, B., Hosseini, M. R., Wood, A., & Bakhshi, J. (2016). An Investigation into using SAP-PS as a Multidimensional Project Control System (MPCS). *International Journal of Enterprise Information Systems*, *12*(2), 66–81. doi:10.4018/IJEIS.2016040105

Malega, P. (2017). Small and Medium Enterprises in the Slovak Republic: Status and Competitiveness of SMEs in the Global Markets and Possibilities of Optimization. In M. Vemić (Ed.), *Optimal Management Strategies in Small and Medium Enterprises* (pp. 102–124). Hershey, PA: IGI Global. doi:10.4018/978-1-5225-1949-2.ch006

Malewska, K. M. (2017). Intuition in Decision-Making on the Example of a Non-Profit Organization. In V. Potocan, M. Ünğan, & Z. Nedelko (Eds.), *Handbook of Research on Managerial Solutions in Non-Profit Organizations* (pp. 378–399). Hershey, PA: IGI Global. doi:10.4018/978-1-5225-0731-4.ch018

Maroofi, F. (2017). Entrepreneurial Orientation and Organizational Learning Ability Analysis for Innovation and Firm Performance. In N. Baporikar (Ed.), *Innovation and Shifting Perspectives in Management Education* (pp. 144–165). Hershey, PA: IGI Global. doi:10.4018/978-1-5225-1019-2.ch007

Martins, P. V., & Zacarias, M. (2017). A Web-based Tool for Business Process Improvement. *International Journal of Web Portals*, *9*(2), 68–84. doi:10.4018/IJWP.2017070104

Matthies, B., & Coners, A. (2017). Exploring the Conceptual Nature of e-Business Projects. *Journal of Electronic Commerce in Organizations*, *15*(3), 33–63. doi:10.4018/JECO.2017070103

McKee, J. (2018). Architecture as a Tool to Solve Business Planning Problems. In M. Khosrow-Pour, D.B.A. (Ed.), Encyclopedia of Information Science and Technology, Fourth Edition (pp. 573-586). Hershey, PA: IGI Global. doi:10.4018/978-1-5225-2255-3.ch050

McMurray, A. J., Cross, J., & Caponecchia, C. (2018). The Risk Management Profession in Australia: Business Continuity Plan Practices. In N. Bajgoric (Ed.), *Always-On Enterprise Information Systems for Modern Organizations* (pp. 112–129). Hershey, PA: IGI Global. doi:10.4018/978-1-5225-3704-5.ch006

Meddah, I. H., & Belkadi, K. (2018). Mining Patterns Using Business Process Management. In R. Hamou (Ed.), *Handbook of Research on Biomimicry in Information Retrieval and Knowledge Management* (pp. 78–89). Hershey, PA: IGI Global. doi:10.4018/978-1-5225-3004-6.ch005

Mendes, L. (2017). TQM and Knowledge Management: An Integrated Approach Towards Tacit Knowledge Management. In D. Jaziri-Bouagina & G. Jamil (Eds.), *Handbook of Research on Tacit Knowledge Management for Organizational Success* (pp. 236–263). Hershey, PA: IGI Global. doi:10.4018/978-1-5225-2394-9.ch009

Mnjama, N. M. (2017). Preservation of Recorded Information in Public and Private Sector Organizations. In P. Jain & N. Mnjama (Eds.), *Managing Knowledge Resources and Records in Modern Organizations* (pp. 149–167). Hershey, PA: IGI Global. doi:10.4018/978-1-5225-1965-2.ch009

Mokoqama, M., & Fields, Z. (2017). Principles of Responsible Management Education (PRME): Call for Responsible Management Education. In Z. Fields (Ed.), *Collective Creativity for Responsible and Sustainable Business Practice* (pp. 229–241). Hershey, PA: IGI Global. doi:10.4018/978-1-5225-1823-5.ch012

Muniapan, B. (2017). Philosophy and Management: The Relevance of Vedanta in Management. In P. Ordóñez de Pablos (Ed.), *Managerial Strategies and Solutions for Business Success in Asia* (pp. 124–139). Hershey, PA: IGI Global. doi:10.4018/978-1-5225-1886-0.ch007

Muniapan, B., Gregory, M. L., & Ling, L. A. (2016). Marketing Education in Sarawak: Looking at It from the Employers' Viewpoint. In B. Smith & A. Porath (Eds.), *Global Perspectives on Contemporary Marketing Education* (pp. 112–130). Hershey, PA: IGI Global. doi:10.4018/978-1-4666-9784-3.ch008

Murad, S. E., & Dowaji, S. (2017). Using Value-Based Approach for Managing Cloud-Based Services. In A. Turuk, B. Sahoo, & S. Addya (Eds.), *Resource Management and Efficiency in Cloud Computing Environments* (pp. 33–60). Hershey, PA: IGI Global. doi:10.4018/978-1-5225-1721-4.ch002

Mutahar, A. M., Daud, N. M., Thurasamy, R., Isaac, O., & Abdulsalam, R. (2018). The Mediating of Perceived Usefulness and Perceived Ease of Use: The Case of Mobile Banking in Yemen. *International Journal of Technology Diffusion*, *9*(2), 21–40. doi:10.4018/IJTD.2018040102

Naidoo, V. (2017). E-Learning and Management Education at African Universities. In N. Baporikar (Ed.), *Management Education for Global Leadership* (pp. 181–201). Hershey, PA: IGI Global. doi:10.4018/978-1-5225-1013-0.ch009

Naidoo, V., & Igbinakhase, I. (2018). Opportunities and Challenges of Knowledge Retention in SMEs. In N. Baporikar (Ed.), *Knowledge Integration Strategies for Entrepreneurship and Sustainability* (pp. 70–94). Hershey, PA: IGI Global. doi:10.4018/978-1-5225-5115-7.ch004

Nayak, S., & Prabhu, N. (2017). Paradigm Shift in Management Education: Need for a Cross Functional Perspective. In N. Baporikar (Ed.), *Management Education for Global Leadership* (pp. 241–255). Hershey, PA: IGI Global. doi:10.4018/978-1-5225-1013-0.ch012

Ndede-Amadi, A. A. (2016). Student Interest in the IS Specialization as Predictor of the Success Potential of New Information Systems Programmes within the Schools of Business in Kenyan Public Universities. *International Journal of Information Systems and Social Change*, *7*(2), 63–79. doi:10.4018/IJISSC.2016040104

Nedelko, Z., & Potocan, V. (2016). Management Practices for Processes Optimization: Case of Slovenia. In G. Alor-Hernández, C. Sánchez-Ramírez, & J. García-Alcaraz (Eds.), *Handbook of Research on Managerial Strategies for Achieving Optimal Performance in Industrial Processes* (pp. 545–561). Hershey, PA: IGI Global. doi:10.4018/978-1-5225-0130-5.ch025

Nedelko, Z., & Potocan, V. (2017). Management Solutions in Non-Profit Organizations: Case of Slovenia. In V. Potocan, M. Üngan, & Z. Nedelko (Eds.), *Handbook of Research on Managerial Solutions in Non-Profit Organizations* (pp. 1–22). Hershey, PA: IGI Global. doi:10.4018/978-1-5225-0731-4.ch001

Nedelko, Z., & Potocan, V. (2017). Priority of Management Tools Utilization among Managers: International Comparison. In V. Wang (Ed.), *Encyclopedia of Strategic Leadership and Management* (pp. 1083–1094). Hershey, PA: IGI Global. doi:10.4018/978-1-5225-1049-9.ch075

Nedelko, Z., Raudeliūnienė, J., & Črešnar, R. (2018). Knowledge Dynamics in Supply Chain Management. In N. Baporikar (Ed.), *Knowledge Integration Strategies for Entrepreneurship and Sustainability* (pp. 150–166). Hershey, PA: IGI Global. doi:10.4018/978-1-5225-5115-7.ch008

Nguyen, H. T., & Hipsher, S. A. (2018). Innovation and Creativity Used by Private Sector Firms in a Resources-Constrained Environment. In S. Hipsher (Ed.), *Examining the Private Sector's Role in Wealth Creation and Poverty Reduction* (pp. 219–238). Hershey, PA: IGI Global. doi:10.4018/978-1-5225-3117-3.ch010

Nycz, M., & Półkowski, Z. (2016). Business Intelligence as a Modern IT Supporting Management of Local Government Units in Poland. *International Journal of Knowledge and Systems Science*, *7*(4), 1–18. doi:10.4018/IJKSS.2016100101

Obaji, N. O., Senin, A. A., & Olugu, M. U. (2016). Supportive Government Policy as a Mechanism for Business Incubation Performance in Nigeria. *International Journal of Information Systems and Social Change*, *7*(4), 52–66. doi:10.4018/IJISSC.2016100103

Obicci, P. A. (2017). Risk Sharing in a Partnership. In *Risk Management Strategies in Public-Private Partnerships* (pp. 115–152). Hershey, PA: IGI Global. doi:10.4018/978-1-5225-2503-5.ch004

Obidallah, W. J., & Raahemi, B. (2017). Managing Changes in Service Oriented Virtual Organizations: A Structural and Procedural Framework to Facilitate the Process of Change. *Journal of Electronic Commerce in Organizations*, *15*(1), 59–83. doi:10.4018/JECO.2017010104

Ojasalo, J., & Ojasalo, K. (2016). Service Logic Business Model Canvas for Lean Development of SMEs and Start-Ups. In N. Baporikar (Ed.), *Handbook of Research on Entrepreneurship in the Contemporary Knowledge-Based Global Economy* (pp. 217–243). Hershey, PA: IGI Global. doi:10.4018/978-1-4666-8798-1.ch010

Ojo, O. (2017). Impact of Innovation on the Entrepreneurial Success in Selected Business Enterprises in South-West Nigeria. *International Journal of Innovation in the Digital Economy*, *8*(2), 29–38. doi:10.4018/IJIDE.2017040103

Okdinawati, L., Simatupang, T. M., & Sunitiyoso, Y. (2017). Multi-Agent Reinforcement Learning for Value Co-Creation of Collaborative Transportation Management (CTM). *International Journal of Information Systems and Supply Chain Management*, *10*(3), 84–95. doi:10.4018/IJISSCM.2017070105

Ortner, E., Mevius, M., Wiedmann, P., & Kurz, F. (2016). Design of Interactional Decision Support Applications for E-Participation in Smart Cities. *International Journal of Electronic Government Research*, *12*(2), 18–38. doi:10.4018/IJEGR.2016040102

Pal, K. (2018). Building High Quality Big Data-Based Applications in Supply Chains. In A. Kumar & S. Saurav (Eds.), *Supply Chain Management Strategies and Risk Assessment in Retail Environments* (pp. 1–24). Hershey, PA: IGI Global. doi:10.4018/978-1-5225-3056-5.ch001

Palos-Sanchez, P. R., & Correia, M. B. (2018). Perspectives of the Adoption of Cloud Computing in the Tourism Sector. In J. Rodrigues, C. Ramos, P. Cardoso, & C. Henriques (Eds.), *Handbook of Research on Technological Developments for Cultural Heritage and eTourism Applications* (pp. 377–400). Hershey, PA: IGI Global. doi:10.4018/978-1-5225-2927-9.ch018

Parry, V. K., & Lind, M. L. (2016). Alignment of Business Strategy and Information Technology Considering Information Technology Governance, Project Portfolio Control, and Risk Management. *International Journal of Information Technology Project Management*, *7*(4), 21–37. doi:10.4018/IJITPM.2016100102

Pashkova, N., Trujillo-Barrera, A., Apostolakis, G., Van Dijk, G., Drakos, P. D., & Baourakis, G. (2016). Business Management Models of Microfinance Institutions (MFIs) in Africa: A Study into Their Enabling Environments. *International Journal of Food and Beverage Manufacturing and Business Models*, *1*(2), 63–82. doi:10.4018/IJFBMBM.2016070105

Patiño, B. E. (2017). New Generation Management by Convergence and Individual Identity: A Systemic and Human-Oriented Approach. In N. Baporikar (Ed.), *Innovation and Shifting Perspectives in Management Education* (pp. 119–143). Hershey, PA: IGI Global. doi:10.4018/978-1-5225-1019-2.ch006

Pawliczek, A., & Rössler, M. (2017). Knowledge of Management Tools and Systems in SMEs: Knowledge Transfer in Management. In A. Bencsik (Ed.), *Knowledge Management Initiatives and Strategies in Small and Medium Enterprises* (pp. 180–203). Hershey, PA: IGI Global. doi:10.4018/978-1-5225-1642-2.ch009

Pejic-Bach, M., Omazic, M. A., Aleksic, A., & Zoroja, J. (2018). Knowledge-Based Decision Making: A Multi-Case Analysis. In R. Leon (Ed.), *Managerial Strategies for Business Sustainability During Turbulent Times* (pp. 160–184). Hershey, PA: IGI Global. doi:10.4018/978-1-5225-2716-9.ch009

Perano, M., Hysa, X., & Calabrese, M. (2018). Strategic Planning, Cultural Context, and Business Continuity Management: Business Cases in the City of Shkoder. In A. Presenza & L. Sheehan (Eds.), *Geopolitics and Strategic Management in the Global Economy* (pp. 57–77). Hershey, PA: IGI Global. doi:10.4018/978-1-5225-2673-5.ch004

Pereira, R., Mira da Silva, M., & Lapão, L. V. (2017). IT Governance Maturity Patterns in Portuguese Healthcare. In S. De Haes & W. Van Grembergen (Eds.), *Strategic IT Governance and Alignment in Business Settings* (pp. 24–52). Hershey, PA: IGI Global. doi:10.4018/978-1-5225-0861-8.ch002

Perez-Uribe, R., & Ocampo-Guzman, D. (2016). Conflict within Colombian Family Owned SMEs: An Explosive Blend between Feelings and Business. In J. Saiz-Álvarez (Ed.), *Handbook of Research on Social Entrepreneurship and Solidarity Economics* (pp. 329–354). Hershey, PA: IGI Global. doi:10.4018/978-1-5225-0097-1.ch017

Pérez-Uribe, R. I., Torres, D. A., Jurado, S. P., & Prada, D. M. (2018). Cloud Tools for the Development of Project Management in SMEs. In R. Perez-Uribe, C. Salcedo-Perez, & D. Ocampo-Guzman (Eds.), *Handbook of Research on Intrapreneurship and Organizational Sustainability in SMEs* (pp. 95–120). Hershey, PA: IGI Global. doi:10.4018/978-1-5225-3543-0.ch005

Petrisor, I., & Cozmiuc, D. (2017). Global Supply Chain Management Organization at Siemens in the Advent of Industry 4.0. In L. Saglietto & C. Cezanne (Eds.), *Global Intermediation and Logistics Service Providers* (pp. 123–142). Hershey, PA: IGI Global. doi:10.4018/978-1-5225-2133-4.ch007

Pierce, J. M., Velliaris, D. M., & Edwards, J. (2017). A Living Case Study: A Journey Not a Destination. In N. Silton (Ed.), *Exploring the Benefits of Creativity in Education, Media, and the Arts* (pp. 158–178). Hershey, PA: IGI Global. doi:10.4018/978-1-5225-0504-4.ch008

Radosavljevic, M., & Andjelkovic, A. (2017). Multi-Criteria Decision Making Approach for Choosing Business Process for the Improvement: Upgrading of the Six Sigma Methodology. In J. Stanković, P. Delias, S. Marinković, & S. Rochhia (Eds.), *Tools and Techniques for Economic Decision Analysis* (pp. 225–247). Hershey, PA: IGI Global. doi:10.4018/978-1-5225-0959-2.ch011

Radovic, V. M. (2017). Corporate Sustainability and Responsibility and Disaster Risk Reduction: A Serbian Overview. In M. Camilleri (Ed.), *CSR 2.0 and the New Era of Corporate Citizenship* (pp. 147–164). Hershey, PA: IGI Global. doi:10.4018/978-1-5225-1842-6.ch008

Raghunath, K. M., Devi, S. L., & Patro, C. S. (2018). Impact of Risk Assessment Models on Risk Factors: A Holistic Outlook. In K. Strang, M. Korstanje, & N. Vajjhala (Eds.), *Research, Practices, and Innovations in Global Risk and Contingency Management* (pp. 134–153). Hershey, PA: IGI Global. doi:10.4018/978-1-5225-4754-9.ch008

Raman, A., & Goyal, D. P. (2017). Extending IMPLEMENT Framework for Enterprise Information Systems Implementation to Information System Innovation. In M. Tavana (Ed.), *Enterprise Information Systems and the Digitalization of Business Functions* (pp. 137–177). Hershey, PA: IGI Global. doi:10.4018/978-1-5225-2382-6.ch007

Rao, Y., & Zhang, Y. (2017). The Construction and Development of Academic Library Digital Special Subject Databases. In L. Ruan, Q. Zhu, & Y. Ye (Eds.), *Academic Library Development and Administration in China* (pp. 163–183). Hershey, PA: IGI Global. doi:10.4018/978-1-5225-0550-1.ch010

Ravasan, A. Z., Mohammadi, M. M., & Hamidi, H. (2018). An Investigation Into the Critical Success Factors of Implementing Information Technology Service Management Frameworks. In K. Jakobs (Ed.), *Corporate and Global Standardization Initiatives in Contemporary Society* (pp. 200–218). Hershey, PA: IGI Global. doi:10.4018/978-1-5225-5320-5.ch009

Renna, P., Izzo, C., & Romaniello, T. (2016). The Business Process Management Systems to Support Continuous Improvements. In W. Nuninger & J. Châtelet (Eds.), *Handbook of Research on Quality Assurance and Value Management in Higher Education* (pp. 237–256). Hershey, PA: IGI Global. doi:10.4018/978-1-5225-0024-7.ch009

Rezaie, S., Mirabedini, S. J., & Abtahi, A. (2018). Designing a Model for Implementation of Business Intelligence in the Banking Industry. *International Journal of Enterprise Information Systems, 14*(1), 77–103. doi:10.4018/IJEIS.2018010105

Riccò, R. (2016). Diversity Management: Bringing Equality, Equity, and Inclusion in the Workplace. In J. Prescott (Ed.), *Handbook of Research on Race, Gender, and the Fight for Equality* (pp. 335–359). Hershey, PA: IGI Global. doi:10.4018/978-1-5225-0047-6.ch015

Romano, L., Grimaldi, R., & Colasuonno, F. S. (2017). Demand Management as a Success Factor in Project Portfolio Management. In L. Romano (Ed.), *Project Portfolio Management Strategies for Effective Organizational Operations* (pp. 202–219). Hershey, PA: IGI Global. doi:10.4018/978-1-5225-2151-8.ch008

Rostek, K. B. (2016). Risk Management: Role and Importance in Business Organization. In D. Jakóbczak (Ed.), *Analyzing Risk through Probabilistic Modeling in Operations Research* (pp. 149–178). Hershey, PA: IGI Global. doi:10.4018/978-1-4666-9458-3.ch007

Rouhani, S., & Savoji, S. R. (2016). A Success Assessment Model for BI Tools Implementation: An Empirical Study of Banking Industry. *International Journal of Business Intelligence Research, 7*(1), 25–44. doi:10.4018/IJBIR.2016010103

Ruan, Z. (2016). A Corpus-Based Functional Analysis of Complex Nominal Groups in Written Business Discourse: The Case of "Business". *International Journal of Computer-Assisted Language Learning and Teaching*, *6*(2), 74–90. doi:10.4018/IJCALLT.2016040105

Ruhi, U. (2018). Towards an Interdisciplinary Socio-Technical Definition of Virtual Communities. In M. Khosrow-Pour, D.B.A. (Ed.), Encyclopedia of Information Science and Technology, Fourth Edition (pp. 4278-4295). Hershey, PA: IGI Global. doi:10.4018/978-1-5225-2255-3.ch371

Ryan, J., Doster, B., Daily, S., & Lewis, C. (2016). A Case Study Perspective for Balanced Perioperative Workflow Achievement through Data-Driven Process Improvement. *International Journal of Healthcare Information Systems and Informatics*, *11*(3), 19–41. doi:10.4018/IJHISI.2016070102

Safari, M. R., & Jiang, Q. (2018). The Theory and Practice of IT Governance Maturity and Strategies Alignment: Evidence From Banking Industry. *Journal of Global Information Management*, *26*(2), 127–146. doi:10.4018/JGIM.2018040106

Sahoo, J., Pati, B., & Mohanty, B. (2017). Knowledge Management as an Academic Discipline: An Assessment. In B. Gunjal (Ed.), *Managing Knowledge and Scholarly Assets in Academic Libraries* (pp. 99–126). Hershey, PA: IGI Global. doi:10.4018/978-1-5225-1741-2.ch005

Saini, D. (2017). Relevance of Teaching Values and Ethics in Management Education. In N. Baporikar (Ed.), *Management Education for Global Leadership* (pp. 90–111). Hershey, PA: IGI Global. doi:10.4018/978-1-5225-1013-0.ch005

Sambhanthan, A. (2017). Assessing and Benchmarking Sustainability in Organisations: An Integrated Conceptual Model. *International Journal of Systems and Service-Oriented Engineering*, *7*(4), 22–43. doi:10.4018/IJSSOE.2017100102

Sambhanthan, A., & Potdar, V. (2017). A Study of the Parameters Impacting Sustainability in Information Technology Organizations. *International Journal of Knowledge-Based Organizations*, *7*(3), 27–39. doi:10.4018/IJKBO.2017070103

Sánchez-Fernández, M. D., & Manríquez, M. R. (2018). The Entrepreneurial Spirit Based on Social Values: The Digital Generation. In P. Isaias & L. Carvalho (Eds.), *User Innovation and the Entrepreneurship Phenomenon in the Digital Economy* (pp. 173–193). Hershey, PA: IGI Global. doi:10.4018/978-1-5225-2826-5.ch009

Sanchez-Ruiz, L., & Blanco, B. (2017). Process Management for SMEs: Barriers, Enablers, and Benefits. In M. Vemić (Ed.), *Optimal Management Strategies in Small and Medium Enterprises* (pp. 293–319). Hershey, PA: IGI Global. doi:10.4018/978-1-5225-1949-2.ch014

Sanz, L. F., Gómez-Pérez, J., & Castillo-Martinez, A. (2018). Analysis of the European ICT Competence Frameworks. In V. Ahuja & S. Rathore (Eds.), *Multidisciplinary Perspectives on Human Capital and Information Technology Professionals* (pp. 225–245). Hershey, PA: IGI Global. doi:10.4018/978-1-5225-5297-0.ch012

Sarvepalli, A., & Godin, J. (2017). Business Process Management in the Classroom. *Journal of Cases on Information Technology*, *19*(2), 17–28. doi:10.4018/JCIT.2017040102

Satpathy, B., & Muniapan, B. (2016). Ancient Wisdom for Transformational Leadership and Its Insights from the Bhagavad-Gita. In U. Aung & P. Ordoñez de Pablos (Eds.), *Managerial Strategies and Practice in the Asian Business Sector* (pp. 1–10). Hershey, PA: IGI Global. doi:10.4018/978-1-4666-9758-4.ch001

Saygili, E. E., Ozturkoglu, Y., & Kocakulah, M. C. (2017). End Users' Perceptions of Critical Success Factors in ERP Applications. *International Journal of Enterprise Information Systems*, *13*(4), 58–75. doi:10.4018/IJEIS.2017100104

Saygili, E. E., & Saygili, A. T. (2017). Contemporary Issues in Enterprise Information Systems: A Critical Review of CSFs in ERP Implementations. In M. Tavana (Ed.), *Enterprise Information Systems and the Digitalization of Business Functions* (pp. 120–136). Hershey, PA: IGI Global. doi:10.4018/978-1-5225-2382-6.ch006

Seidenstricker, S., & Antonino, A. (2018). Business Model Innovation-Oriented Technology Management for Emergent Technologies. In M. Khosrow-Pour, D.B.A. (Ed.), Encyclopedia of Information Science and Technology, Fourth Edition (pp. 4560-4569). Hershey, PA: IGI Global. doi:10.4018/978-1-5225-2255-3.ch396

Senaratne, S., & Gunarathne, A. D. (2017). Excellence Perspective for Management Education from a Global Accountants' Hub in Asia. In N. Baporikar (Ed.), *Management Education for Global Leadership* (pp. 158–180). Hershey, PA: IGI Global. doi:10.4018/978-1-5225-1013-0.ch008

Sensuse, D. I., & Cahyaningsih, E. (2018). Knowledge Management Models: A Summative Review. *International Journal of Information Systems in the Service Sector*, *10*(1), 71–100. doi:10.4018/IJISSS.2018010105

Sensuse, D. I., Wibowo, W. C., & Cahyaningsih, E. (2016). Indonesian Government Knowledge Management Model: A Theoretical Model. *Information Resources Management Journal, 29*(1), 91–108. doi:10.4018/irmj.2016010106

Seth, M., Goyal, D., & Kiran, R. (2017). Diminution of Impediments in Implementation of Supply Chain Management Information System for Enhancing its Effectiveness in Indian Automobile Industry. *Journal of Global Information Management, 25*(3), 1–20. doi:10.4018/JGIM.2017070101

Seyal, A. H., & Rahman, M. N. (2017). Investigating Impact of Inter-Organizational Factors in Measuring ERP Systems Success: Bruneian Perspectives. In M. Tavana (Ed.), *Enterprise Information Systems and the Digitalization of Business Functions* (pp. 178–204). Hershey, PA: IGI Global. doi:10.4018/978-1-5225-2382-6.ch008

Shaikh, A. A., & Karjaluoto, H. (2016). On Some Misconceptions Concerning Digital Banking and Alternative Delivery Channels. *International Journal of E-Business Research, 12*(3), 1–16. doi:10.4018/IJEBR.2016070101

Shams, S. M. (2016). Stakeholder Relationship Management in Online Business and Competitive Value Propositions: Evidence from the Sports Industry. *International Journal of Online Marketing, 6*(2), 1–17. doi:10.4018/IJOM.2016040101

Shamsuzzoha, A. (2016). Management of Risk and Resilience within Collaborative Business Network. In R. Addo-Tenkorang, J. Kantola, P. Helo, & A. Shamsuzzoha (Eds.), *Supply Chain Strategies and the Engineer-to-Order Approach* (pp. 143–159). Hershey, PA: IGI Global. doi:10.4018/978-1-5225-0021-6.ch008

Shaqrah, A. A. (2018). Analyzing Business Intelligence Systems Based on 7s Model of McKinsey. *International Journal of Business Intelligence Research, 9*(1), 53–63. doi:10.4018/IJBIR.2018010104

Sharma, A. J. (2017). Enhancing Sustainability through Experiential Learning in Management Education. In N. Baporikar (Ed.), *Management Education for Global Leadership* (pp. 256–274). Hershey, PA: IGI Global. doi:10.4018/978-1-5225-1013-0.ch013

Shetty, K. P. (2017). Responsible Global Leadership: Ethical Challenges in Management Education. In N. Baporikar (Ed.), *Innovation and Shifting Perspectives in Management Education* (pp. 194–223). Hershey, PA: IGI Global. doi:10.4018/978-1-5225-1019-2.ch009

Sinthupundaja, J., & Kohda, Y. (2017). Effects of Corporate Social Responsibility and Creating Shared Value on Sustainability. *International Journal of Sustainable Entrepreneurship and Corporate Social Responsibility*, *2*(1), 27–38. doi:10.4018/IJSECSR.2017010103

Škarica, I., & Hrgović, A. V. (2018). Implementation of Total Quality Management Principles in Public Health Institutes in the Republic of Croatia. *International Journal of Productivity Management and Assessment Technologies*, *6*(1), 1–16. doi:10.4018/IJPMAT.2018010101

Smuts, H., Kotzé, P., Van der Merwe, A., & Loock, M. (2017). Framework for Managing Shared Knowledge in an Information Systems Outsourcing Context. *International Journal of Knowledge Management*, *13*(4), 1–30. doi:10.4018/IJKM.2017100101

Soares, E. R., & Zaidan, F. H. (2016). Information Architecture and Business Modeling in Modern Organizations of Information Technology: Professional Career Plan in Organizations IT. In G. Jamil, J. Poças Rascão, F. Ribeiro, & A. Malheiro da Silva (Eds.), *Handbook of Research on Information Architecture and Management in Modern Organizations* (pp. 439–457). Hershey, PA: IGI Global. doi:10.4018/978-1-4666-8637-3.ch020

Sousa, M. J., Cruz, R., Dias, I., & Caracol, C. (2017). Information Management Systems in the Supply Chain. In G. Jamil, A. Soares, & C. Pessoa (Eds.), *Handbook of Research on Information Management for Effective Logistics and Supply Chains* (pp. 469–485). Hershey, PA: IGI Global. doi:10.4018/978-1-5225-0973-8.ch025

Spremic, M., Turulja, L., & Bajgoric, N. (2018). Two Approaches in Assessing Business Continuity Management Attitudes in the Organizational Context. In N. Bajgoric (Ed.), *Always-On Enterprise Information Systems for Modern Organizations* (pp. 159–183). Hershey, PA: IGI Global. doi:10.4018/978-1-5225-3704-5.ch008

Steenkamp, A. L. (2018). Some Insights in Computer Science and Information Technology. In *Examining the Changing Role of Supervision in Doctoral Research Projects: Emerging Research and Opportunities* (pp. 113–133). Hershey, PA: IGI Global. doi:10.4018/978-1-5225-2610-0.ch005

Studdard, N., Dawson, M., Burton, S. L., Jackson, N., Leonard, B., Quisenberry, W., & Rahim, E. (2016). Nurturing Social Entrepreneurship and Building Social Entrepreneurial Self-Efficacy: Focusing on Primary and Secondary Schooling to Develop Future Social Entrepreneurs. In Z. Fields (Ed.), *Incorporating Business Models and Strategies into Social Entrepreneurship* (pp. 154–175). Hershey, PA: IGI Global. doi:10.4018/978-1-4666-8748-6.ch010

Sun, Z. (2016). A Framework for Developing Management Intelligent Systems. *International Journal of Systems and Service-Oriented Engineering*, *6*(1), 37–53. doi:10.4018/IJSSOE.2016010103

Swami, B., & Mphele, G. T. (2016). Problems Preventing Growth of Small Entrepreneurs: A Case Study of a Few Small Entrepreneurs in Botswana Sub-Urban Areas. In N. Baporikar (Ed.), *Handbook of Research on Entrepreneurship in the Contemporary Knowledge-Based Global Economy* (pp. 479–508). Hershey, PA: IGI Global. doi:10.4018/978-1-4666-8798-1.ch020

Tabach, A., & Croteau, A. (2017). Configurations of Information Technology Governance Practices and Business Unit Performance. *International Journal of IT/Business Alignment and Governance*, *8*(2), 1–27. doi:10.4018/IJITBAG.2017070101

Talaue, G. M., & Iqbal, T. (2017). Assessment of e-Business Mode of Selected Private Universities in the Philippines and Pakistan. *International Journal of Online Marketing*, *7*(4), 63–77. doi:10.4018/IJOM.2017100105

Tam, G. C. (2017). Project Manager Sustainability Competence. In *Managerial Strategies and Green Solutions for Project Sustainability* (pp. 178–207). Hershey, PA: IGI Global. doi:10.4018/978-1-5225-2371-0.ch008

Tambo, T. (2018). Fashion Retail Innovation: About Context, Antecedents, and Outcome in Technological Change Projects. In I. Management Association (Ed.), Fashion and Textiles: Breakthroughs in Research and Practice (pp. 233-260). Hershey, PA: IGI Global. doi:10.4018/978-1-5225-3432-7.ch010

Tambo, T., & Mikkelsen, O. E. (2016). Fashion Supply Chain Optimization: Linking Make-to-Order Purchasing and B2B E-Commerce. In S. Joshi & R. Joshi (Eds.), *Designing and Implementing Global Supply Chain Management* (pp. 1–21). Hershey, PA: IGI Global. doi:10.4018/978-1-4666-9720-1.ch001

Tandon, K. (2016). Innovative Andragogy: The Paradigm Shift to Heutagogy. In S. Tiwari & L. Nafees (Eds.), *Innovative Management Education Pedagogies for Preparing Next-Generation Leaders* (pp. 238–257). Hershey, PA: IGI Global. doi:10.4018/978-1-4666-9691-4.ch014

Tantau, A. D., & Frăţilă, L. C. (2018). Information and Management System for Renewable Energy Business. In *Entrepreneurship and Business Development in the Renewable Energy Sector* (pp. 200–244). Hershey, PA: IGI Global. doi:10.4018/978-1-5225-3625-3.ch006

Teixeira, N., Pardal, P. N., & Rafael, B. G. (2018). Internationalization, Financial Performance, and Organizational Challenges: A Success Case in Portugal. In L. Carvalho (Ed.), *Handbook of Research on Entrepreneurial Ecosystems and Social Dynamics in a Globalized World* (pp. 379–423). Hershey, PA: IGI Global. doi:10.4018/978-1-5225-3525-6.ch017

Trad, A., & Kalpić, D. (2016). The E-Business Transformation Framework for E-Commerce Architecture-Modeling Projects. In I. Lee (Ed.), *Encyclopedia of E-Commerce Development, Implementation, and Management* (pp. 733–753). Hershey, PA: IGI Global. doi:10.4018/978-1-4666-9787-4.ch052

Trad, A., & Kalpić, D. (2016). The E-Business Transformation Framework for E-Commerce Control and Monitoring Pattern. In I. Lee (Ed.), *Encyclopedia of E-Commerce Development, Implementation, and Management* (pp. 754–777). Hershey, PA: IGI Global. doi:10.4018/978-1-4666-9787-4.ch053

Trad, A., & Kalpić, D. (2018). The Business Transformation Framework, Agile Project and Change Management. In M. Khosrow-Pour, D.B.A. (Ed.), Encyclopedia of Information Science and Technology, Fourth Edition (pp. 620-635). Hershey, PA: IGI Global. doi:10.4018/978-1-5225-2255-3.ch054

Trad, A., & Kalpić, D. (2018). The Business Transformation and Enterprise Architecture Framework: The Financial Engineering E-Risk Management and E-Law Integration. In B. Sergi, F. Fidanoski, M. Ziolo, & V. Naumovski (Eds.), *Regaining Global Stability After the Financial Crisis* (pp. 46–65). Hershey, PA: IGI Global. doi:10.4018/978-1-5225-4026-7.ch003

Turulja, L., & Bajgoric, N. (2018). Business Continuity and Information Systems: A Systematic Literature Review. In N. Bajgoric (Ed.), *Always-On Enterprise Information Systems for Modern Organizations* (pp. 60–87). Hershey, PA: IGI Global. doi:10.4018/978-1-5225-3704-5.ch004

van Wessel, R. M., de Vries, H. J., & Ribbers, P. M. (2016). Business Benefits through Company IT Standardization. In K. Jakobs (Ed.), *Effective Standardization Management in Corporate Settings* (pp. 34–53). Hershey, PA: IGI Global. doi:10.4018/978-1-4666-9737-9.ch003

Vargas-Hernández, J. G. (2017). Professional Integrity in Business Management Education. In N. Baporikar (Ed.), *Management Education for Global Leadership* (pp. 70–89). Hershey, PA: IGI Global. doi:10.4018/978-1-5225-1013-0.ch004

Vasista, T. G., & AlAbdullatif, A. M. (2017). Role of Electronic Customer Relationship Management in Demand Chain Management: A Predictive Analytic Approach. *International Journal of Information Systems and Supply Chain Management, 10*(1), 53–67. doi:10.4018/IJISSCM.2017010104

Vergidis, K. (2016). Rediscovering Business Processes: Definitions, Patterns, and Modelling Approaches. In P. Papajorgji, F. Pinet, A. Guimarães, & J. Papathanasiou (Eds.), *Automated Enterprise Systems for Maximizing Business Performance* (pp. 97–122). Hershey, PA: IGI Global. doi:10.4018/978-1-4666-8841-4.ch007

Vieru, D., & Bourdeau, S. (2017). Survival in the Digital Era: A Digital Competence-Based Multi-Case Study in the Canadian SME Clothing Industry. *International Journal of Social and Organizational Dynamics in IT, 6*(1), 17–34. doi:10.4018/IJSODIT.2017010102

Vijayan, G., & Kamarulzaman, N. H. (2017). An Introduction to Sustainable Supply Chain Management and Business Implications. In M. Khan, M. Hussain, & M. Ajmal (Eds.), *Green Supply Chain Management for Sustainable Business Practice* (pp. 27–50). Hershey, PA: IGI Global. doi:10.4018/978-1-5225-0635-5.ch002

Vlachvei, A., & Notta, O. (2017). Firm Competitiveness: Theories, Evidence, and Measurement. In A. Vlachvei, O. Notta, K. Karantininis, & N. Tsounis (Eds.), *Factors Affecting Firm Competitiveness and Performance in the Modern Business World* (pp. 1–42). Hershey, PA: IGI Global. doi:10.4018/978-1-5225-0843-4.ch001

von Rosing, M., Fullington, N., & Walker, J. (2016). Using the Business Ontology and Enterprise Standards to Transform Three Leading Organizations. *International Journal of Conceptual Structures and Smart Applications, 4*(1), 71–99. doi:10.4018/IJCSSA.2016010104

von Rosing, M., & von Scheel, H. (2016). Using the Business Ontology to Develop Enterprise Standards. *International Journal of Conceptual Structures and Smart Applications, 4*(1), 48–70. doi:10.4018/IJCSSA.2016010103

Walczak, S. (2016). Artificial Neural Networks and other AI Applications for Business Management Decision Support. *International Journal of Sociotechnology and Knowledge Development, 8*(4), 1–20. doi:10.4018/IJSKD.2016100101

Wamba, S. F., Akter, S., Kang, H., Bhattacharya, M., & Upal, M. (2016). The Primer of Social Media Analytics. *Journal of Organizational and End User Computing, 28*(2), 1–12. doi:10.4018/JOEUC.2016040101

Wang, C., Schofield, M., Li, X., & Ou, X. (2017). Do Chinese Students in Public and Private Higher Education Institutes Perform at Different Level in One of the Leadership Skills: Critical Thinking?: An Exploratory Comparison. In V. Wang (Ed.), *Encyclopedia of Strategic Leadership and Management* (pp. 160–181). Hershey, PA: IGI Global. doi:10.4018/978-1-5225-1049-9.ch013

Wang, F., Raisinghani, M. S., Mora, M., & Wang, X. (2016). Strategic E-Business Management through a Balanced Scored Card Approach. In I. Lee (Ed.), *Encyclopedia of E-Commerce Development, Implementation, and Management* (pp. 361–386). Hershey, PA: IGI Global. doi:10.4018/978-1-4666-9787-4.ch027

Wang, J. (2017). Multi-Agent based Production Management Decision System Modelling for the Textile Enterprise. *Journal of Global Information Management, 25*(4), 1–15. doi:10.4018/JGIM.2017100101

Wiedemann, A., & Gewald, H. (2017). Examining Cross-Domain Alignment: The Correlation of Business Strategy, IT Management, and IT Business Value. *International Journal of IT/Business Alignment and Governance, 8*(1), 17–31. doi:10.4018/IJITBAG.2017010102

Wolf, R., & Thiel, M. (2018). Advancing Global Business Ethics in China: Reducing Poverty Through Human and Social Welfare. In S. Hipsher (Ed.), *Examining the Private Sector's Role in Wealth Creation and Poverty Reduction* (pp. 67–84). Hershey, PA: IGI Global. doi:10.4018/978-1-5225-3117-3.ch004

Wu, J., Ding, F., Xu, M., Mo, Z., & Jin, A. (2016). Investigating the Determinants of Decision-Making on Adoption of Public Cloud Computing in E-government. *Journal of Global Information Management, 24*(3), 71–89. doi:10.4018/JGIM.2016070104

Xu, L., & de Vrieze, P. (2016). Building Situational Applications for Virtual Enterprises. In I. Lee (Ed.), *Encyclopedia of E-Commerce Development, Implementation, and Management* (pp. 715–724). Hershey, PA: IGI Global. doi:10.4018/978-1-4666-9787-4.ch050

Yablonsky, S. (2018). Innovation Platforms: Data and Analytics Platforms. In *Multi-Sided Platforms (MSPs) and Sharing Strategies in the Digital Economy: Emerging Research and Opportunities* (pp. 72–95). Hershey, PA: IGI Global. doi:10.4018/978-1-5225-5457-8.ch003

Yusoff, A., Ahmad, N. H., & Halim, H. A. (2017). Agropreneurship among Gen Y in Malaysia: The Role of Academic Institutions. In N. Ahmad, T. Ramayah, H. Halim, & S. Rahman (Eds.), *Handbook of Research on Small and Medium Enterprises in Developing Countries* (pp. 23–47). Hershey, PA: IGI Global. doi:10.4018/978-1-5225-2165-5.ch002

Zanin, F., Comuzzi, E., & Costantini, A. (2018). The Effect of Business Strategy and Stock Market Listing on the Use of Risk Assessment Tools. In *Management Control Systems in Complex Settings: Emerging Research and Opportunities* (pp. 145–168). Hershey, PA: IGI Global. doi:10.4018/978-1-5225-3987-2.ch007

Zgheib, P. W. (2017). Corporate Innovation and Intrapreneurship in the Middle East. In P. Zgheib (Ed.), *Entrepreneurship and Business Innovation in the Middle East* (pp. 37–56). Hershey, PA: IGI Global. doi:10.4018/978-1-5225-2066-5.ch003

About the Contributors

Mambo Mupepi is the President of Grand Change Inc, an international change management consultancy firm. Research interests include Organizational Change Extensive experience acquired in Europe, Africa and US and is associated with various organizations. Publications include *Effective Talent Management for Organizational success* (IGI Global 2017), *Can the Usage of Social Media Increase the Gregariousness of the Family to Grow Successful Family-Owned Businesses?* (IGI Global 2017), *British Imperialism in Zimbabwe: Narrating the Organizational Development of the First Chimurenga* (Cognella 2015), and many other refereed articles and book chapters.

Robert Costello has been a researcher within the field of online learning, and in particular personalised & adaptive learning while incorporating learning theories and Adaptive Information Retrieval (AIR). His research trends do vary to incorporate Higher Education, which has mostly involved tailoring system designs for community collaboration, mLearning and gamification within Higher Education. Over the last 13 years he has taught a variety of computing modules in Further Education to Higher Education. Currently he is a HE Programme leader for Newcastle College University Centre for Level 6 BSc Hons Top-Up degrees.

* * *

Kevin Barrons currently is a faculty member in the Seidman College of Business where he teaches management information systems courses. Dr. Barrons research is focused on the Strategic Information Technology and Applications. In addition to this, he has reviewed the guiding practices for successful learning outcomes in teams.

Ditte Kolbaek has many years' experience in practice as she was manager of Organizational learning in the global IT company Oracle (EMEA) in eight years during which she and her team developed and implemented Proactive Review as a process of problem solving, learning from experience and innovation. Ditte Kolbaek holds a PhD in organizational learning based on her work in Oracle, and she has published several articles and books about proactive reviews. In 2018 she edited a book about online leadership and collaboration titled "Online Collaboration and Communication in Contemporary Organizations" with 20 authors from 11 countries. The book is published by IGI Global.

Sérgio Maravilhas is a Lecturer at UNIFACS, Brazil. Having two Post-Docs, one from UFBA about Patents and innovation and another one from UNIFACS about FABLABS, both with PNPD/CAPES Grants. He has a PhD in Information and Communication in Digital Platforms (UA+UP), a Master in Information Management (FEUP and Sheffield University, UK), a Postgraduate Course in ICT (FEUP), a Specialization in Innovation and Technological Entrepreneurship (FEUP and North Carolina State University, USA) and a 5 years Degree in Philosophy, Educational Branch (FLUP). A Teacher and Trainer since 1998, worked at ESE-IPP as a Supervisor at the Internet@School project between 2002/2005, and a university teacher since 2005 at Aveiro University (DEGEI), and since 2010 at ULP and IESFF in Masters and MBA levels. Teaches Marketing, Research Methods, Creative Processes in Innovation, Intellectual and Industrial Property, Technology Watch, Information Management and Organizational Behaviour in universities and he's a trainer in ICT, Sales, Negotiation and Neuro-Linguistic Programming (NLP). Publishes and attends conferences mainly in the subjects of patent information, innovation, marketing, web 2.0, webradio and sustainability.

Index

O

P

R

S

T

U

V

W

Z

www.ingramcontent.com/pod-product-compliance
Lightning Source LLC
LaVergne TN
LVHW081328300926
849161LV00008B/1912